NEGOTIATING THE DISABLED BODY

EARLY CHRISTIANITY AND ITS LITERATURE

David G. Horrell, General Editor

Number 23

NEGOTIATING THE DISABLED BODY

Representations of Disability
in Early Christian Texts

Anna Rebecca Solevåg

SBL PRESS

Atlanta

Copyright © 2018 by Anna Rebecca Solevåg

Library of Congress Cataloging-in-Publication Data

Names: Solevåg, Anna Rebecca, 1973– author.
Title: Negotiating the disabled body : representations of disability in early Christian texts / by Anna Rebecca Solevåg.
Description: Atlanta : SBL Press, [2018] | Series: Early Christianity and its literature ; number 23 | Includes bibliographical references and index.
Identifiers: LCCN 2018033041 (print) | LCCN 2018044032 (ebook) | ISBN 9780884143260 (ebk.) | ISBN 9780884143253 | ISBN 9780884143253 (hbk. : alk. paper) | ISBN 9781628372212 (pbk. : alk. paper)
Subjects: LCSH: People with disabilities—Religious aspects—Christianity. | Christian literature, Early—History and criticism. | Bible. New Testament—Criticism, interpretation, etc. | People with disabilities in the Bible.
Classification: LCC BT732.7 (ebook) | LCC BT732.7 .S647 2018 (print) | DDC 261.8/32409—dc23
LC record available at https://lccn.loc.gov/2018033041

Printed on acid-free paper.

In memoriam
William Quinton Matheson (1926–2013)
Rachel Sarah Beckett (1954–2016)

CONTENTS

Acknowledgments

This research project started six years ago, when I received a postdoctoral research grant from the Norwegian Research Council (NFR). I want to thank NFR for the generous funding and the School of Mission and Theology (now VID Specialized University) for hosting me as a postdoc. VID proved to be a wonderful work environment that I am now happy to call my academic home. During the project I was also able to spend a semester at the Graduate Theological Union in Berkeley, CA. I am grateful to Marion Grau (Church Divinity School of the Pacific) and Annette Weissenrieder (San Francisco Theological Seminary) for inviting me and hosting me while there.

What would academia be without scholar friends with whom to discuss ideas and who are willing to read half-baked texts? Marianne Bjelland Kartzow, Marion Grau, and Tina Dykesteen Nilsen are sisters in spirit whose input I value deeply, and I am thankful for deep conversations, constructive critique, and solid support. I received valuable comments on chapter drafts from Thomas Arentzen, Zoro Dube, Inger Marie Lid, Marianne Bjelland Kartzow, Christina Petterson, Rikard Roitto, Katy Valentine, Peggy Vernieu, and Annette Weissenrieder. Thanks, guys, and remember I owe you one! I also want to thank Hugo Lundhaug for help with the Coptic text of the Berlin Codex and Tina Dykesteen Nilsen for help with Hebrew transliteration. Finally, I want to thank the librarians at VID for their patience and professionalism: Nina, Dina, and Solveig, you rock!

Luckily, life is more than scholarship. I am so blessed to have a husband whose love lifts me and whose practical skills make my life much less complicated. Thank you, Vidar, for your support and faith in me. I am also grateful to my children, Torbjørn and Silje, and my daughter-in-law, Henriette, for cheering me on. This book is dedicated to the memory of my father, William Quinton Matheson, and my sister, Rachel Sarah Beckett, who passed away over the past few years. Both are dearly loved and deeply missed.

Abbreviations

Primary Sources

Act Pet.	Coptic Act of Peter, Berlin Codex
Act. Verc.	Actus Vercellences
Acts Pet.	Acts of Peter
Ant.	Josephus, *Jewish Antiquities*
Aph.	Hippocrates, *Aphorisms*
1 Apol.	Justin Martyr, *First Apology*
Art.	Plutarch, *Artaxerxes*
Carm.	Catullus, *Carmina*
Caus. mor.	Hippocrates, *De causis morborum*
Chaer.	Chariton, *De Chaerea et Callirhoe*
Claud.	Suetonius, *Claudius*
Curios.	Plutarch, *De curiositate*
De laude	Plutarch, *De laude ipsius*
Descr.	Pausanias, *Descriptions of Greece*
Dig.	Ulpian, *Digest*
Dom.	Suetonius, *Domitianus*
Ep.	Horace, *Epistles*
Epid.	Hippocrates, *Epidemics*
Eth. nic.	Aristotle, *Nichomachean Ethics*
Flat.	Hippocrates, *De flatibus*
Frag.	Aristophanes, *Fragments*
Frag.	Papias, *Fragments*
Gen. an.	Aristotle, *On the Generation of Animals*
Gos. Thom.	Gospel of Thomas
Gyn.	Soranus, *Gynecology*
Hist.	Polybius, *Historiae*; Tacitus, *Historiae*
Hist. eccl.	Eusebius, *Ecclesiastical History*
Hist. Aug.	Historia Augusta

Loc. aff.	Galen, *On the Affected Parts*
LXX	Septuagint
Mart. Pet.	Martyrdom of Peter
Mart. Pol.	Martyrdom of Polycarp
Metam.	Apuleius, *The Golden Ass*
Meth. med.	Galen, *De methodo medendi*
Mor.	Plutarch, *Moralia*
Morb. sacr.	Hippocrates, *The Sacred Disease*
Mul.	Hippocrates, *Female Diseases*
Noct. att.	Aulus Gellius, *Attic Nights*
Od.	Horace, *Odes*
Op.	Hesiod, *Works and Days*
Per.	Plutarch, *Pericles*
Philops.	Lucian, *Philopseudes*
Pol.	Aristotle, *Politics*
Progn.	Hippocrates, *Prognostic*
r.	reign
Res.	Pseudo-Justin, *De resurrectione*
Sev.	Historia Augusta, Severus Alexander
Sign. diut.	Aretaeus, *On the Causes and Symptoms of Chronic Disease*
Superst.	Plutarch, *De superstitione*
Syr. d.	Lucian, *The Goddess of Syria*
T. Sol.	Testament of Solomon
Urb. cond.	Livy, *Ab urbe condita*
Usu part.	Galen, *On the Usefulness of the Parts of the Body*
Vesp.	Suetonius, *Vespasianus*

Secondary Sources

AB	Anchor Bible
AHB	*Ancient History Bulletin*
AHR	*American Historical Review*
AJHR	*Australian Journal of Human Rights*
ALH	*American Literary History*
ANF	Roberts, Alexander, and James Donaldson, eds. *The Ante-Nicene Fathers: Translations of the Writings of the Fathers Down to A.D. 325.* 10 vols. 1885–1887. Christian Classics Ethereal Library, https://www.ccel.org/fathers.html.

ANRW	Temporini, Hildegard, and Wolfgang Haase, eds. *Aufstieg und Niedergang der römischen Welt: Geschichte und Kultur Roms im Spiegel der neueren Forschung.* Part 2, *Principat.* Berlin: de Gruyter, 1972–.
BCT	*Bible and Critical Theory*
BDAG	Danker, Frederick W., Walter Bauer, William F. Arndt, and F. Wilbur Gingrich. *Greek-English Lexicon of the New Testament and Other Early Christian Literature.* 3rd. ed. Chicago: University of Chicago Press, 2000.
BibInt	*Biblical Interpretation*
BibRef	Biblical Refigurations
BINS	Biblical Interpretation Series
BRP	Brill Research Perspectives in Biblical Interpretation
BSac	*Bibliotheca Sacra*
BW	Bible and Women
BZNW	Beihefte zur Zeithschrift für die neutestamentliche Wissenschaft
CBQ	*Catholic Biblical Quarterly*
CTSWWS	Critical Texts in Social Work and the Welfare State
CW	*Classical World*
DSQ	*Disability Studies Quarterly*
ExpTim	*Expository Times*
FCNTECW	A Feminist Companion to the New Testament and Early Christian Writings
FR	*Feminist Review*
Gen. an.	Aristotle, *On the Generation of Animals*
GLQ	*GLQ: A Journal of Lesbian and Gay Studies*
JAAR	*Journal of the American Academy of Religion*
JBL	*Journal of Biblical Literature*
JDR	*Journal of Disability and Religion*
JECS	*Journal of Early Christian Studies*
JFSR	*Journal of Feminist Studies in Religion*
JLA	*Journal of Late Antiquity*
JRDH	*Journal of Religion, Disability, and Health*
JRS	*Journal of Roman Studies*
JSNTSup	Journal for the Study of the New Testament Supplement Series
LCL	Loeb Classical Library
LHBOTS	The Library of Hebrew Bible/Old Testament Studies

LNTS	The Library of New Testament Studies
LSJ	Liddell, Henry George, Robert Scott, Henry Stuart Jones. *A Greek-English Lexicon*. 9th ed. with revised supplement. Oxford: Clarendon, 1996.
Neot	*Neotestamentica*
NRSV	New Revised Standard Version
NTS	*New Testament Studies*
PNA	*Patristica Nordica Annuaria*
PRSt	*Perspectives in Religious Studies*
R&T	*Religion and Theology*
RA	Rewriting Antiquity
Scr	*Scriptura*
SemeiaSt	Semeia Studies
Signs	*Signs: Journal of Women in Society and Culture*
SJDR	*Scandinavian Journal of Disability Research*
SNTSMS	Society for New Testament Studies Monograph Series
SP	Sacra Pagina
WUNT	Wissenschaftliche Untersuchungen zum Neuen Testament

1

INTRODUCTION:
DISABILITY AND EARLY CHRISTIAN LITERATURE

1.1. Bodies and Representations

In ancient Mediterranean cities, statues of gods and rulers would make clear what the ideal body looked like: athletic, able-bodied, symmetrically beautiful with Greco-Roman features, and forever young. Rather than the notion of "normal" that we have in the modern world, it was this golden standard, this idea of perfection that was impressed on the inhabitants of the Roman Empire. Most individual bodies moving through the streets of an ancient city would fall short of this ideal, but some would do so more conspicuously than others. Such bodies, or rather representations of bodies, singled out in texts as different are the focus of this study.

What representations of disability do we find in early Christian literature? What are the meanings ascribed to nonnormative bodies? Can we hear subversive voices? In this book, early Christian textual representations of bodies that are marked as nonnormative or deviant are explored through the lens of disability studies. I suggest that insights from this interdisciplinary field can be helpful for understanding more fully how the disabled body is negotiated in early Christian texts. The case studies presented will reveal a variety of understandings, attitudes, medical frameworks, and taxonomies. These texts are examples of early Christian struggles to come to terms with issues relating to body and dis/ability.

My interest in this line of inquiry grows out of previous studies on issues of embodiment and power relations in early Christianity.[1] In the

---

1. See, e.g., Anna Rebecca Solevåg, *Birthing Salvation: Gender and Class in Early Christian Childbearing Discourse*, BINS (Leiden: Brill, 2013); Solevåg, "Prayer in Acts and the Pastoral Epistles: Intersections of Gender and Class," in *Early Christian Prayer*

same way as the introduction of gender as an analytical category opened up a whole plethora of historical studies, disability as an analytical tool can contribute to insights about cultural categories, ideas of otherness, and social groups' access to or lack of power.[2] Disability historian Catherine J. Kudlick draws on Joan W. Scott's argument for gender as a category of historical analysis when she argues for disability as an equally meaningful lens for historians: "Disability should sit squarely at the center of historical inquiry, both as a subject worth studying in its own right and as one that will provide scholars with a new analytic tool for exploring power itself."[3]

The disabled bodies we meet in early Christian texts are representations.[4] They are literary constructions partaking in discourse, in which negotiation and efforts toward meaning-making are always at play. Rosemarie Garland-Thomson has pointed out that representations of disability do cultural work: "Disability is a representation, a cultural interpretation of physical transformation or configuration, and a comparison of bodies that structures social relations and institutions."[5] The discourse on

---

and Identity Formation, ed. Reidar Hvalvik and Karl Olav Sandnes (Tübingen: Mohr Siebeck, 2014); Solevåg, "Salvation as Slavery, Marriage and Birth: Does the Metaphor Matter?," in *Bodies, Borders, Believers: Ancient Texts and Present Conversations; Essays in Honor of Turid Karlsen Seim on Her Seventieth Birthday*, ed. Anne Hege Grung, Marianne Bjelland Kartzow, and Anna Rebecca Solevåg (Eugene, OR: Pickwick, 2015); Solevåg, "Listening for the Voices of Two Disabled Girls in Early Christian Literature," in *Children and Everyday Life in the Roman World*, ed. Christian Laes and Ville Vuolanto (London: Routledge, 2017): 287–99; Solevåg, "Hysterical Women? Gender and Disability in Early Christian Narrative," in *Disability in Antiquity*, ed. Christian Laes, RA (London: Routledge, 2017).

2. Joan W. Scott, "Gender: A Useful Category of Historical Analysis," *AHR* 91.5 (1986): 77–97.

3. Catherine J. Kudlick, "Disability History: Why We Need Another 'Other,'" *AHR* 108 (2003): 765.

4. Drawing on insights from Michel Foucault and the linguistic turn in historiography, scholars of early Christianity have studied the discursive constructions and negotiations around power and gender. See, e.g., Elizabeth A. Clark, *History, Theory, Text: Historians and the Linguistic Turn* (Cambridge: Harvard University Press, 2004); Caroline Vander Stichele and Todd C. Penner, *Contextualizing Gender in Early Christian Discourse: Thinking beyond Thecla* (Edinburgh: T&T Clark, 2009); Jorunn Økland, *Women in Their Place: Paul and the Corinthian Discourse of Gender and Sanctuary Space*, JSNTSup 269 (London: T&T Clark, 2004); Judith Perkins, *The Suffering Self: Pain and Narrative Representation in the Early Christian Era* (London: Routledge, 1995).

5. Rosemarie Garland-Thomson, *Extraordinary Bodies: Figuring Physical Disability in American Culture and Literature* (New York: Columbia University Press, 1997), 6.

disability is not isolated but is part of other discourses about embodiment in early Christianity, as will be developed later in this chapter. Discourses on health care and medicine are one such overlap. Another concerns ideas about beauty and perceived correlations between looks and morality, which in turn is connected to discourses on gender, class, and race. Yet another revolves around themes of sexual renunciation and other ascetic practices meant to discipline the body. Disability is thus a lens that can be used to reveal ideas about embodiment in early Christian discourse more widely understood. I employ an intersectional perspective, drawing on the cross-disciplinary confluence of theoretical frameworks from feminist and gender, queer, race, class, and postcolonial studies. The central notion of intersectionality is that mutually reinforcing vectors of power and oppression, such as race, gender, class, and sexuality, must be taken into account in order to understand the complexity of hierarchical relations.[6] Every person belongs to more than one category, and various oppressive mechanisms can work together to create new hierarchies and systems of discrimination.[7]

If representations of disability are cultural interpretations, can we detect any patterns in the meaning-making efforts around nonnormative bodies? According to David T. Mitchell and Sharon L. Snyder, "Disability inaugurates the act of interpretation."[8] Efforts to narrate disability are attempts to bring the body's unruliness under control. Mitchell and Snyder have introduced the term *narrative prosthesis* to refer to "both the prevalence of disability representations and the myriad meanings ascribed to it."[9] In early Christian discourse, such efforts toward interpretation of unruly and extraordinary bodies appear in a multitude of ways, from healing narratives to stories about disabling, from theologizing to using disability as invective. Early Christian texts show a fascinating variety in how they negotiate disability. It is the multiple, polyphonous, contradicting ways in which this happens that I present in this work.

---

6. Jennifer C. Nash, "Re-thinking Intersectionality," *FR* 89 (2008): 2; Paulina de los Reyes and Diana Mulinari, *Intersektionalitet: Kritiska reflektioner över (o)jämlikhetens landskap* (Stockholm: Liber, 2005), 24–25.

7. Marianne Bjelland Kartzow, *Destabilizing the Margins: An Intersectional Approach to Early Christian Memory* (Eugene, OR: Pickwick, 2012), 15.

8. David T. Mitchell and Sharon L. Snyder, *Narrative Prosthesis: Disability and the Dependencies of Discourse* (Ann Arbor: University of Michigan Press, 2001), 6.

9. Mitchell and Snyder, *Narrative Prosthesis*, 4.

My primary criterion in the selection of texts has been *variation* in several different respects. First, I have chosen texts from a variety of genres and from works within the New Testament as well as noncanonical literature. The case studies range from gospel stories and apocryphal narratives to Pauline letters and patristic expositions. Second, I have looked for intersectional variation. In other words, I have chosen characters and literary representations that display and negotiate various intersections of gender, status, ethnicity, age, dis/ability, and so on. The case studies are also chosen on the basis of a variety of disability categories and will present characters that are designated with terms such as *blind, deaf, mute, lame, demon-possessed, mad*, and *eunuch*. The last category can be understood as a category of reproductive disability, as I will argue. Finally, this study introduces a selection of current disability studies concept and frameworks that I find useful for an analysis of early Christian disability discourse. I have selected the concept of narrative prosthesis, the framework of gaze and stare, stigma theory, monster theory, and crip theory and employ these in the case studies. In each chapter, I forefront one such concept in order to explore its analytical potential for early Christian texts.

1.2. Disability as an Analytical Category

Disability studies is a field with intellectual roots in the social sciences, humanities, and rehabilitation sciences.[10] Similar to feminist approaches and critical race studies, it stands at the intersection of political activism and academia. Beginning in the 1960s and 1970s, people with disabilities began to organize and collectively protest their confinement in institutions, their poverty, and the discrimination they encountered.[11] They challenged the orthodox view that the causes of the widespread economic and social deprivation disabled people experienced were located within the individual and his or her impairment.[12] At the core of disability studies is a critique of the so-called *medical model* of disability and other "property

---

10. Gary L. Albrecht, Katherine D. Seelman, and Michael Bury, "Introduction: The Formation of Disability Studies," in *The Handbook of Disability Studies*, ed. Gary L. Albrecht, Katherine D. Seelman, and Michael Bury (Thousand Oaks, CA: Sage, 2001), 2.

11. Colin Barnes, Mike Oliver, and Len Barton, introduction to *Disability Studies Today*, ed. Colin Barnes, Mike Oliver and Len Barton (Cambridge: Polity, 2002), 4.

12. Barnes, Oliver and Barton, introduction, 4.

definitions" that see disability as inherent in the person with an impairment.[13] The medical model is the understanding of disability developed within modern medicine, and it is pervasive in the Western world. Discourse within this model focuses on clinical descriptions of bodies and body parts; promotes the intervention of professionals focused on cure, rehabilitation, and adjustment; and is *for/on* rather than *with/by* people with disabilities.[14] It is criticized by disability activists and scholars because it individualizes and pathologizes disability.

As an alternative to the medical model, a *social model* of disability was put forth by scholars within the disability movement. This model focuses on social oppression, cultural discourse, and environmental barriers rather than biological deficit and claims that it is the constrictions and inadequacies of society that disables the individual.[15] Within this paradigm, there is a strict differentiation between impairment and disability. While impairment is "the functional limitation within the individual caused by physical, mental or sensory impairment," disability is "the loss or limitation of opportunities to take part in the normal life of the community on an equal level with others due to physical or social barriers."[16] The model draws on a Marxist understanding of the connection between oppression and economic relations in a capitalistic society, arguing that industrialization and capitalism caused the segregation of the disabled into institutions.[17]

While the social model grew out of a British context, disability activists in North America drew on *identity* as their conceptual framework, arguing for a *minority model* clearly influenced by the civil rights movement. It was argued that people with disabilities constitute a minority position in society, like people of color, that has been denied civil rights, equal access, and protection.[18] Disability was redefined as a social and political category that marked identity and common experience. By identifying as "people with disabilities" or "disabled people," disability was reclaimed by

---

13. Gareth Williams, "Theorizing Disability," in Albrecht, Seelman, and Bury, *Handbook of Disability Studies*, 124–25.

14. Dan Goodley, *Disability Studies: An Interdisciplinary Introduction* (Los Angeles: Sage, 2011), 7.

15. Tom Shakespeare, "The Social Model of Disability," in *The Disability Studies Reader*, ed. Lennard J. Davis (New York: Routledge, 2006), 197.

16. Disabled People's International 1982, cited in Goodley, *Disability Studies*, 8.

17. Michael Oliver, *The Politics of Disablement*, CTSWWS (Basingstoke: Macmillan, 1990), 25–42.

18. Goodley, *Disability Studies*, 12–14.

the community "to identify us as a constituency, to serve our needs for unity and identity, and to function as a basis for political activism."[19]

Within the Nordic countries, disability theorizing has been shaped by the context of strong welfare states, expanded disability services, and the principle of "normalization," that is, community participation. The Nordic *relational model* argues that disability is a person-environment mismatch, that disability is situational or contextual, and that disability is relative.[20] While the social model is a strong version of the environmental turn in disability studies, holding that disability is solely caused by society's failure to adapt, the Nordic approach is more relational and relative and does not rule out the individual body and functional limitations from the discussion.[21] For example, Inger Marie Lid draws on this relational understanding to reflect on disability as an unsurprising aspect of the human condition. She tries to bridge a rigid binary understanding of disabled/nondisabled and dispense with a functionalist view of "normality." If variation in functional ability is an element of human diversity, and if vulnerability is the common ground, mutual dependence should define human relationships.[22]

1.3. The Cultural Model: Historicizing Disability

In the following I present the *cultural model*, which is the model I rely on in this book. The social model's dependency on binaries—medical versus social, impairment versus disability—has been heavily critiqued.[23] Disability scholars drawing on a Foucauldian, postmodern framework argue for a less rigid distinction between impairment and disability. They have pointed to the social construction of both concepts, dismantling the binary in a similar fashion to Judith Butler's critique of the distinction between sex and gender.[24] Michel Foucault's understanding of the

19. Simi Linton, *Claiming Disability: Knowledge and Identity* (New York: New York University Press, 1998), 12.

20. Goodley, *Disability Studies*, 15–16.

21. Jan Tøssebro, "Introduction to the Special Issue of SJDR: Understanding Disability," *SJDR* 6.1 (2004): 4–5.

22. Inger Marie Lid, "Disability as a Human Condition Discussed in a Theological Perspective," *Diaconia* 3 (2012).

23. Helen Meekosha and Russell Shuttleworth, "What's So 'Critical' about Critical Disability Studies?," *AJHR* 15 (2009): 50.

24. Shelley Tremain, "Foucault, Governmentality and Critical Disability Theory,"

connection between power and knowledge has provided the framework to analyze problematic aspects of institutionalization and other practices of care that "reveal technologies and procedures that classify, normalise, manage and control."[25] In particular, the notion of biopower is helpful. Foucault understood biopower as a technology of power that has structured modern society into a normalizing society through regulatory and corrective mechanism. The practices of biopower objectivize people and have "caused the contemporary disabled subject to emerge into discourse and social existence."[26]

The suggestion that the modern subject emerges through particular discourses and institutions contributes to an understanding of disability as a changing historical phenomenon. Thomson ventures that the modern disabled figure is a culturally and historically specific social construction, framed by ideologies of liberal individualism and the moral imperative of work.[27] She argues that disability is not a "self-evident physical condition" or just a personal misfortune. Rather, it is "the attribution of corporeal deviance—not so much a property of bodies as a product of cultural rules about what bodies should be or do."[28] The understanding that disability is a "product of cultural rules" is often referred to as the *cultural model*. This set of perspectives has become formative for a humanities approach to disability studies. Thomson has also introduced the term *normate* to describe the veiled subject position from which the disabled as a figure of otherness is constructed. The normate is constituted by defining the deviant others who make up the normate's boundaries: "Normate, then, is the constructed identity of those who, by way of the bodily configurations and cultural capital they assume, can step into a position of authority and wield the power it grants them."[29]

However, the poststructuralist framework has its limits. For disability theorists, the absence of a palpable, material body is a core concern. As

---

in *Foucault and the Government of Disability*, Corporealities (Ann Arbor: University of Michigan Press, 2005), 9–11. For Butler's critique of the sex/gender binary, see Judith Butler, *Gender Trouble: Feminism and the Subversion of Identity* (New York: Routledge, 1990).

25. Meekosha and Shuttleworth, "What's So 'Critical,'" 57.

26. Tremain, "Foucault, Governmentality and Critical Disability Theory," 5–6.

27. Thomson, *Extraordinary Bodies*, 39–41.

28. Thomson, *Extraordinary Bodies*, 6.

29. Thomson, *Extraordinary Bodies*, 8.

Bill Hughes maintains, "In Foucault's work, the body is a target (of power), an effect, a text upon which to write. This poststructuralist approach to the body tends to transform it into a supracarnal substance. The body is constituted as passive, without agency, the plaything of discourse and text, a surface ripe for inscription."[30] If the body is just a text, what about the experience of physical pain? Tobin Siebers claims that constructionist body theory upholds models that represent pain as either regulatory or resistant and downplays its physicality. Such notions are unrealistic and "contribute to an ideology of ability that marginalizes people with disabilities."[31] He proposes a theory of "complex embodiment" that adjusts social constructionism by focusing on the realism of bodies: "A theory that describes reality as a mediation, no less real for being such, between representation and its social objects."[32] Another critical voice is Lennard J. Davis, who dismisses both the notion of identity, prevalent in the minority model, and the social constructionism of Foucault-inspired disability theory. In an era he views as "dismodern" rather than postmodern, he finds that the experience of the limitations of the body is common ground and argues for "a commonality of bodies within the notion of difference.... We are all nonstandard."[33] Both Siebers and Davis point to weaknesses with the discursive approach that are important to keep in mind and that I will revisit in the chapters to come when I reflect on lived experience of disability in antiquity in relation to the sources.

Scholars working with disability historically find the cultural model useful because it focuses on the historical variations in understandings of disability and the layers of meaning residing in culture.[34] The social model,

30. Bill Hughes, "What Can a Foucauldian Analysis Contribute to Disability Studies?," in *Foucault and the Government of Disability*, ed. Shelley Tremain, Corporealities (Ann Arbor: University of Michigan Press, 2005), 85.

31. Tobin Siebers, "Disability in Theory: From Social Constructionism to the New Realism of the Body," *ALH* 13 (2001): 743–46.

32. Tobin Siebers, *Disability Theory* (Ann Arbor: University of Michigan Press, 2008), 30.

33. Lennard J. Davis, *Bending over Backwards: Disability, Dismodernism, and Other Difficult Positions* (New York: New York University Press, 2002), 31–32.

34. For disability historians drawing on the cultural model, see, e.g., Joshua R. Eyler, "Introduction: Breaking Boundaries, Building Bridges," in *Disability in the Middle Ages: Reconsiderations and Reverberations*, ed. Joshua R. Eyler (Farnham: Ashgate, 2010), 5–6; David M. Turner, *Disability in Eighteenth-Century England: Imagining Physical Impairment* (Hoboken: Taylor & Francis, 2012), 1–2; Julia Watts Belser,

at least in its early conception, lacked a nuanced reflection on how disability operates in other eras, as the focus was on the cultural production of disability within the rise of capitalism. It has been suggested that a moral model or religious model preceded the medical model and dominated in the eras before modernity and industrialization.[35] This is a simplified understanding that has been nuanced by historical studies of disability. Studies of medieval history have shown that the link between sin and illness is not the only lens through which medieval societies viewed disability.[36] Irina Metzler argues that medieval texts display ambiguity concerning the connection between physical impairment and spiritual sin and that a singular "moral model" cannot be imposed on the sources. Alongside the notion of impairment as the result of sin, there was a competing notion of impairment as something requiring physical healing.[37] As the case studies in this book will show, the perspective that "disability is a defect caused by moral lapse or sins" is evident in some of the texts but appears alongside other understandings.[38]

Disability history has developed into a prolific subdiscipline in which insights from disability theory are deployed, developed, and refined through the study of impairment and disability in various historical eras.[39] Kudlick has argued that using disability as an analytical category is crucial for understanding "how Western cultures determine hierarchies and maintain social order."[40] As an approach to historical texts, disability studies offers a lens to ask new questions. How is disability represented in the

---

Rabbinic Tales of Destruction: Gender, Sex and Disability in the Ruins of Jerusalem (Oxford: Oxford University Press, 2018), xxvii–xxix.

35. Oliver, *Politics of Disablement*, 25–29; Goodley, *Disability Studies*, 5–7.

36. Eyler, "Introduction," 3. For studies on disability in the Middle Ages, see, e.g., Irina Metzler, *A Social History of Disability in the Middle Ages: Cultural Considerations of Physical Impairment* (New York: Routledge, 2013); Irina Metzler, ed., *Disability in Medieval Europe: Thinking about Physical Impairment during the High Middle Ages, c. 1100–1400* (London: Routledge, 2006); Tory Vandeventer Pearman, *Women and Disability in Medieval Literature* (Basingstoke: Palgrave Macmillan, 2010); Sebastian Barsch, Anne Klein, and Pieter Verstraete, eds., *The Imperfect Historian: Disability Histories in Europe* (Frankfurt: Peter Lang, 2013); Eyler, *Disability in the Middle Ages*.

37. Metzler, *Disability in Medieval Europe*, 186–87.

38. Quote from Goodley, *Disability Studies*, 7.

39. Cf., e.g., The Disability History Association, which has a website and an online review journal, *H-Disability Reviews*, www.dishist.org.

40. Kudlick, "Disability History," 3.

text? What categories of disability do we find? What kinds of stigmas are attached to certain categories? What kinds of attitudes do we find toward people with different kinds of impairments? What are the motives and factors of integration or exclusion? How is disability utilized for a variety of social ends? How do religious texts, ideas, rituals, and conventions partake in a society's discourse on disability? What is disability's relationship to other identity categories, such as race, class, and gender?

The term *disability* is a modern category, and thus theoretical reflection is called for if we want to use it for other eras. David Turner argues that terms like *disabled* and *people with disabilities* can be used by disability historians in an open-ended way about people who "potentially may have faced restrictions on their ability to carry out everyday activities through injury, disease, congenital malformation, aging or chronic illness, or whose appearance made them liable to be characterized by contemporary cultural ideas associated with non-standard bodies."[41] It is in this open-ended manner I use disability-related terms in reference to ancient texts.

1.3.1. Disability in the Ancient Mediterranean World

It is only in the last two decades that insights from disability studies have been employed in biblical and early Christian studies.[42] Some monograph-length studies have emerged on the Hebrew Bible and the New Testament but not on other early Christian texts, as far as I am aware.[43] Studies from

---

41. Turner, *Disability in Eighteenth-Century England*, 11.

42. For edited works on the Bible, see Sarah J. Melcher, Mikeal C. Parsons, and Amos Yong, eds., *The Bible and Disability: A Commentary* (Waco, TX: Baylor University Press, 2017); Candida R. Moss and Jeremy Schipper, *Disability Studies and Biblical Literature* (New York: Palgrave Macmillan, 2011); Hector Avalos, Sarah J. Melcher, and Jeremy Schipper, *This Abled Body: Rethinking Disabilities in Biblical Studies*, SemeiaSt 55 (Atlanta: Society of Biblical Literature, 2007). See also Joel S. Baden and Candida R. Moss, *Reconceiving Infertility: Biblical Perspectives on Procreation and Childlessness* (Princeton: Princeton Universitety Press, 2015). For edited works on early Christianity, see the articles in the special issue on religion, medicine, disability, and health in *JLA* 8 (2015) and the section on the late ancient world in Laes, *Disability in Antiquity*.

43. On the Hebrew Bible, see Rebecca Raphael, *Biblical Corpora: Representations of Disability in Hebrew Biblical Literature*, LHBOTS (London: Continuum, 2009); Jeremy Schipper, *Disability and Isaiah's Suffering Servant*, ed. James Crossley and Francesca Stavrakopoulou, BibRef (Oxford: Oxford University Press, 2011); Schipper, *Dis-*

a disability perspective on Greek, Roman, Hellenistic, and ancient Jewish cultures are valuable resources in order to contextualize biblical and early Christian discourses on disability.[44] I draw on insights from this expanding field of historical research for methodological insights as well as for the identification and analysis of source material. In a survey essay on religion, medicine, disability, and health in late antiquity, Heidi Marx-Wolf and Kristi Upson-Saia lay out some guidelines for the field that I also find important. First, they point to the danger of imposing modern medical vocabulary and taxonomies. Rather than engaging in retrospective diagnosis, we should continue to refine our understanding of the ancient sources' own classificatory schemes. Second, it is important not to impose modern boundaries between religion, medicine, philosophy, biology, and so on but instead acknowledge the overlap that existed in antiquity. Finally, they warn against scholarship that is singularly attentive to representational and rhetorical aspects of disability and health and hence disregards "the real, lived experience of the sick and impaired."[45] There are very

---

ability Studies and the Hebrew Bible: Figuring Mephibosheth in the David Story (New York: T&T Clark, 2006); Saul M. Olyan, Disability in the Hebrew Bible: Interpreting Mental and Physical Differences (New York: Cambridge University Press, 2008). On the New Testament, see Louise J. Lawrence, Bible and Bedlam: Madness, Sanism, and New Testament Interpretation, LNTS (London: Bloomsbury T&T Clark, 2018); Louise J. Lawrence, Sense and Stigma in the Gospels: Depictions of Sensory-Disabled Characters (Oxford: Oxford University Press, 2013); Louise A. Gosbell, "'The Poor, the Crippled, the Blind, and the Lame': Physical and Sensory Disability in the Gospels of the New Testament" (Ph.D. diss., Macquarie University, 2015). Gosbell's dissertation was subsequently published as a monograph, "The Poor, the Crippled, the Blind, and the Lame": Physical and Sensory Disability in the Gospels of the New Testament (Tübingen: Mohr Siebeck, 2018).

44. See, e.g., Henri-Jacques Stiker, A History of Disability (Ann Arbor: University of Michigan Press, 1999); Robert Garland, The Eye of the Beholder: Deformity and Disability in the Graeco-Roman World (Ithaca: Cornell University Press, 1995); Martha L. Rose, The Staff of Oedipus: Transforming Disability in Ancient Greece (Ann Arbor: University of Michigan Press, 2003); Christian Laes, Chris F. Goodey, and Martha Lynn Rose, eds., Disabilities in Roman Antiquity: Disparate Bodies a Capite ad Calcem (Leiden: Brill, 2013); Laes, Disability in Antiquity; Heidi Marx-Wolf and Kristi Upson-Saia, "The State of the Question: Religion, Medicine, Disability and Health in Late Antiquity," JLA 8 (2015): 306–21; Judith Z. Abrams, Judaism and Disability: Portrayals in Ancient Texts from the Tanach through the Bavli (Washington, D.C.: Gallaudet University Press, 1998); Belser, Rabbinic Tales of Destruction.

45. Marx-Wolf and Upson-Saia, "State of the Question," 266–72, quote at 270.

few sources from antiquity that recount first-person experiences of people with disabilities.[46] Yet the various representations may also prompt our imagination to ponder these multifaceted experiences.[47] On an individual level, people with disabilities may have ascribed different meanings to their bodies and their lives than what prevailed in the cultural discourse. The lack of sources can serve as an inspiration to explore creative ways in which to engage with plausible experiences of people with disabilities. This does not necessarily involve any historical reconstruction or claims about a reality behind the text, but it can involve pointing to plausible scenarios as well as discursive openings in the narratives themselves.

In the following I briefly sketch the discursive field of disability and its overlap with other ancient discourses. First, I present some of the terms and categories connected to impairment and disability that occur in ancient sources. An important task for a disability studies approach to ancient texts is, in my view, to determine the degree of overlap, as well as difference, between ancient and modern categories.[48] Second, I look at ancient Mediterranean ideas about health and medicine and introduce the medical anthropological model of health care systems as a helpful framework for understanding ancient discourses on disability and illness. Third, I discuss how discourses on disability overlapped with other discourses on the body. Using insights from intersectionality, I introduce the notion of *kyriarchy*, coined by Elisabeth Schüssler Fiorenza, which I find useful for understanding the complex power structures of the ancient Mediterranean. Finally, the ancient pseudoscience of *physiognomy* is presented. Physiognomy was a popular method of "reading" bodies and attributing deviance. In several of the case studies in this book, physiognomic reasoning is embedded in the textual representation of disability.

1.4. Labeling Difference: Taxonomies of Disability

As noted above, disability is a modern category. There is no term for disabled in Greek, Latin, or Hebrew. There are, however, other types of categorizations, and this section tries to delineate some ancient Mediterranean

---

46. Christian Laes, "Introduction: Disabilities in the Ancient World: Past, Present and Future," in Laes, *Disability in Antiquity*, 3.

47. Lawrence, *Sense and Stigma in the Gospels*, 2. See also Marx-Wolf and Upson-Saia, "State of the Question," 270–72.

48. Olyan, *Disability in the Hebrew Bible*, 12–13.

taxonomies of disability. The Greek and Latin vocabularies of disability are quite vague and general. The terminology of disability did not belong to the domain of medicine, as the Hippocratic doctors treated curable diseases, not permanent conditions.[49] Martha L. Rose observes that the Greeks did not have a category of physical disability "in which people were a priori banned from carrying out certain roles and compartmentalized into certain others."[50] She maintains that it is a modern assumption to conclude from the classical Greek ideal of the perfect body that all disabled people who deviated from this norm were uniformly reviled.

Nicolas Vlahogiannis takes a somewhat different stance, arguing that able-bodiedness should be the primary point of reference for disability in antiquity because the ideal of the perfect body loomed large in ancient discourse. This notion is reflected in language, with word pairs that emphasize "the constraints imposed by the physical state" both in Greek (δυνατός/ἀδύνατος) and Latin (firmus/infirmus).[51] Vlahogiannis thus gives a broad definition of disability in antiquity that incorporates "appearance and socially ascribed abnormalities, such as polydactylism, left-handedness, old age, obesity, impotence, and even those who are socially ill-positioned, such as beggars, the poor, the homeless, the ugly and the diseased."[52] Within this broad category, disabled persons were sometimes considered according to their appearance, other times according to their social situation, and other times again with a view to their particular impairments.[53] In other words, disability overlaps with deformity in the ancient context, as physical abnormalities and bodily malfunction are not always kept apart.[54] Christian Laes has pointed out that infirmity may be a more appropriate term than disability for premodern society, arguing that "infirmity was a highly fluid, differentiating category, often used ad hoc and mostly defined in the context of a person's social role."[55]

---

49. Rose, *Staff of Oedipus*, 11.

50. Rose, *Staff of Oedipus*, 2.

51. Nicholas Vlahogiannis, "Disabling Bodies," in *Changing Bodies, Changing Meanings: Studies on the Human Body in Antiquity*, ed. Dominic Montserrat (London: Routledge, 1998), 16.

52. Vlahogiannis, "Disabling Bodies," 17.

53. Evelyne Samama, "The Greek Vocabulary of Disabilities," in Laes, *Disability in Antiquity*, 121–38.

54. Garland, *Eye of the Beholder*, 5; Nicole Kelley, "Deformity and Disability in Greece and Rome," in Avalos, Melcher, and Schipper, *This Abled Body*, 34–35.

55. Laes, "Introduction," 4.

The notion of an overarching category of infirmity or disability may also be found in the Bible. According to Rebecca Raphael, the categories of blind, deaf, and lame are often grouped in the Hebrew Bible, constituting a "trilogy of disability."[56] This trilogy turns up in legal material, narrative, prophecy, and poetry and shows that an abstract concept of disability underlies the Hebrew texts:

> The grouping of "blind and deaf" and "blind and lame," but never "deaf and lame" [is] evidence of higher-level concepts. Blindness and deafness are both sensory impairments, and blindness and lameness both affect mobility; deafness and lameness do not share the same kind of obvious common feature. In short, the linguistic and textual evidence does support the existence of abstractions that grouped various impairments together, even though a single term does not exist.[57]

In the New Testament, there is a similar grouping of disability categories that point to the existence of a higher-level concept of infirmity or disability. In the gospels, references to Jesus's healing activities list different impairments, including deafness, muteness, blindness, lameness, leprosy, demon possession, and different forms of weaknesses and illnesses (see, e.g., Matt 4:23–24; 15:30; Luke 7:21–22). Matthew presents the following list of infirmities: "Great crowds came to him, bringing with them the lame [χωλούς], the maimed [κυλλούς], the blind [τυφλούς], the mute [κωφούς], and many others (Matt 15:30)."[58] John uses the term ἀσθενέω as an overarching term for various disabilities when he describes the group gathered by the Bethesda pool: "In these lay many invalids [ἀσθενούντων]—blind, lame, and paralyzed" (John 5:3). This term can also refer to sickness, which shows that notions of illness and disability sometimes overlapped.[59] Likewise, the term ἀσθένεια denotes disease and sickness as well as want of strength.[60]

Lame, blind, and deaf, as well as some of the other categories of physical disability mentioned above, seem, on a surface level, similar to categories we operate with in the modern world. However, the meanings ascribed to them are in fact quite distinct and alien from a modern perspective, as

---

56. Raphael, *Biblical Corpora*, 13–14.
57. Raphael, *Biblical Corpora*, 14–15.
58. Unless noted, quotations from the Bible are from NRSV.
59. BDAG, s.v. "ἀσθενέω": "be sick"; LSJ, s.v. "ἀσθενέω": "to be week, feebly, sickly."
60. BDAG and LSJ, s.v. "ἀσθένεια."

I will elaborate in the case studies. One example is the term κωφός, which can refer to being mute, deaf, or both.[61] Muteness and deafness were often understood in terms of mental incapacity or demon possession.[62] Laes has argued that in an oral culture like the ancient Mediterranean, speech and hearing were closely connected to each other and were extremely important for taking part in society.[63]

Demon possession is a less obvious category of disability from a modern perspective.[64] Most people in the ancient world believed that the gods could cause disability and illness, either directly through divine intervention or by the more specialized means of possession.[65] Δαιμόνιον is the Greek term for an inferior divine being, and the polytheistic religions of the era held that gods, lesser gods, and spirits could possess a person for good or for evil.[66] Nevertheless, exorcism was not a culturally sanctioned form of healing, and demon possession was often discredited as superstition (Lucian, *Philops.* 8–16; Plutarch, *Superst.* 7 [168c]).[67] Demon possession occurs frequently in Jewish and early Christian sources. These religious traditions had a dualistic world view and connected demon possession with Satan and evil forces (see, e.g., Mark 3:22–27).[68]

Infertility or barrenness should be understood as a category of disability in the ancient Mediterranean.[69] Infertility was a condition that car-

---

61. BDAG and LSJ, s.v. "κωφός."

62. Rose, *Staff of Oedipus*, 72, 76–77.

63. Christian Laes, "Silent History? Speech Impairment in Roman Antiquity," in Laes, Goodey, and Rose, *Disabilities in Roman Antiquity*, 153–55.

64. For studies on demon possession in early Christianity, see, e.g., Lawrence, *Bible and Bedlam*; Gregory A. Smith, "How Thin Is a Demon?," *JECS* 16 (2008); David Brakke, *Demons and the Making of the Monk: Spiritual Combat in Early Christianity* (Cambridge: Harvard University Press, 2006); Dale B. Martin, *Inventing Superstition: From the Hippocratics to the Christians* (Cambridge: Harvard University Press, 2004); Eric Sorensen, *Possession and Exorcism in the New Testament and Early Christianity* (Tübingen: Mohr Siebeck, 2002); Jonathan Z. Smith, "Towards Interpreting Demonic Powers in Hellenistic and Roman Antiquity," *ANRW* 16.1:425–39.

65. Hector Avalos, *Health Care and the Rise of Christianity* (Peabody, MA: Hendrickson, 1999), 62–63.

66. Sorensen, *Possession and Exorcism*, 75–91; Dale B. Martin, *The Corinthian Body* (New Haven: Yale University Press, 1995), 153–55.

67. Sorensen, *Possession and Exorcism*, 6–7.

68. Sorensen, *Possession and Exorcism*, 118–19.

69. Martha L. Edwards, "The Cultural Context of Deformity in the Greek World:

ried notable stigma in Israelite culture.[70] Raphael observes that female infertility is a prominent disability motif in Genesis.[71] The motif also occurs in other parts of the Hebrew Bible, and it is women, not men, who are labeled as barren in unfruitful marriages.[72] The eunuch, however, is the male equivalent to the barren woman.[73] Greco-Roman childbearing discourse also emphasized women's role as childbearers. The institution of marriage was for the procreation of children, and medical writings considered the female body primarily in terms of reproductive capacity.[74] In this context, too, infertile women and eunuchs were juxtaposed (Aulus Gellius, *Noct. att.* 4.2.6–11). In the New Testament as well, infertility surfaces as a primarily female disability (e.g., Mark 5:25–29; Luke 1:7).[75] The cultural expectation that women would reproduce was severed in the early Christian ascetic tradition, where imminent eschatological expectation overshadowed the pressure to procreate.[76]

1.5. In Search of Healing: Ancient Health Care Systems

References to impairments and people with disabilities can be found in a variety of written sources from antiquity, and often healing and treatment are not concerns in the texts. Nevertheless, ancient medical writings and ancient ideas about health and healthcare are one aspect of ancient disability discourse that is reflected in the material I will present and deserves a brief introduction here.[77] The ancient art of medicine developed in Greece during the classical era. The treatment of illness was professionalized, and

---

Let There Be a Law That No Deformed Child Shall Be Reared," *AHB* 10.3–4 (1996): 91; Schipper, *Disability and Isaiah's Suffering Servant*, 21.

70. Baden and Moss, *Reconceiving Infertility*, 39–41.

71. Raphael, *Biblical Corpora*, 58, 81.

72. Baden and Moss, *Reconceiving Infertility*, 27–35.

73. Baden and Moss, *Reconceiving Infertility*, 135–36.

74. Solevåg, *Birthing Salvation*, 43–76.

75. I have suggested that in early Christian texts a "female dyad of disability," encompassing reproductive disabilities and madness/demon possession, compliments the biblical trilogy of disability observed by Raphael. Solevåg, "Hysterical Women?," 323.

76. Baden and Moss, *Reconceiving Infertility*, 206–8; Solevåg, *Birthing Salvation*, 168–85.

77. For an introduction to Classical medicine, see Vivian Nutton, *Ancient Medicine* (London: Routledge, 2004).

in addition to seeing patients, doctors tried to systematize and share their knowledge through writing.[78] The Hippocratic collection of medical treatises consists of about sixty or so preserved works that date, mostly, to the fifth and fourth centuries BCE.[79] Aristotle, too, wrote on medicine and shows familiarity with Hippocratic writings.[80] In the Roman Empire in the first century, there was an established guild of professional—mostly Greek—doctors trained in the Hippocratic tradition. Medical treatises and tracts from this time period include the medical writings of Aretaeus (first century CE), the gynecological treatise by Soranus (first to second century CE), the Latin encyclopedic compilation on the art of medicine by Celsus (second century CE), and the vast oeuvre of Galen (ca. 129–216 CE), the most famous doctor of his time. The medical writers tried to systematize knowledge about the body and its functions and dysfunctions, out of which they could deduce a prognosis and give advice on treatment. But the medical writers were also interested in the cause of illness and disease. They specifically argued against popular belief in the gods as the progenitors of illness and developed elaborate theories about how illness was caused either by imbalances originating within the body or by external factors such as nutrition, exercise, or climate.[81]

Most people were not familiar with the medical writers' theories, and it was common to attribute illness to divine intervention or ideas about pollution, such as demon possession. It is thus possible to delineate between two quite distinct ways of understanding both cause and cure for various illnesses in the ancient Mediterranean. In one paradigm, the cause of illness is ascribed to divine intervention, based in an etiology of invasion, and in the other, it is ascribed to natural causes, based in a system of balance both within the body and with its immediate surroundings.[82] This difference in understandings of health and illness may be conceptualized using the framework of health care system from medical anthropology.[83] Scholars who have applied this framework to early

---

78. Philip J. van der Eijk, *Medicine and Philosophy in Classical Antiquity: Doctors and Philosophers on Nature, Soul, Health and Disease* (Cambridge: Cambridge University Press, 2005), 32.

79. Nutton, *Ancient Medicine*, 60.

80. Van der Eijk, *Medicine and Philosophy in Classical Antiquity*, 14.

81. Nutton, *Ancient Medicine*, 70–71.

82. Martin, *Corinthian Body*, 146–59.

83. See Arthur Kleinman, *Patients and Healers in the Context of Culture: An*

Christianity differentiate between a popular health care sector, a professional sector, and a folk sector that often blend into the two others.[84] In
my opinion, the boundaries between folk and popular are not very clear
in antiquity, but I find a clear difference between the folk/popular sectors,
on the one side, and the professional sector, on the other. The professional sector is represented by the Hippocratic doctors with their theories
and writings. Over against this professionalized knowledge there were
the popular beliefs and ideas about illness as invasion. Within this folk/
popular sector of ancient health care, there were healers and exorcists. As
noted above, many people in the ancient world believed not only that the
gods could cause illness but also that they could heal. Asclepius came to
be seen as the healing god par excellence. In the Asclepian cult, healing
came about through incubation in the temple, where the devotee would
spend the night and receive visions from the god as a sign of healing.[85]

In daily life, however, these sectors were not separate but intersected.
Depending on a person's level of education and social setting, they could
be acquainted with the scholarly idea of the physical causes of illness, or
they could be more familiar with various etiologies of divine intervention in illness, demon possession among them. A person with an illness
or disability might seek healing within the family framework; from folk
healers; at an Asclepian temple or some other sanctuary; or, if they had the
access and economy to do so, from a professional doctor.[86] This overlap of
ideas and notions can also be seen in the New Testament, for example, in
the woman with the flow of blood who came to Jesus, a folk healer, after
unsuccessful treatment by professional doctors (Mark 5:26).

1.6. Disability and Kyriarchy: Intersecting Power Structures

As noted above, my approach to early Christian texts draws on the theoretical framework of intersectionality. Marianne Bjelland Kartzow argues

---

Exploration of the Borderland between Anthropology, Medicine, and Psychiatry (Berkeley: University of California Press, 1980), 50.

84. John J. Pilch, *Healing in the New Testament: Insights from Medical and Mediterranean Anthropology* (Minneapolis: Fortress, 2000), 62–70; Elaine M. Wainwright,
Women Healing/Healing Women: The Genderization of Healing in Early Christianity,
ed. Philip R. Davies, Bible World (London: Equinox, 2006), 35.

85. Nutton, *Ancient Medicine*, 104.

86. Avalos, *Health Care and the Rise of Christianity*, 77–78.

that intersectionality should be used "to destabilize ancient and new power structures and ways of organizing identity."[87] She has also introduced the helpful notion of "asking the other question" to ancient texts. This means to examine the intersectional reasoning of the text and to ask about the categories that are not made explicit: "When class is mentioned, it is relevant to ask about gender; when ethnicity or race is at work, it is relevant to ask about class."[88] Used in this way, intersectionality can serve as a tool to unpack the rhetoric of a given text and fill in gaps and silences.[89]

To determine what it meant to be disabled in antiquity, it is necessary to ask what other identity categories and power hierarchies intersected with disability in order to affect a person's social location. Schüssler Fiorenza argues that recognizing the role of the *kyrios/paterfamilias*—the male householder—is a key to understand the intersecting power structures of antiquity. Not all men were equal in power, and the prototypical powerful man was the male head of the household. The Greek *oikonomia* tradition defined three main relationships in the household: between husband and wife, between father and children, and between owner and slaves (Aristotle, *Pol.* 1253b). In view of this, gender, generation, and the distinction between slave and free were important identity markers in Greco-Roman society.[90] Schüssler Fiorenza's coinage of the terms *kyriarchy/kyriarchal/ kyriocentric* "underscores that domination is not simply a matter of patriarchal, gender-based dualism but of more comprehensive, interlocking, hierarchically ordered structures of discrimination."[91] The household was understood as the microcosm of empire, and the emperor was configured as a *paterfamilias* for all his subordinates.[92] In a multicultural society like the Roman Empire, ethnic and racial divisions also played a significant role, as did the differentiation between center and periphery, Rome and

---

87. Kartzow, *Destabilizing the Margins*, 16.

88. Marianne Bjelland Kartzow, " 'Asking the Other Question': An Intersectional Approach to Galatians 3:28 and the Colossian Household Code," *BibInt* 18 (2010): 371.

89. Kartzow, *Destabilizing the Margins*, 19.

90. Solevåg, *Birthing Salvation*, 49–51.

91. Elisabeth Schüssler Fiorenza, *Rhetoric and Ethic: The Politics of Biblical Studies* (Minneapolis: Augsburg Fortress, 1999), ix.

92. Elisabeth Schüssler Fiorenza, "Introduction: Exploring the Intersections of Race, Gender, Status, and Ethnicity in Early Christian Studies," in *Prejudice and Christian Beginnings: Investigating Race, Gender, and Ethnicity in Early Christian Studies*, ed. Elisabeth Schüssler Fiorenza and Laura Salah Nasrallah (Minneapolis: Fortress, 2009), 11–12.

the colonies. Romanness and Greekness were considered cultures superior to the various barbarians on the outside of the empire and to other ethnic groups within.[93] In other words, gender, age, class, citizenship, wealth, and ethnicity were all relevant factors in evaluating and negotiating a person's social location.

Ideas about ability and disability operated within this kyriarchal matrix. Ancient Greece and Rome were cultures that revered the strong, unblemished body. In Greece it was the young, male athlete's body that was the perceived pinnacle of bodily strength and perfection, whereas in Rome it was the well-trained, victorious soldier's. In this idea of bodily perfection, the young, able-bodied, upper-class male of Roman or Greek descent was the norm (Aristotle, *Pol.* 1252–1260). Bodily perfection was thus entangled with ideas about masculinity. Manliness tied in with strength, courage, and self-control.[94] Proper speech was also an important part of male comportment and self-fashioning.[95] Just like bodily perfection was conceived of in terms of masculinity, weakness in body was gendered female. Women were considered weak because of their sex. Aristotle states in *On the Generation of Animals* that women are characterized by inability (ἀδυναμία) as men are characterized by ability (766a; see also 728a). Galen, too, claims that women are a less developed, somewhat truncated version of humankind, imperfect (ἀτελές) and mutilated (ἀνάπηρον) in comparison to men (Galen, *Usu part.* 14.2). Hence, the category of *woman* reverberated with the category of *sick*, as both were related to weakness (ἀσθένεια).

---

93. For studies on race and ethnicity, see Denise Kimber Buell, *Why This New Race: Ethnic Reasoning in Early Christianity* (New York: Columbia University Press, 2005); Gay L. Byron, *Symbolic Blackness and Ethnic Difference in Early Christian Literature* (London: Routledge, 2002). The power relations between center and periphery are central to postcolonial studies. See, e.g., Stephen D. Moore, *Empire and Apocalypse: Postcolonialism and the New Testament* (Sheffield: Sheffield Phoenix, 2006).

94. For studies on masculinity, see, e.g., Maud W. Gleason, *Making Men: Sophists and Self-Presentation in Ancient Rome* (Princeton: Princeton University Press, 1995); Craig A. Williams, *Roman Homosexuality: Ideologies of Masculinity in Classical Antiquity* (Oxford: Oxford University Press, 1999); Stephen D. Moore and Janice Capel Anderson, *New Testament Masculinities* (Atlanta: Society of Biblical Literature, 2003); Colleen M. Conway, *Behold the Man: Jesus and Greco-Roman Masculinity* (Oxford: Oxford University Press, 2008); Peter-Ben Smit, "Masculinity and the Bible: Survey, Models and Perspectives," *BRP* 2 (2017): 1–97.

95. Gleason, *Making Men*, 83.

Class and economy were also factors that influenced the construction of disability as well as the lived experience. People with economic means were able to negotiate their impairments very differently than less affluent people. For example, they could rely on slaves for transportation, nursing, and other menial tasks.[96] There is evidence that people with various disabilities were involved in a wide range of economic activities.[97] Still, many disabled were cared for by their family.[98] Although some people with disabilities undoubtedly had to rely on begging in order to survive, it is contested how common this was. Although the blind beggar is a literary trope, it does not mean that it was a common means of survival.[99] As Robert Garland has noted, slaves had a high risk of becoming disabled, either through hard work and neglect or by being deliberately maimed.[100] Physical disability likely decreased the financial value of slaves and may have impeded their manumission.[101] Sick and disabled slaves who no longer held economic value were sometimes left in temples or at religious healing sites (Suetonius, *Claud.* 25.2). However, there was also a market for slaves with deformed bodies. During the Roman Empire it became fashionable among affluent households to display their wealth through a collection of "human curiosities," such as hunchbacks, dwarfs and "imbeciles."[102] Plutarch claims that the demand for such slaves was so great that there was a separate monster market in Rome exclusively offering such human "goods" (*Curios.* 10 [520c]).

Yet another intersection is that between race and disability. Historians, poets, and ethnographers described races distant from the perceived center of the world as degenerate and monstrous.[103] Moreover, the Greek medical writings were quite preoccupied with geography and its influence

---

96. Garland, *Eye of the Beholder*, 30.

97. Rose, *Staff of Oedipus*, 40–42; Garland, *Eye of the Beholder*, 32–35.

98. Garland, *Eye of the Beholder*, 39.

99. Garland assumes so, but Trentin and Rose warn against conflating literary tropes with the lives of ordinary people. See Garland, *Eye of the Beholder*, 39; Lisa Trentin, "Exploring Visual Impairment in Roman Antiquity," in Laes, Goodey, and Rose, *Disabilities in Roman Antiquity* (Leiden: Brill, 2013), 108–10; Rose, *Staff of Oedipus*, 90–92.

100. Garland, *Eye of the Beholder*, 22.

101. Katy Valentine, "Reading the Slave Girl of Acts 16:16–18 in Light of Enslavement and Disability," *BibInt* 26 (2018): 356.

102. Garland, *Eye of the Beholder*, 46–47.

103. Garland, *Eye of the Beholder*, 159–64.

on health and the body. Landscape and climate were regarded as an external influence that could cause disease; hence different ethnic groups were understood to be prone to different diseases due to their geographical location. Moreover, the races themselves had certain inherent traits which, with the exception of the Romans and the Greeks, were pathologized.[104]

Disability was also connected to age.[105] Old age was sometimes described negatively as a time of bodily deterioration as well as mental decline.[106] Old men were considered to be less masculine, or at least in danger of becoming effeminate if they retreated from the public (male) space.[107] On the other hand, old age was also associated with wisdom, virtue, maturity, and reason.[108] There are clear gender differences in descriptions of the elderly and their dis/abilities in early Christian sources. Whereas older men are often presented as strong and fit despite their age (e.g., Mart. Pol. 7; 13), and thus natural leaders for the community (e.g., 1 Tim 5:17; Jas 5:14; 1 Pet 5:5), widows are presented as a quintessentially needy category of women and often as ailing in body (e.g., Acts 4:1; 1 Tim 5:5; Acts Verc. 21).

1.7. Physiognomy: Reading the Body to Reveal the Soul

The ancient pseudoscience of physiognomy claimed that outward appearance signified inner moral features and that a person's physical traits could be deciphered to reveal the corresponding moral qualities. Physiognomic reasoning overlaps with disability discourse in several of the case studies in this book.[109] Throughout history, people with disabilities have been

---

104. Nutton, *Ancient Medicine*, 75–76.

105. Rose, *Staff of Oedipus*, 23–24.

106. Tim G. Parkin, *Old Age in the Roman World: A Cultural and Social History* (Baltimore: Johns Hopkins University Press, 2003), 244–45.

107. Marianne Bjelland Kartzow, *Gossip and Gender: Othering of Speech in the Pastoral Epistles* (Berlin: de Gruyter, 2009), 185–86.

108. Barclay, John M. G., "There Is Neither Young Nor Old? Early Christianity and Ancient Ideologies of Age," *NTS* 53 (2007): 233. See also Karen King, "Images of Aging and Immortality in Ancient Christianity," in *Metamorphoses: Resurrection, Body and Transformative Practices in Early Christianity*, ed. Turid Karlsen Seim and Jorunn Økland (Berlin: de Gruyter, 2009).

109. For the use of physiognomy in early Christian texts, see, e.g., Mikeal C. Parsons, *Body and Character in Luke and Acts: The Subversion of Physiognomy in Early Christianity* (Grand Rapids: Baker Academic, 2006); Chad Hartsock, *Sight and Blind-*

particularly vulnerable to physiognomic interpretations. Mitchell and Snyder have shown how disability has been read physiognomically in narratives from antiquity until today.[110] Disabled bodies exhibit a difference that make them ripe for interpretation, they argue: "If the 'external effect' led directly to a knowledge of the 'internal faculty,' then those who inhabited bodies deemed 'outside the norm' proved most ripe for a scrutiny of their moral or intellectual content."[111]

The physiognomic handbooks were written to help the would-be physiognomer decipher the signs of body and face. A handful of these have been preserved, including the rhetorician Polemon's *Physiognomy* (second century CE) and one attributed to Aristotle.[112] Polemon begins his *Physiognomy* thus:

> Know that the eyes are the gateway to the heart, from which arises the cares of the soul and appear the secrets of the conscience.... I shall now describe to you the external form of the eyes, their shapes, indications and signs, such as will suffice you to practice physiognomy, for they are among the witnesses that provide the truest information for physiognomy as regards the knowledge you seek about good and bad.[113]

In minute detail, these handbooks describe different features, such as narrow or wide foreheads, different eye colors, and shape of the nose, and explain what the corresponding personality traits are. The handbooks focus on the eyes and the face, but they also describe signs for the rest of the body, as well as voice and gait. The physiognomer was also expected to decipher the connection between certain bodily features and their resem-

---

ness in Luke-Acts: The Use of Physical Features in Characterization, BINS (Leiden: Brill, 2008); Karl Olav Sandnes, *Belly and Body in the Pauline Epistles*, SNTSMS 120 (Cambridge: Cambridge University Press, 2002); J. Albert Harrill, "Invective against Paul (2 Cor 10:10), the Physiognomics of the Ancient Slave Body, and the Greco-Roman Rhetoric of Manhood," in *Antiquity and Humanity: Essays on Ancient Religion and Philosophy*, ed. Adela Yarbro Collins and Margaret M. Mitchell (Tübingen: Mohr Siebeck, 2001).

110. Mitchell and Snyder, *Narrative Prosthesis*, 57–61.

111. Mitchell and Snyder, *Narrative Prosthesis*, 59.

112. For texts, translations, and introductory essays, see Simon Swain, ed. *Seeing the Face, Seeing the Soul: Polemon's Physiognomy from Classical Antiquity to Medieval Islam* (Oxford: Oxford University Press, 2007).

113. George Boys-Stones, "Physiognomy and Ancient Psychological Theory," in Swain, *Seeing the Face, Seeing the Soul*, 341.

blance to different animals and their innate characteristic.[114] Within this body of literature race and ethnicity were connected with moral qualities, and the perceived degeneracy of all races other than the Greeks is quite clear in the racial stereotyping that the physiognomies offer.[115]

According to Polemon, "fast-moving eyes indicate evil, wicked conjecture, and lack of truth"; "if the feet are very fleshy and soft, they indicate weakness, softness, and laxity"; and "largeness of the stomach and great fleshiness, especially if it has softness and droop, indicates much movement, drunkenness, and love of sexual intercourse."[116] The taxonomy is clear: good-looking men are good, but those with nonnormative bodies betray a deviant soul. Masculinity and male self-presentation are highly important in the physiognomic writings, as Maud Gleason has demonstrated. These handbooks were written to help men of the ruling class differentiate between the masculine—and hence morally good—man and the effeminate; they were "a tool for decoding the signs of gender deviance."[117] Gait and voice were particularly important signs to look for in terms of gender deviance. According to Polemon, "You should learn [the signs of masculinity and femininity] from the gaze, the movement, and the voice."[118] The handbooks also draw on class and ethnic stereotypes and explain how to distinguish the capable male not only from the effeminate but also from the slavish.[119]

1.8. Reading Early Christian Texts with a Disability Studies Lens

Biblical scholars drawing on disability studies do not follow one particular methodology. The emphasis varies, from attention to terminology and literary representation, to critique of normate tendencies in previous scholarship, to constructive rereadings in an effort to "reclaim the identity of those stigmatized as 'other.'"[120] The perspectives and concepts I have pre-

---

114. Robert Hoyland, "A New Edition and Translation of the Leiden Polemon," in Swain, *Seeing the Face, Seeing the Soul*, 385.

115. Simon Swain, "Polemon's *Physiognomy*," in Swain, *Seeing the Face, Seeing the Soul*, 197.

116. Hoyland, "New Edition and Translation of the Leiden Polemon," 347, 397, 405.

117. Gleason, *Making Men*, 58.

118. Hoyland, "New Edition and Translation of the Leiden Polemon," 393.

119. Harrill, "Invective Against Paul," 119.

120. See, respectively, Laes, "Introduction," 8; Raphael, *Biblical Corpora*, 21–26;

sented in this chapter provide some guiding principles in my own analysis of the texts.

An important contribution of this volume is to bring the analysis of disability in ancient texts into dialogue with particular concepts and insights from disability studies. I think concepts such as Mitchell and Snyder's theory of narrative prosthesis, Erving Goffman's notion of *stigma*, and Susan Sontag's analysis of illness as metaphor can serve as useful lenses when reading early Christian texts on disability. Putting such modern frameworks in conversation with ancient texts may also help develop and fine-tune these interpretive tools.

In an effort to contextualize the text within its ancient location, I pay attention to the disability terminology in the texts. I examine terms for disabilities, illnesses, and sometimes healing in order to understand how people with nonnormative bodies are labeled. I understand these terms and labels as embedded in discourse and engaged for a variety of purposes. Hence, I also search for hints of taxonomic efforts and ask how representations of disability function within the literary framework. Is disability used for a particular literary purpose? Which medical or etiological frameworks does the text rely on in its presentation of disability?

I also try to probe the lived experience of disability by asking questions about the social location of characters with disabilities. An important aspect of my approach is to bring intersectional perspectives to bear in studies of illness and disability in early Christian texts. What difference does it make when we ask questions about gender, sexuality, age, class, ethnicity, and so on in conjunction with dis/ability? In some cases, I also take an interest in the research history of the texts I study. Can we see traces of a normate biases in previous scholarship?

These guiding principles should not be seen not as steps in a fixed methodological approach but more as areas of inquiry that may be combined in different ways to provide a meaningful mapping of a text's negotiation of disability. It is an open-ended approach that explores the multiple ways in which a disability studies lens may be used.[121]

Schipper, *Disability and Isaiah's Suffering Servant*, 10–12; Lawrence, *Sense and Stigma in the Gospels*, 1–2.

121. For a concluding discussion of disability studies approaches to the Bible, see §8.3.

1.8.1. Outline of the Book

The chapters are organized around particular case studies. In each chapter I introduce a text or a set of texts together with a particular theoretical concept from disability studies that I find useful for the analysis. In the first three chapters I focus on healing narratives, since early Christian stories about miraculous healing have been important for theological reflection around disability throughout Christian history.[122] In chapter 2 I look at two healing stories from the Gospel of Mark: the lame man with the four helpers (2:1–10) and the demon-possessed Syro-Phoenician girl (7:24–30). I introduce Mitchell and Snyder's theory of narrative prosthesis as a model for understanding the literary work of disability in texts and explore the various designations and meanings of these characters' disabilities. I show how a disability studies approach opens up for new questions, digging deeper into the intersectional aspects of living with various disabilities and how it may have varied according to age, gender, class, and ethnicity.

The Gospel of John has only three healing stories, which are the focus of chapter 3. I argue that the royal official's son (4:46–54), the man by the Bethesda pool (5:1–15), and the man born blind (9:1–41) represent different categories of illness (fever) and disability (mobility impairment and blindness) as well as a range of social locations. I draw on Sontag's discussion of metaphors of illness as a helpful framework to understand the highly symbolic, metaphorical use of disability that John represents. John's symbolic use of blindness in particular draws on a cultural script that aligns blindness with ignorance and lack of insight. I show how John introduces different terms for and ideas about disability and illness than the Synoptics, and I also show that the use of disability in the narrative is quite different from Mark's.

In contrast to John, where only men are healed, women are the primary characters in the healing narratives in the Acts of Peter. Chapter 4

---

122. See, e.g., Nancy L. Eiesland, *The Disabled God: Toward a Liberatory Theology of Disability* (Nashville: Abingdon, 1994), 70–75; Jennifer L. Koosed and Darla Schumm, "Out of the Darkness: Examining the Rhetoric of Blindness in the Gospel of John," in *Disability in Judaism, Christianity, and Islam: Sacred Texts, Historical Traditions, and Social Analysis*, ed. Darla Schumm and Michael Stoltzfus (New York: Palgrave Macmillan, 2011); Julia Watts Belser and Melanie S. Morrison, "What No Longer Serves Us: Resisting Ableism and Anti-Judaism in New Testament Healing Narratives," *JFSR* 27.2 (2011): 153–70.

analyzes references to and uses of disability in this second-century apoc-ryphal work. Acts of Peter is chosen due to its stories of unhealing as well as healing, and the attention devoted to women and their sexuality within the context of disability. I look at four instances of un/healing of women: Peter's healing and unhealing of his lame daughter (Act Pet.); the dis-abling punishment of a Christ-believing woman, Rufina, who is caught in adultery (Act. Verc. 2); the healing of a group of blind widows (Act. Verc. 20–21); and a vision of the dismemberment and killing of a female demon (Act. Verc. 22). I draw on the concept of "the male gaze," developed by feminist classics scholars, and Garland-Thomson's concept of "staring" in order to tease out the gendered aspects of disability in the narrative.

In the final three chapters I look at representations of disability in tex-tual contexts that are not preoccupied with healing. In all these chapters, the overlap between discourses of disability and masculinity come to the fore. I argue that the normate male in antiquity is able-bodied and that *disability invective*, accusations about a deviant body, was used in ancient rhetoric. Goffman's notion of stigma frames chapter 5, which explores accusations against Jesus that he was demon-possessed (e.g., Mark 3:19–30; Matt 12:22) and Paul's efforts to defend himself against accusations of madness in the Corinthian correspondence (esp. 2 Cor 11). The chap-ter also discusses the categories of madness and demon possession as two alternative etiologies that explain deviant behavior, based in different sec-tors of the ancient health care system.

In chapter 6 I examine the church father Papias's description of the death of Judas (*Frag.* 4.2–3) to show how disability is used as a category of invective. Papias draws on medical insights as well as physiognomy to car-icature Judas as disabled and effeminate. He uses the culturally assigned location of blindness and dropsy—as disabilities and illnesses that reveal moral character—to construct a deviant body that fits his deviant soul. Here I introduce monster theory as a useful theoretical framework to understand the text.

The final analytical chapter (ch. 7) employs Robert McRuer's crip theory and cripping as a process of critique to read the eunuch figure in antiquity. The eunuch category may be understood as a reproductive disability, and the inclusion of this category thus broadens the variety of disabilities discussed in this book. The two New Testament passages that employ the term (Matt 19:12; Acts 8:24–30) are analyzed with a view to how bodily signs were reinterpreted as part of early Christian discourse on inclusion and exclusion. In the conclusion (ch. 8), I reflect on the long lines through history that connect notions about disability from early Christianity to postmodern culture. I also draw together the various readings and perspectives, pointing to some common themes and suggesting some potentials for future research.

Healings as Narrative Prosthesis in Mark

2.1. Introduction: Narrative Prosthesis

In this chapter I examine the representations of disability in two healing stories from Mark: the man with the four helpers (2:1–12) and the Syro-Phoenician woman's daughter (7:24–30). First, I discuss the labels that these disabled characters are given—"paralyzed" and "demon-possessed"—but also try to determine these narrative characters' social location through an intersectional lens. Second, I examine how disability functions in these narratives, using the concept of narrative prosthesis, which I will introduce below. I suggest that Mark deploys disability in a particular way that has both likenesses and differences to the way disability functions in other gospels or early Christian narratives.

Mitchell and Snyder have observed that disability has an unusual literary history. Whereas racial and sexual minorities have been invisible in the dominant culture's literature, disabled peoples' social invisibility has occurred despite the pervasive use of disabled characters in literature since antiquity.[1] Why this never-ending fascination with the representation of disability? Mitchell and Snyder have proposed that "disability has been used throughout history as a crutch upon which literary narratives lean for their representational power, disruptive potentiality, and analytical insight."[2] They call this literary dependency on disability *narrative prosthesis*. According to Mitchell and Snyder, there are two ways in which a disabled character can serve as a prosthetic for the narrative: first, as a *narrative element* that somehow resolves the problem of deviance; second, as a *metaphorical device* drawing on physiognomic reasoning.

---

1. Mitchell and Snyder, *Narrative Prosthesis*, 6.
2. Mitchell and Snyder, *Narrative Prosthesis*, 49.

In the first trajectory, disability supplies the impetus to tell a story. As Mitchell and Snyder say, "The very need for a story is called into being when something has gone amiss with the known world.... Stories compensate for an unknown or unnatural deviance that begs an explanation."[3] In other words, the story reveals a need to resolve or correct the problem of disability. It is an effort at meaning-making: "Because disability represents that which goes awry in the normalizing bodily scheme, narratives sought to unravel the riddle of anomaly's origins."[4] Such stories follow a simple narrative structure: first, a deviance is exposed; second, an explanation of origin or consequences is called for; third, the deviance is brought to the center of the story; and fourth, the story rehabilitates the deviance in some manner. The repair of deviance can happen in different ways: through some sort of cure, through rescue from social censure, through the extermination of the deviant character as a purification of the social body, or through a revaluation of modes of being.[5] The healing stories in the gospels follow such a prosthetic narrative scheme. For example, the story of the man born blind (John 9:1–7) starts with the disciples' question: "Rabbi, who sinned?" (John 9:2). The observation of a blind man requires an explanation and serves as the impetus for the ensuing narrative, which ends with the rehabilitation of the problem of the man's lack of sight through a miraculous healing.

In the second trajectory, disability is used to reveal the moral character of the person or represent a negative moral trait more generally. Going back to the ancient pseudoscience of physiognomy, disability has been interpreted as an external symptom of an inner, moral deviance, according to Mitchell and Snyder. Disability has thus been used by writers to allow a metaphorical play between macro- and microregisters of meaning.[6] An example from the gospels is the Q saying about the eye as the lamp of the body: "The eye is the lamp of the body. So, if your eye is healthy, your whole body will be full of light; but if your eye is unhealthy, your whole body will be full of darkness. If then the light in you is darkness, how great is the darkness!" (Matt 6:22–23 // Luke 11:34–36).[7] Sight and health are here metaphorically connected to moral superiority, while a sick eye

---

3. Mitchell and Snyder, *Narrative Prosthesis*, 53.

4. Mitchell and Snyder, *Narrative Prosthesis*, 59.

5. Mitchell and Snyder, *Narrative Prosthesis*, 53–54.

6. Mitchell and Snyder, *Narrative Prosthesis*, 60–62.

7. For a disability perspective reading of this saying, see Candida R. Moss, "Mark

serves as a metaphor for lack of understanding and moral judgment. In the following chapters I will give examples of such metaphorical and physiognomic uses of disability.

Mitchell and Snyder use the concept to read a number of literary works from different times and cultures, such as Sophocles's *Oedipus Rex*, Shakespeare's *King Lear*, and Herman Melville's *Moby Dick*. They argue that all these stories are examples of the same phenomenon: they are stories that seek to *prostheticize*—to resolve or correct—a deviance that seems improper in a social context.[8] As noted, the healing stories in early Christian gospels and acts fit neatly into Mitchell and Snyder's description. These narratives follow a particular prostheticizing script in which the problem of disability is resolved through a miraculous act of healing. The healing gives credit to God, instigates conversion, and thus functions as a narrative device that drives the story forward. This pattern has been observed by biblical scholars drawing on Mitchell and Snyder's theory, and it will be part of my argument as well.[9] However, the various prosthetic uses in healing stories and other literary representations of disability raise the question of whether or not the term narrative prosthesis is a sharp enough analytical tool. It seems to me that most stories that involve disabled characters can be labeled as narratively prosthetic. It is the various ways that this prostheticizing happens that is interesting and needs to be more closely mapped. In some texts the metaphorical trajectory is most clearly at play; in other instances it is the narrative drive that is more apparent. Moreover, the metaphorical trajectory can project inwardly in a physiognomic move, but it can also project outwardly, beyond the individual character, as I will show in this chapter. In subsequent chapters, I will also comment on the fact that the metaphorical trajectory of narrative prosthesis is not limited to narrative texts but can be found in rhetorical and argumentative texts as well (see §5.3 and ch. 6).

---

and Matthew," in Melcher, Parsons, and Yong, *Bible and Disability*, 281–82. On blindness as a metaphor in the gospels, see discussion in ch. 3.

8. Mitchell and Snyder, *Narrative Prosthesis*, 53.

9. See, e.g., Raphael, *Biblical Corpora*, 53–54; Lawrence, *Sense and Stigma in the Gospels*, 32–33.

2.1.1. Markan Healings

In Mark, Jesus's healings are foregrounded and appear early in comparison to the other canonical gospels. Already in the first chapter, Mark narrates three explicit healing incidents: the possessed in the synagogue (1:23–27), Peter's feverish mother-in-law (1:30–31), and the leper (1:40–44). A fourth, the healing of the paralytic, follows immediately after (2:1–12).[10] The stories are interspersed with comments on how the word about Jesus's healing activity spread and people flocked to see him (see 1:28, 32–33, 45; 2:2). Mark also adds two summary statements that emphasize Jesus's healing activity (1:34, 39). Luke follows Mark in placing these four healings at the beginning of Jesus's ministry but inserts the birth narrative before them and breaks the sequence of healing stories up by interjecting the calling of the disciples (see Luke 4–5). In the Gospel of Matthew, the first healing story does not occur until chapter 8, after the Sermon on the Mount. There is, however, a summary statement about Jesus's preaching and healing activity in 4:23–24.

In Mark, Jesus heals the demon-possessed (1:23–26; 5:2–13; 7:25–30; 9:14–27) alongside other sick and disabled people, such as a leprous person (1:40–45), two men with some sort of paralysis (2:3–12; 3:1–5), a terminally ill child (5:23, 35–42), a woman with gynecological problems (5:25–34), a deaf-mute (7:31–37), and blind people (8:22–25; 10:46–52). According to Elaine M. Wainwright, Jesus is cast as a folk healer in contrast to professional healers by the Markan storyteller.[11]

The two passages I will analyze are quite different from one another, in terms of both content and placement within the framework of Mark's narrative. The first, the story of the paralyzed man with four helpers (Mark 2:1–12), occurs early in the gospel, as the final healing in the series that inaugurates Jesus's ministry. In the second, Jesus heals a Syro-Phoenician girl who is demon-possessed (7:24–30). The story is one of four healing stories in Mark concerned with demon possession. This story is the only healing from a distance in this gospel. Jesus heals both men and women, girls and boys in Mark, and the two passages I have chosen thus repre-

---

10. I use *Mark* as a designation of the anonymous author of the Gospel of Mark. For more on the authorship of Mark, see Adela Yarbro Collins, *Mark: A Commentary*, Hermeneia (Minneapolis: Fortress, 2007), 2–6.

11. Wainwright, *Women Healing/Healing Women*, 102–4.

sent a variety in terms of disability, age, gender, ethnicity, and perhaps also class, as I will argue.

2.2. "Take Your Mat and Go to Your Home": The Man with the Four Helpers (Mark 2:1–12)

The story about the man with the four helpers occurs in all the Synoptic Gospels (Mark 2:1–12 // Matt 9:2–8 // Luke 5:17–26). In Mark, the passage starts with Jesus in a home (ἐν οἴκῳ, 2:1) teaching the word (ὁ λόγος, 2:2).[12] Unable to get through the throng of people gathered to see Jesus, a paralyzed man (παραλυτικός, 2:3) is lowered by four helpers through the ceiling to get to Jesus. Upon seeing their faith, Jesus forgives the man his sins (2:5). This action causes grumbling among a group of scribes who are present because only God can forgive sins. Although they are only thinking "in their hearts" that Jesus is blaspheming, Jesus senses this and confronts them with a question: "Which is easier, to say to the paralytic, 'Your sins are forgiven,' or to say, 'Stand up and take your mat and walk'?" (2:9). Jesus then heals the man in order to show that he does indeed have the authority to forgive sins: "So that you may know that the Son of Man has authority on earth to forgive sins" (2:10).

The character in the story is called "the paralytic" (ὁ παραλυτικός) throughout the story and is thus identified by and through his disability. This is similar to how other disabled characters are labeled in Mark. They are usually just referred to as "a leper" (λεπρός, Mark 1:40), "a deaf (man)" (7:32), or "a blind (man)" and very seldom have a name or a family connection.[13] Within the disability movement, such designations have been criticized and some disability activists argue for the use of *people-first* language.[14] Referring to a "person *with* a disability" rather than "a disabled person" underscores that disability is one characteristic

---

12. Presumably in Peter's home, which seems to be Jesus base at the beginning of Mark (cf. 1:29), Joel Marcus, *Mark 1–8: A New Translation with Introduction and Commentary*, AB 27A (Garden City, NY: Doubleday, 2000), 215.

13. The only named individual with a disability is Bartimeus (Mark 10:46–52). It is perhaps significant that he becomes a follower of Jesus (10:52). It can also be argued that Peter's mother-in-law and Jairus's daughter are named, as they are at least identifiable individuals with a family connection. For the difference in labeling between male and female persons with disabilities in early Christian narrative, see Solevåg, "Hysterical Women?," 317.

14. Goodley, *Disability Studies*, 12–13.

of that individual but not the defining variable.[15] A person should not be reduced to his or her disability, and as part of this case study I make an effort to flesh out other aspects of this character. Yet strictly adhering to people-first language is hardly in itself liberating. I refer to the character in this story and literary figures throughout the book in a variety of ways in an effort to, in Thomson's words, reveal "both the cultural work and the limits of language."[16]

It is clear that the term παραλυτικός refers to some kind of mobility impairment. The man lies on a mat (κράβαττον, 2:9, 11) and is carried by four helpers (αἰρόμενον ὑπὸ τεσσάρων, 2:3). The word παραλυτικός is an adjective constructed from the verb παραλύω, which means "to undo, disable, or enfeeble."[17] Within the New Testament, the term occurs only in Mark and Matthew. In Mark, it is just the man with the four helpers who is referred to as παραλυτικός. In Matthew it appears in a summary statement about Jesus's ministry (4:24), in the parallel version of this story (9:1–8), and in the story about the centurion with the sick servant (8:6). This adjective does not occur in the Greek literary corpus outside of early Christian usage that derives from these Matthean and Markan passages. A more common term for a person with some sort of bodily paralysis is the perfect passive participle of παραλύω, παραλελυμένος. This term occurs in the Hippocratic collection as well as in Aristotle and Galen.[18] Παραλελυμένος is also the term Luke uses in his version of our story, a fact that has been used to support the argument that Luke was a doctor.[19] That claim remains uncertain, but it has been shown that the author of Luke is influenced by medical terminology and had some knowledge of ancient medicine.[20]

Another common Greek term for a person with a mobility impairment is χωλός. This term designates a spectrum of afflictions, from being entirely lame to having a limp or other sort of slight mobility challenge.[21]

---

15. Linton, *Claiming Disability*, 13.

16. Rosemarie Garland-Thomson, "Feminist Disability Studies," *Signs* 30 (2005): 1559.

17. LSJ, s.v. "παραλύω."

18. See, e.g., Hippocrates, *Epid.* 1.26; Aristotle, *Eth. nic.* 1102b; Galen, *Caus. mor.* 7.30.7–31.

19. Wendy Cotter, *The Christ of the Miracle Stories: Portrait through Encounter* (Grand Rapids: Baker Academic, 2010), 89.

20. Annette Weissenrieder, *Images of Illness in the Gospel of Luke: Insights of Ancient Medical Texts* (Tübingen: Mohr Siebeck, 2003), 335, 357.

21. Rose, *Staff of Oedipus*, 13.

In the New Testament, χωλός occurs frequently (e.g., Matt 11:5; 15:30–31; Mark 9:45; Luke 7:22; Acts 3:2). This seems to be the term used about congenital mobility impairments. For example, there are two healing stories in Acts in which a man lame from birth is healed by the apostles. Both these men are designated χωλός (χωλὸς ἐκ κοιλίας μητρός, Acts 3:2; 14:8). Whereas χωλός is a more generic, colloquial term, παραλύω and παράλυσις are medical terms, frequently used in the medical corpus. The medical writer Aretaeus has a chapter on παράλυσις in his book *On the Causes and Symptoms of Chronic Disease*:

> There are six causes of paralytic disorders; for they arise from a wound, a blow, exposure to cold, indigestion, venery, intoxication. But so likewise the vehement affections of the soul, such as astonishment, fear, dejection of spirits, and, in children, frights. Great and unexpected joy has also occasioned paralysis [παρὲλυσε], as, likewise, unrestrained laughter, even unto death. These, indeed, are the primary causes; but the ultimate and vital cause is refrigeration of the innate heat. It suffers from humidity, or dryness, and is more incurable than the other; but if also in connection with a wound, and complete cutting asunder of a nerve, it is incurable. … When the affections are confirmed, they are made manifest by loss of motion, insensibility of heat and cold; and also of plucking the hair, of tickling, and of touching. (*Sign. diut.* 1.7 [Adams])

Aretaeus mentions a variety of causes for paralysis. The Hippocratic paradigm of imbalance and the influence of the surroundings on a person's health can be seen in his mention of sleep, climate, intake of food and drink, emotional stress, and so on.[22]

Why has Mark chosen to call this particular man παραλυτικός? What is different about him, so that the more common χωλός is not used? Perhaps he has symptoms similar to Aretaeus's description? The centurion's sick servant in Matthew is also labeled παραλυτικός. Whatever has afflicted the centurion's slave, it seems to be a recent development and the person is said to be in great pain: "Lord, my servant is lying at home paralyzed [παραλυτικός], in terrible distress" (Matt 8:6). Although it is impossible to say with any certainty, the label given to the man with the four helpers may point toward an impairment that was recently acquired, painful, and perhaps more serious than the general designation χωλός would imply.

---

22. Rose, *Staff of Oedipus*, 13

The fact that he is carried on a stretcher points in this direction. A person labeled χωλός might only have a limp and thus have the ability to walk her- or himself, perhaps with a cane or crutch.

2.2.1. Fleshing Out a Paralytic

In the following I will widen the focus to other aspects of this Markan character. How could a first-century Greco-Roman writer like Mark imagine the social location and behavior of a person with a mobility impairment, one he decides to designate παραλυτικός? I argue that this character is portrayed as resourceful in several respects.

First, Mark presents this character as a man with four helpers. Together with his helpers, he is able to get up on the roof, dismantle it, and be lowered into the room where Jesus is. After he is healed, Jesus says "take your mat and go to your home [εἰς τὸν οἶκόν σου]." In other words, the man has a house to return to.[23] Is he a householder, a master of his own household? One might get closer to an answer by probing the identity of his four helpers. These characters are only referred to by their number (αἰρόμενον ὑπὸ τεσσάρων, Mark 2:3). Joel Marcus refers to these helpers as friends and incorporates this understanding into his translation: "And a paralytic was brought to him, carried by four of his friends." Marcus also seems to assume that the man is poor, noting the BDAG reference to κράββατος as "the poor person's bed."[24] However, κράββατος is a quite general term denoting a piece of furniture to lie on.[25]

In antiquity, friendship was a social relation based on equality. In contrast to familial or patron-client relationships, which were hierarchical, indeed kyriarchical, friendship between free men was based on reciprocity and equality in social position.[26] It seems unlikely, therefore, that friends would carry a fellow free male, as this was typically a task

---

23. Cf. the man by the Bethesda pool (John 5:1–9), who does not seem to have a home; see §3.3.

24. Marcus, *Mark 1–8*, 215–16. The identity of the helpers is vague also in Matthew and Luke's version, and the same assumption by commentators can be found here. See, e.g., David F. Watson, "Luke-Acts," in Melcher, Parsons, Yong, *Bible and Disability*, 310.

25. LSJ, s.v. "κράββατος": "couch, mattress, pallet." BDAG, s.v. "κράββατος": "mattress, pallet, the poor man's bed."

26. David Konstan, *Friendship in the Classical World* (Cambridge: Cambridge University Press, 1997), 90–92.

for slaves. In Greco-Roman society, wealthy people would rely on their slaves for their mobility needs whether they were disabled or not. Litters (*lecticae*) and sedan chairs (*sellae*) carried by slaves were a common sight in ancient cities.[27] The wealthiest had particular slaves set aside for the task of carrying their owners. Called *lecticarii*, these were often the tallest, strongest, and most handsome of their male slaves.[28] Litters, cots, and stretchers were used for transporting the sick and injured as well as people permanently unable to walk.[29] Inscriptional evidence from the Asclepian cult tells of a suppliant, Epidaurus, who came to the temple on a stretcher (κλίνη) and of another one, Diaetus, who was carried by his servants to the temple and was assisted by them while he was there.[30] Plutarch mentions a lame engineer of siege engines, Artemos, who acquired the nickname Periphoretus because he was carried everywhere on a litter (φορεῖων, *Per.* 27.3–4). These examples show that a person with a mobility impairment was not excluded from traveling or holding an occupation as long as they were affluent or important enough to have slaves to carry them. For someone less affluent who had mobility needs, family members might serve such a function.

It seems plausible that the four helpers in Mark's story are presented as slaves or perhaps family members, rather than friends. I argue that the man in our story is constructed by Mark as a householder affluent enough to rely on servants for his transportation needs. Although no family is mentioned, it was quite uncommon for a Jewish man not to be married. As I have argued above, the term παραλυτικός may signal that the impairment was recently acquired rather than congenital. If the figure Mark constructed is an affluent householder, the reader might assume that he has a wife and children, as well as slaves.

---

27. The litter, *lectica* (Greek, φορεῖων or σκιμπόδιον), was carried by up to eight slaves. See William Smith, *A Dictionary of Greek and Roman Antiquities* (London: John Murray, 1914), s.v. "lectica."

28. Smith, *Dictionary of Greek and Roman Antiquities*, s.v. "lectica."

29. Rose, *Staff of Oedipus*, 25. See also Smith, *Dictionary of Greek and Roman Antiquities*, s.v. "lectica": "Shortly after the introduction of these *lecticae* among the Romans, and during the latter period of the Republic, they appear to have been very common, though they were chiefly used in journeys, and in the city of Rome itself only by ladies and invalids."

30. Emma J. Edelstein and Ludwig Edelstein, *Asclepius: Collection and Interpretation of the Testimonies*, 2 vols. (Baltimore: Johns Hopkins University Press, 1998), 1:236–37.

Second, the plot—dismantling the roof and lowering the man down—requires courage and self-confidence. But by whom: the man seeking healing or his helpers? Several commentators seem to assume the latter, implying that the disabled character is rather passive. Marcus notes that the paralytic's "helpless condition is underlined by the fact that he has been carried on a stretcher by four of his friends."[31] The friends, on the other hand, are considered creative and courageous: "The boundary is crossed through a bold move by the paralytic's friends."[32] Adela Yarbro Collins likewise assumes that the scheme is implemented on the helpers' initiative rather than by the man on the mat: "They take extraordinary means to overcome the obstacle posed by the crowd blocking their access to Jesus."[33] Even though the man with the four helpers needs assistance to carry the scheme out, Mark does not indicate whose idea it was to dismantle the roof. It is possible that Mark intended the reader to understand that the disabled man himself was the brain behind the scheme and the one who instructed the four helpers to carry it out. Marcus and Collins fill in gaps in the story with assumptions about the ingenuity of the friends without considering the possibility that the man on the mat had a say in the matter.

By rereading this story with an awareness of the assumptions about people with disabilities as poor and passive, one might discern the contours of a character that seems quite self-confident. He is not afraid to be at the center of attention but lets his helpers take apart someone else's house and takes center stage as he is lowered down in front of Jesus and the crowds. Contrast this bold-faced action to the behavior of the woman suffering from hemorrhages, who sneaks up on Jesus from behind, silently touching the hem of his garment (Mark 5:27). It seems that a certain social status is reflected in this spectacular performance. In fact, the paralytic's behavior is similar to Jairus's. Both these men confront Jesus with their petitions in front of a large crowd (Mark 5:21). Jairus is confident about addressing Jesus because of his status in the community as a synagogue leader. Similarly, the man with the four helpers seems confident enough about his standing in the community to face the crowds and disturb Jesus's preaching.

Third, the roof scheme shows creativity and ingenuity. Public spaces have often been designed with a normate bias, thus limiting disabled

---

31. Marcus, *Mark 1–8*, 220.
32. Marcus, *Mark 1–8*, 220.
33. Collins, *Mark*, 184–85.

people's access to these spaces.[34] People with disabilities thus often need to think outside the box in order to maneuver the physical world. The invention and production of prosthetics is one example of this creativity. Although we know that prosthetics were crafted and used in antiquity, they are not mentioned at all in the Hippocratic corpus, and very seldom in the medical literature overall. Rose argues that the reason for this is that prosthetics were individually crafted items, not medically prescribed implements.[35] Hence, it may well have been the lame man himself that skillfully crafted his own access to the place he wanted to be.

I suggest, then, that the man we meet in Mark 2:1–11 is presented as a quite resourceful person. Having a home and (at least) four servants, he is portrayed as somewhat affluent. We do not know anything about his family, but the impairment described would not exclude him from having a wife and children, nor from having a profession. His determination and audacity in getting to Jesus suggests that he has some respect and authority in the community. Finally, he is resourceful in engineering his own access to a seemingly inaccessible space. This is perhaps a novel picture of the man with the four helpers in Mark. I think it is important to read narratives with disabled characters without making the assumption that all such characters in the New Testament are presented in the same way— as belonging to the social category of the destitutely poor.[36] As I hope to show in this book, reading with an intersectional lens reveals a much more complex picture. The disabled body is negotiated in a number of ways in early Christian texts.

2.2.2. Disability and Sin

Since the reader has already encountered several healing stories by the time she gets to Mark 2:1, the expectation after the paralytic is lowered through the ceiling is that Jesus will proceed to heal him. He does not. He forgives the man his sins—to the provocation of the scribes (Mark 2:7). Why does Jesus forgive the man his sins? Does the Markan Jesus connect

---

34. Accessibility is one on the guiding principles of the United Nations Convention on the Rights of Persons with Disabilities; see article 9: www.un.org/development/desa/disabilities/convention-on-the-rights-of-persons-with-disabilities.html.

35. Rose, *Staff of Oedipus*, 26.

36. As argued by Staffan Bengtsson, "The Two-Sided Coin: Disability, Normalcy and Social Categorization in the New Testament," *SJDR* 18 (2016): 1–11.

disability and sin? Is the man disabled because he has sinned, according to this story? The narrator does not make the connection clear. The man has not asked for forgiveness (note, by the way, that neither has he asked for healing). Is he perceived as particularly sinful, compared to the other people gathered, due to his condition? Sin was associated with sickness in first-century Palestine and could thus be viewed as an obstacle to healing.[37] This sentiment can be seen in John 9:2, when the disciples ask Jesus, "Rabbi, who sinned, this man or his parents, that he was born blind?" If this is the underlying sentiment in Mark, Jesus first needs to forgive him his sins in order to be able to heal him. It is possible that Mark leans in this direction, since only the paralytic is forgiven his sins, not the helpers (5:5). However, this may also be explained by the fact that the paralytic is a more central figure in the story.

Alternatively, Mark may not be positing a causal link between Jesus's forgiveness of sins and his healing action.[38] The fact that the Markan Jesus gives priority to forgive the man his sins before he heals him may instead be interpreted as a sign that Jesus is not primarily interested in this person as a paralytic but sees him, to adopt the language of twentieth-century disability activism, from a people-first perspective. When Jesus addresses the man, he calls him "child" (τέκνον, 2:5). Thus, Jesus frames him as first and foremost a child of God, or perhaps, as Collins suggests, a pupil in a sage-student relationship.[39] As a human being, this person with a mobility impairment is under the human condition of sin—a condition everyone needs to repent from (Mark 1:15). When Jesus forgives the man his sins, the reader may understand this as a sign of the inbreaking of the kingdom of God: the forgiveness of sins is an act that everyone who encounters Jesus may seek.

How about the reverse side of the sin/disability connection? Candida Moss argues that "bodily wholeness and faith in Jesus are intimately connected" in Mark. She posits that according to the Markan Jesus, "your faith makes you well."[40] A closer look might reveal some nuances to this picture. Among the fourteen healing stories in Mark, Jesus only remarks on the faith of two characters that are healed: the woman with the flow of blood (5:25–34) and the blind Bartimeus (10:46–52). Jesus says to both of

---

37. Marcus, *Mark 1–8*, 221.
38. Marcus, *Mark 1–8*, 221.
39. Collins, *Mark*, 185.
40. Moss, "Mark and Matthew," 284.

them: "Your faith has made you well" (ἡ πίστις σου σέσωκέν σε, 5:34; 10:52).
More often, however, it is a helper or family member whose faith is being
tested or commented upon by the narrator (e.g., the four helpers of the
paralyzed man in 2:5, the father Jairus in 5:23, 36, the Syro-Phoenician
mother in 7:29, and the father of the demon-possessed boy in 9:17–24).[41]
Moss herself suggests that the seeming connection between disability and
sin in Mark is disrupted in the saying on autoamputation in 9:42–48. The
saying "treats disability not as the consequence of sin but as its preventa-
tive" and also "admits that disabled bodies are accepted in the kingdom of
God."[42] These examples show that even within the Gospel of Mark, there
are multiple ways of configuring disability and sin. The various connections between sin and disability I have traced so far show that the notion of
a premodern moral model that unambiguously connects disability and sin
is too simple (see §1.3). However, the fact that sin becomes a topic in this
passage also underscores Mitchell and Snyder's point that disabled bodies
provoke efforts at meaning-making and that perceived deviance requires
an explanation. As I will come back to in the conclusion to this chapter,
this healing story serves as a narrative prosthesis, resolving "a deviance
marked as improper to a social context."[43]

2.3. A Demon-Possessed Girl and Her Persuasive Mother (Mark 7:24–30)

I now move on to explore another healing narrative in Mark, the story
about the Syro-Phoenician woman and her demon-possessed daughter
(Mark 7:24–30). In this passage a woman approaches Jesus and pleads for
the healing of her little daughter. An unusual characteristic of this healing
narrative is that the person healed, the daughter, is quite peripheral in the
narration.[44] The girl is the topic of Jesus and the woman's conversation, but
Jesus never meets her, and there is no scene in which she is present. She is

---

41. On the connection between faith and healing, see Anna Rebecca Solevåg,
"'Leap, Ye, Lame for Joy': The Dynamics of Disability in Conversion," in *The Complexity of Conversion*, ed. Valerie Nicolet Anderson and Marianne Bjelland Kartzow (Sheffield: Sheffield Phoenix, forthcoming).

42. Moss, "Mark and Matthew," 294.

43. Mitchell and Snyder, *Narrative Prosthesis*, 53.

44. Sharon H. Ringe, "A Gentile Woman's Story, Revisited: Rereading Mark 7.24–
31a," in *A Feminist Companion to Mark*, ed. Amy-Jill Levine with Marianne Blickenstaff (London: Sheffield Academic, 2001), 87.

also very quiet—although the woman speaks, the daughter does not. This story is the only healing from a distance that occurs in Mark.[45]

Jesus has just traveled from the Jewish region of Galilee and has entered "the region of Tyre" (7:24). This was a rural area where both Jews and Syro-Phoenicians resided, a borderland between the fully Jewish Galilee to the south and the fully Hellenized city of Tyre to the north. Tyre was a port city and the capital of the Roman province of Syria. In this borderland space, a woman seeks out Jesus in a private home and throws herself at his feet. Like the man with the four helpers, she enters a house and demands Jesus's attention. Whereas the man with his helpers seems to rely on spectacle rather than speech, the woman employs both speech and bodily gestures.[46] The man does not seem to humble himself before Jesus, nor does he explicitly ask—much less plead—for healing. The woman, on the other hand, throws herself at the feet of Jesus, a typical gesture of kyriarchal submission, and calls him master (κύριε, 7:28). The woman wants healing for her daughter, and she begs Jesus for it.

The daughter's affliction is first called an "unclean spirit" (πνεῦμα ἀκάθαρτον, 7:25) and is subsequently referred to as "the demon" (τὸ δαιμόνιον, 7:26, 29, 30). As noted in the introduction, the belief that demon possession could cause illness and disability was widespread in Jewish as well as other ancient Mediterranean cultures (see §1.4). The exchange between the woman and Jesus clearly invokes categories of gender, ethnicity, and class.[47] The woman is doubly designated as both Greek and Syro-Phoenician (ἦν Ἑλληνίς Συροφοινίκισσα τῷ γένει, 7:26). This is the only occurrence in Mark of the label Ἑλληνίς, and it is the first time the narrator has pointed out the ethnicity of a character. Jesus has traveled outside of Jewish territory also earlier in Mark. In 5:1–20 he goes to "the country of the Gerasenes" (5:1), probably the city of Gerasa, one of the

---

45. As Harrocks has noted, there are similarities, including healing from a distance, with the officer in Capernaum. This passage occurs in the three other gospels but not in Mark (Matt 8:5–13 // Luke 7:1–10 // John 4:46–53). See Rebecca Harrocks, "Jesus' Gentile Healings: The Absence of Bodily Contact and the Requirement of Faith," in *The Body in Biblical, Christian, and Jewish Texts*, ed. Joan E. Taylor (London: Bloomsbury, 2015).

46. For the significance of gestures and bodily *habitus* in this story, see Jennifer A. Glancy, "Jesus, the Syrophoenician Woman and Other First Century Bodies," *BibInt* 18 (2010).

47. Glancy, "Jesus, the Syrophoenician Woman," 350–51.

Hellenistic Decapolis cities east of Galilee.[48] Interestingly, in that story, too, he interacts with a person possessed by an unclean spirit. Mark possibly suggests a connection between ethnicity and demon possession, as I will discuss below.

The ethnic designation as Greek probably signals that the woman belonged to the culturally privileged class of Greek-speaking city-dwellers in Tyre.[49] Thus, some scholars argue that she is portrayed as being of higher status, as more affluent and politically connected than Jesus, who is a wandering Jewish preacher whose closest friends are fishermen.[50] However, in a Jewish context, the term Ἑλληνίς, Greek, could also designate religious status. According to several commentators of this passage, it served a similar function as the term τὰ ἔθνη, "the nations," as a religious designation for gentiles as opposed to Jews.[51] As we have no other information about this family, such as who else it consists of apart from the mother and daughter, it is difficult to determine exactly what the woman's social position is relative to that of Jesus.[52] Is she portrayed as rich and well connected, or is she labeled by Mark as a (religiously) inferior outsider? Sharon H. Ringe embodies this paradox in her own scholarly development. In an essay from the 1980s she argued that the woman was a poor widow, while in a recent essay she vouches for the woman's affluent status.[53]

By subjugating herself on the ground and calling him master, the Syro-Phoenician woman shows Jesus deference in alignment with kyriarchal codes of behavior, in which women were subordinated to men who were free and were thus (in contrast to slaves) masters over their own bodies and often also of their own households. Jennifer A. Glancy has pointed out that lowering oneself before another person was the most common visual marker for submission to superior power and authority in Roman antiquity.[54] She regards the encounter between Jesus and the Syro-Phoenician woman as a "corporal performance of social identity."[55] It is one of

---

48. Collins, *Mark*, 266–67.

49. Ringe, "Gentile Woman's Story," 86.

50. According to Mark, the first four disciples Jesus calls are fishermen: Simon (Peter), his brother Andrew, and the brothers James and John Zebedee (Mark 1:16–19).

51. Collins, *Mark*, 364; Marcus, *Mark 1–8*, 462.

52. For a more thorough discussion on the intersectional dimensions of this mother-daughter family, see Solevåg, "Listening for the Voices."

53. Ringe, "Gentile Woman's Story, Revisited," 91 n. 25

54. Glancy, "Jesus, the Syrophoenician Woman," 353.

55. Glancy, "Jesus, the Syrophoenician Woman," 344.

the basic insights of intersectionality that power and status are not always clear-cut and that many factors mutually influence each other.[56] Identities are complex, and in encounters between people, identity and status are negotiated. The woman's ambivalent position is underscored by her actions: she falls at his feet, but when Jesus presents her with a riddle, she is not afraid to talk back (7:27–28). She enters into discussion with him as if he was her equal, and she wins the argument.

2.3.1. A Distant Daughter

As already noted, the girl is not present at the encounter between Jesus and the woman, but at home. This recalls the story of Jairus's daughter from Mark 5:21–43, where Jairus approaches Jesus in public while the sick daughter is at home. There are other similarities between these stories as well. In both, a parent seeks out Jesus and pleas for a child who is ill, throwing her- or himself to the ground in the process. Both girls are referred to as θυγάτριον, the diminutive of θυγάτηρ, daughter. Jairus's daughter is twelve, and we may assume that the Syro-Phoenician girl is no older. She is later referred to as παιδίον, which means little or young child.[57] The term would not refer to a girl after she had entered puberty and was thus considered of marriageable age, usually between the age of twelve and fourteen.[58] Notwithstanding these similarities between Jairus's daughter and our story, they develop quite differently. Jesus comes home with Jairus, and the story ends with a very moving scene in which he takes the daughter's hand, talks to her, and raises her in the presence of her parents (5:41–42). In contrast, Jesus seems unwilling to help the Syro-Phoenician girl, and although he finally heals her, there is no meeting between the two. Glancy puts the difference succinctly: "Jesus responds positively to one petitioner. He recoils from the other."[59] The difference between these two encounters serves as a reminder of the importance of an intersectional perspective on disability. Not all ill or disabled people in the gospels' healing stories are the same. Rebecca Harrocks has observed that Jesus does not touch

---

56. Kartzow, *Destabilizing the Margins*, 10.

57. LSJ, s.v. "παιδίον."

58. Cornelia B. Horn and J. W. Martens, *"Let the Little Children Come to Me":
Childhood and Children in Early Christianity* (Washington, DC: Catholic University of America Press, 2009), 18.

59. Glancy, "Jesus, the Syrophoenician Woman," 358.

any non-Jews in the healing stories in the Synoptics.[60] While healings of Jews may be with or without touch, there are no healings of non-Jews in which touch is involved. Thus the distance between healer and healed in this story may have to do with ethnicity.

2.3.2. Scavenging Dogs or Cute Puppies?

The dog metaphor that Jesus uses has puzzled many readers of this passage. According to Jesus, there are some, the children, who need to be prioritized when food is limited, and there are others, the dogs, who do not deserve to be fed (Mark 7:27). The children are usually understood to be a metaphor for the Jews and the dogs a metaphor of the non-Jewish population in the area, the gentiles.[61] This is the interpretation Matthew inserts explicitly into his version of the story, in which Jesus says: "I was sent only to the lost sheep of the house of Israel" (15:24).

The term *dog* was used metaphorically as a pejorative epithet in Greco-Roman as well as Jewish culture.[62] In antiquity, dogs were bred and reared for hunting, as guard and shepherd dogs, and as pets.[63] Loose dogs roaming the streets and scavenging the gutters for food must have been a common sight in ancient cities. Dogs were associated with voracious appetites, were regarded as scavengers, and were perceived to defile the sacred, arouse fear, and behave shamelessly. According to Mark D. Nanos, the sentiment was that dogs would "parade about naked, defecate, conduct sexual behavior, and generally carry on without regard for human conventions of modesty and prudence."[64] When used about women, the epithet *dog* denoted shamelessness and sexual immodesty in particular.[65] According to Hesiod's creation myth, Pandora had a mind like a bitch (κύνεόν τε

---

60. Harrocks, "Jesus's Gentile Healings," 83–84.

61. Collins, *Mark*, 366; Marcus, *Mark 1–8*, 464.

62. Mark D. Nanos, "Paul's Reversal of Jews Calling Gentiles 'Dogs' (Phillipians 3:2): 1600 Years of an Ideological Tale Wagging an Exegetical Dog?," *BibInt* 17 (2009); Alan H. Cadwallader, "When a Woman Is a Dog: Ancient and Modern Ethology Meet the Syrophoenician Women," *BCT* 1.4 (2005); Ringe, "Gentile Woman's Story," 90.

63. Douglas Brewer, Terence Clark, and Adrian Philipps, *Dogs in Antiquity: Anubis to Cerberus; The Origins of the Domestic Dog* (Warminster: Aris and Philipps, 2001), 87–94. For dogs as pets for children, see Keith Bradley, "The Sentimental Education of the Roman Child: The Role of Pet Keeping," *Latomus* 57 (1998): 523–57.

64. Nanos, "Paul's Reversal of Jews Calling Gentiles 'Dogs,'" 458–59.

65. LSJ, s.v. "κύων." See also Cadwallader, "When a Woman Is a Dog," 35.2.

νόον, *Op.* 67).[66] Aristophanes claimed that both women and dogs were ill-tempered (γυνή καὶ κύων ἀκράχολος, *Frag.* 594).

Nevertheless, similarity to dogs could also be used to describe positive traits, for example, as tenacity and loyalty in people who functioned as guardians.[67] Moreover, dogs were often the pets of children, and affectionate bonds between dogs and children are described in literature and portrayed in images from antiquity.[68] A combination of good and bad characteristics is apparent in the description of doglike traits in Polemon's *Physiognomy*: "The dog is tame, loyal, patient, ready to help, protective, desirous, alert to what should be defended, cheating when necessary, courageous at home and submissive away from home, loathing the stranger, covetous, miserly, stubborn, prattling, gluttonous, dirty, bad-natured, lacking in modesty, and mundane."[69]

Dogs were associated with doctors in general and Asclepius in particular.[70] In the iconography of the Asclepian cult, the healing god was usually depicted with snakes, but also with dogs.[71] In inscriptions at Asclepian sanctuaries, dogs are accredited for healing supplicants.[72] Ingvild Sælid Gilhus notes that dogs as well as pigs are associated with demons in the gospels.[73] Revelation draws on the derogatory connotations of κύων: "Outside are the dogs and sorcerers [οἱ κύνες καὶ οἱ φάρμακοι] and fornicators and murderers and idolaters, and everyone who loves and practices falsehood" (Rev 22:15). Note that dogs and sorcerers (φάρμακοι) are here mention in the same quotation, perhaps alluding to the link between dogs and various healing practices.

---

66. For a discussion of the use of the label "dog" to denote female immodesty, see Solevåg, *Birthing Salvation*, 45, 192–94.

67. Nanos, "Paul's Reversal of Jews Calling Gentiles 'Dogs,'" 457.

68. Bradley, "Sentimental Education of the Roman Child"; Elaine M. Wainwright, "Of Dogs and Women: Ethology and Gender in Ancient Healing; The Canaanite Woman's Story—Matt 15:21–28," in *Miracles Revisited: New Testament Miracle Stories and Their Concepts of Reality*, ed. Stefan Alkier and Annette Weissenrieder (Berlin: de Gruyter, 2013), 64–65.

69. Swain, *Seeing the Face, Seeing the Soul*, 385.

70. Wainwright, "Of Dogs and Women," 67.

71. Edelstein and Edelstein, *Asclepius*, 1:345, 362.

72. Edelstein and Edelstein, *Asclepius*, 1:233–34. See also Nutton, *Ancient Medicine*, 110; Ingvild Sælid Gilhus, *Animals, Gods and Humans: Changing Attitudes to Animals in Greek, Roman and Early Christian Ideas* (London: Routledge, 2006), 109.

73. Gilhus, *Animals, Gods and Humans*, 170.

2.3.3. Disability and Ethnicity as Animality

The dog-riddle adds a metaphorical layer of meaning to the conversation. The encounter is framed not only as one between two individuals but also as one between two groups. Jesus insinuates that her request is for one less worthy group, the dogs, to receive priority before a more deserving group, the children. The healing request has become a discussion about identity, inclusion, and power. Dong Hyeon Jeong suggests that "colonial neurosis" lies behind Jesus's animalizing retort to the woman's request.[74] According to Gerd Theissen, the Syro-Phoenician population, residing in the cities, was economically better off than the rural Jewish population of the area. He suggests that the Hellenized city-dwellers may often have taken bread out of the mouths of the Jews "when they used their financial means to buy up the grain supply in the countryside."[75] Jesus is insinuating that the woman and her daughter are dogs and that they are asking for something that is not theirs. The mother's answer shifts Jesus's zero-sum argument. She accepts the invective, but she also turns it around when she says that "even the dogs [τὰ κυνάρια] under the table eat the children's crumbs" (7:28). Bread, which is the food the dogs and the children are fighting over in the riddle, was in fact the most common feed for domesticated dogs in antiquity.[76]

Mark uses the diminutive of κύων, κυνάριον, in this passage. Although some argue that Mark uses diminutives interchangeably with the regular form, I suggest that the diminutive serves a purpose in the story.[77] Κυνάριον connects with the two other diminutives in the story, θυγάτριον and παιδίον (perhaps even δαιμόνιον, which grammatically is a diminutive). All of these diminutives refer to the Syro-Phoenician daughter. Thus, they seem to denote age as well as size and allow for the reading of κυνάριον as "puppy." The woman reduces the harshness of the metaphor by using the

---

74. Dong Hyeon Jeong, "The Animal Masks of the Syrophoenician Woman and the Markan Jesus: Reading Mark 7:24–30 through a Postcolonial Animality Lens" (paper presented at the Society of Biblical Literature Annual Meeting, Boston, 20 November 2017), 3.

75. Gerd Theissen, *The Gospels in Context: Social and Political History in the Synoptic Tradition* (London: T&T Clark, 2004), 79. See also Ringe, "Gentile Woman's Story," 84–86.

76. Brewer, Clark, and Philipps, *Dogs in Antiquity*, 96.

77. See, e.g., Collins, *Mark*, 367.

diminutive to alter the metaphorical meaning of the dog image. From the image of scavenger dogs that need to be kept at bay to protect the children and their food, she creates another scenario of a well-functioning symbiosis between children and dogs or puppies: children eat sloppily, but the dogs pick up whatever they drop. Or perhaps she even hints at an affectionate relationship, in which children slip the puppies under the table their leftover food. All these images are within the range of associations that could be invoked with reference to dogs in antiquity.

Theissen's suggestion is a feasible historical background for the saying. The political and economic situation gave way to a sentiment that Syro-Phoenicians were like dogs who stole bread from the children, the Jews. However, there may be another aspect to the riddle. I suggest that the daughter's illness is part of what gives meaning to the metaphor. The story about the Syro-Phoenician mother and daughter can be read in light of Mitchell and Snyder's theory of narrative prosthesis. Mitchell and Snyder point to the use of physiognomic reasoning in literature.[78] The ancient notion of physiognomy connected certain bodily features with particular moral traits using both ethnographic and zoological markers (see §1.7). In this story the Syro-Phoenician daughter's disability is used metaphorically, by combining the terms *dog*, *Syro-Phoenician*, and *demon-possessed*.

As already noted, the daughter has no voice in this story. She never speaks or makes a sound. In the three other stories about the demon-possessed in Mark, the demon screams. The possessed man in the temple screams at Jesus and reveals that he knows who Jesus is (1:26). The Gerasene demoniac similarly screams at Jesus with a loud voice (5:6–10). According to Mark, this man needed to be restrained with chains, as he was violent and would injure himself (5:4–5). Finally, in 9:14–29, Jesus heals a boy possessed by a "spirit of muteness" (πνεῦμα ἄλαλον, 9:17). The exorcism of this boy is quite violent: the boy screams and convulses and afterward lies lifeless on the ground, seemingly dead (9:26). These descriptions of the speech patterns and behavior of demon-possessed people show that a certain kind of erratic and violent behavior could categorize a person as demon-possessed. The dog metaphor employed in 7:24 reverberates with these characteristics of demon possession. The nonverbal orality on either side of the spectrum of socially accepted speech, that is, either irrational screaming or mute silence; the erratic behavior; and

---

78. Mitchell and Snyder, *Narrative Prosthesis*, 60.

the possible need for chaining all link the demon-possessed with animal characteristics. As already noted, muteness and deafness were connected with mental incapacity and demon possession in antiquity (see §1.4). Both demon possession and madness are illnesses that are used as pejorative tropes in rhetorical discourse, a feature of disability rhetoric that will be further explored in chapter 5.

In the story about the Syro-Phoenician girl, the disabled girl is used for her representational value. The textual interest is not in her but in the social meaning that is ascribed to her body. Both disability and ethnicity are animalized and used to other the girl and her mother. The daughter's doglike demon possession is seen as a characteristic of the mother and daughter's ethnic group. Her nonconforming body reveals hidden truths that point beyond herself. She represents the Syro-Phoenicians, who must be healed from their insanity and given the life-giving crumbs (or words) of Jesus. But in pointing beyond herself, the Syro-Phoenician girl also dissolves, both as a character and as a subject.

2.4. Conclusion: Mark's Literary Dependency on Disability

According to Mitchell and Snyder, narrative prosthesis can work either as a *narrative element* that resolves the problem of deviance or as a *metaphorical device*, drawing on physiognomic reasoning. The two healing stories presented follow a prosthetic narrative scheme of naming a deviance, demanding an explanation, homing in on the deviant character, and finally resolving the problem. In both stories, Jesus's healing resolves the problem of a nonnormative body. The second trajectory of Mitchell and Snyder's theory, disability as a metaphorical device, operates quite differently in the two stories. I argued that the discussion on the forgiveness of sin that follows the healing of the lame man is an example of this: the efforts at meaning-making and moralizing that disability often provokes in narrative. The metaphorical move here is from outer to inner, from a macro- to a microlevel, which may be called a *physiognomic* move. The man's disability provokes a discussion about his sinfulness, although it is contested exactly what the connection is. In the other story, however, the metaphorical aspect to the girl's disability projects beyond the individual disabled character to represent an entire ethnic group. Here the metaphorical move is from a macro- to a metalevel, which may be called a *symbolic* move. These nuances in the literary use of disability are not differentiated in Mitchell and Snyder's label *narrative prosthesis*, although they note these various uses. The various ways in which metaphorical meaning is ascribed to disabled characters will be part of the discussion in the following chapters. Mitchell and Snyder developed their theory of narrative prosthesis particularly for studies of narrative literary works (and also film), but the multidirectional metaphorical aspect of narrative prosthesis (the physiognomic and the symbolic moves) is not tied to a narrative genre. As I will discuss in chapters 5 and 6, symbolic as well as physiognomic moves are deployed in disability discourse also in rhetorical texts.

The use of disability as a narrative element is not only something that can be recognized in each individual healing narrative in Mark, it is quite important to the structure of this gospel overall. As noted earlier, the healing of the paralyzed man is the culmination of a series of healing stories at the beginning of Mark. Given the way Mark has chosen to construct his narrative, without any birth or childhood narratives, more hinges on the healing stories in the beginning of the Gospel for Mark than for the other gospel writers. Throughout Mark 1 this series of events connected to healing leads to Jesus's escalating fame. It is the fame caused by Jesus's healing activity that is the reason for the enormous crowd at the beginning of Mark 2. In the first chapter, the reader hardly hears a word of Jesus's preaching, his εὐαγγέλιον (1:1), except its initial proclamation in 1:15: "The time is fulfilled, and the kingdom of God has come near; repent, and believe in the good news." Mark does not reveal what Jesus teaches in the synagogue, only the mode—with authority (ὡς ἐξουσίαν ἔχων, 1:22). The demon-possessed man disturbs his teaching and the exorcism takes center stage. When the demon-possessed man starts to scream at Jesus, Jesus rebukes him (ἐπιτιμάω, 1:25), and everyone agrees that his is a new teaching with authority (διδαχὴ καινὴ κατ᾽ ἐξουσίαν, 1:27). Similarly, in the story about the paralytic, Jesus is in a house preaching the word to the crowd gathered, but nothing is said about the content of his preaching. Again, he is interrupted, this time by the man with the four helpers.[79] In fact, when Jesus says to the scribes that the Son of Man has power on earth to forgive sins (ἐξουσία, 2:10), this is the first preaching we hear that expands on the content of Jesus's good news. However, this proclamation about Jesus's power resonates with the powerful acts we have already seen through the four healing miracles. Jesus explicitly points out that this is

---

79. As Collins also notes (*Mark*, 184).

the reason he performs the healing of the paralytic: to prove that he has power, even the godly power to forgive sins.

Several commentators have observed that Mark links Jesus's authority closely to his healing ability. Mary Ann Tolbert remarks that Jesus's ability to heal the paralytic illustrates his authority to forgive sins: "Jesus's teaching is identified with his actions; his words and his deeds are one."[80] Similarly, Tat-siong Benny Liew notes how Mark omits the content of Jesus teaching in favor of healing at the beginning of Mark and argues that this links Jesus's authority inseparably to his healing power.[81] According to Liew, it is Jesus's ability to heal and his command over unclean spirits that is his authority.[82] This may also explain why demon possession is the most common disability in Mark. No other disability is so clearly connected to power. Theissen takes such observations about the link between healing and authority in Mark further by showing how fundamental it is for the structure of the gospel. He argues that the miracle motifs in Matthew and Luke are less important for the structure of the gospels because these gospel writers have added a biographical arc that carries some of the weight of the narrative.[83] In Matthew and Luke, the birth narratives support the christological claim, but in Mark the weight rests on the miracle stories strategically positioned at the beginning of the gospel.

When Mark deploys disabled characters as a narrative prosthesis to support his christological claim, he not only presents Jesus in a specific way—as first and foremost a powerful healer—but he also constructs and presents disabled characters. Often, commentators fail to notice this. Warren Carter calls this an invisibilizing tendency and argues that contemporary interpreters often "screen out" the disabled bodies in the gospel texts in favor of symbolic and spiritualized readings.[84] Without developed models to analyze the purpose and function of disability, readers tend to compartmentalize impairment as an isolated and individual condition of

---

80. Mary Ann Tolbert, *Sowing the Gospel: Mark's World in Literary-Historical Perspective* (Minneapolis: Fortress, 1989), 136.

81. Tat-siong Benny Liew, *Politics of Parousia: Reading Mark Inter(con)textually* (Leiden: Brill, 1999), 105.

82. Liew, *Politics of Parousia*, 105.

83. Gerd Theissen, *The Miracle Stories of the Early Christian Tradition* (Edinburgh: T&T Clark, 1983), 213, 21–22.

84. Carter, "'Blind, Lame and Paralyzed,'" 130.

existence.[85] Mitchell and Snyder's theory is helpful in order to understand Mark's deployment of disabled characters as an example of a wider literary phenomenon: how literary discourse depends on disability as a narrative prosthesis.[86] Mark hinges Jesus's claim to authority almost exclusively on the healing miracles at the beginning of his gospel. In other words, Mark is completely dependent on disabled characters to get his overarching message across. Without any deaf, blind, lame, leprous, and possessed people to heal, Jesus's special character, in fact, his divinity, is not revealed at all. Disability is the crutch the narrative needs in order to show that God is great.

85. Mitchell and Snyder, *Narrative Prosthesis*, 51.
86. Mitchell and Snyder, *Narrative Prosthesis*, 51.

3
JOHN AND THE SYMBOLIC SIGNIFICANCE OF DISABILITY

3.1. Introduction: Illness as Metaphor

In this chapter I continue to explore early Christian healing narratives by turning to the healing stories in the Gospel of John. There are some noteworthy differences from Mark. First, John has only three healing stories in his gospel: the healing of the royal official's son (4:46–54), the man with a "weakness" (ἀσθένεια) at the Bethesda pool (5:1–15), and the man born blind (9:1–41). Second, a symbolic level of meaning is always close at hand in John, and so also in the healing narratives. Finally, I will also argue that John has a different view on the etiology of illness, drawing more on professionalized understandings of medicine.

As discussed in the previous chapter, a central point in Mitchell and Snyder's theory of narrative prosthesis is that literary representations of disability often use disabled bodies to invoke symbolic meanings. Narratives often posit a physiognomic relationship between the internal and the external body in which "either the 'deviant' body deforms subjectivity or 'deviant' subjectivity violently erupts upon the surface of its bodily container."[1]

Sontag has explored the use of metaphors in relation to illness. She reveals how different illnesses invoke different metaphorical associations and thus shape cultural discourse. Her arguments complement Mitchell and Snyder when she she points out how the use of metaphors stigmatizes illnesses and those who experience them in particular ways.[2] She has shown how certain illnesses and their metaphors become dominant at certain points in history and how they change over time. For example,

---

1. Mitchell and Snyder, *Narrative Prosthesis*, 58.
2. Susan Sontag, *Illness as Metaphor and Aids and Its Metaphors* (London: Penguin Books, 2002), 91–101.

literary references to tuberculosis proliferated in the nineteenth and early twentieth century. The symbolic meanings associated with consumption, as it was called, invoked innocence, youth, romance, and passion, and death from tuberculosis was often described as painless and passive.[3] Sontag compares the Victorian preoccupation with tuberculosis with the place cancer held in the second half of the twentieth century, and to some extent still does. The language used to describe cancer draws on military metaphors, such as invasion, attack, and siege, as well as the notion of demonic possession (malignant, benign).[4] Moreover, cancer talk also invokes economic catastrophe with terms like unregulated, abnormal, and incoherent growth. The tumor is often described as out of control: cancer cells are "cells that have shed the mechanism which 'restrain' growth."[5]

Sontag also shows that illness imagery is invoked in political polemic by equating disease with societal disorder. She warns about the dangers of such politicized illness discourse, pointing out that the concept of disease is never innocent: "The use of cancer in political discourse encourages fatalism and justifies 'severe' measures—as well as strongly reinforcing the widespread notion that disease is necessarily fatal."[6] Sontag detected the same oscillation between the personal and the societal in the discourse concerning HIV in the 1980s.[7] AIDS was described as a plague invading both the individual body and global society, and the rhetoric clearly encompassed racist, xenophobic, and homophobic fears: "AIDS seems to foster ominous fantasies about a disease that is a marker of both individual and social vulnerabilities. The virus invades the body; the disease … is described as invading the whole society."[8]

I find Sontag's perspectives useful for a reading of illness and disability in the Gospel of John. There are certain similarities between the way John adds a layer of metaphorical meaning to his healing narratives and the patterns Sontag has detected in modern illness discourse. Sontag's warning that illness metaphors are never innocent is useful also for biblical scholarship. As I will show, modern interpreters of John have had a tendency to buy into John's symbolic universe wholesale, without realizing the implications

---

3. Sontag, *Illness as Metaphor*, 12–26.
4. Sontag, *Illness as Metaphor*, esp. 65–70.
5. Sontag, *Illness as Metaphor*, 64.
6. Sontag, *Illness as Metaphor*, 84.
7. Sontag, *Illness as Metaphor*, 130–50.
8. Sontag, *Illness as Metaphor*, 151.

it may have for understandings of disability and the danger of stigmatizing people with disabilities in the process.

3.1.1. John and the Symbolic

In the following, I examine each of John's three healing stories.[9] Whereas the first seems to be about a short-term illness, the two other stories concern "long-term, non-urgent physical or sensory impairment," what might today be called disabilities.[10] I choose to include the first for several reasons. First, the healing of the royal official's son is interesting because it is the only one of John's healings that has a synoptic parallel. Second, it is included because this story, together with the two other healing stories, gives an understanding of the terms for and ideas about illness and disability that occur in the Fourth Gospel. Finally, the three narratives are connected in John's literary logic. They constitute three of the seven signs that John presents in his Book of Signs, which is the first main part of his gospel.[11] John calls Jesus's miracles σημεῖα, "signs."[12] They signify that Jesus is sent from the Father, from God. The signs have a dubious status in John, as simultaneously embellished and diminished: believers are rebuked for depending on signs (e.g., 4:48; 6:26; 20:29), but at the same time, Jesus's signs lead people to believe in him (e.g., 2:11; 4:53; 12:11; 20:30–31) and confirm his identity (e.g., 7:31; 9:16; 10:41–42).[13] In contrast to the Synoptics, Jesus does not perform any exorcisms in John. Demon possession is only mentioned in some instances where Jesus himself is accused of being possessed (see §5.2). John's universe is highly dualistic. Throughout the gospel, polar opposites are presented as value-laden sets of contrasts: light/darkness, life/death, good/evil, from above/from below, heaven/earth, spirit/flesh, and so on.[14] In this chapter, I look at the vocabulary that is used for illness, disability, and healing in the three stories in John,

---

9. I use *John* as a designation of the anonymous author of the Gospel of John. For the composition of John, see Paul N. Anderson, *The Riddles of the Fourth Gospel: An Introduction to John* (Minneapolis: Fortress, 2011), 96–114.

10. Gosbell, *"The Poor, the Crippled, the Blind, and the Lame,"* 278.

11. Anderson, *Riddles of the Fourth Gospel*, 9–11.

12. Koosed and Schumm, "Out of the Darkness," 79.

13. Anderson, *Riddles of the Fourth Gospel*, 31–32.

14. Anderson, *Riddles of the Fourth Gospel*, 36–37.

and I explore the symbolic layer of meaning that John incorporates into the narrative.

John frequently refers to "the Jews" (οἱ Ἰουδαῖοι) as adversaries of Jesus. This group is hard to distinguish from the Pharisees (see, e.g., John 9:13–34), as the terms seem to be used interchangeably. The reception history of this usage has undergirded anti-Semitism. I use quotes ("the Jews") to signal that this group is John's narrative construct.[15]

3.2. The Royal Official's Son (John 4:46–54)

This story is quite short, which differentiates it from the healing stories in John 5 and 9. A royal official (τις βασιλικός, 4:46) approaches Jesus, asking for healing for his son who is ill (ἠσθένει, 4:46) and at the point of death (ἤμελλεν γὰρ ἀποθνήσκειν, 4:47). The sick child is not present; the focus of the story is the dialogue between Jesus and the official, who believes Jesus's words when he says "your son will live" (4:50). The man's faith stands in contrast to the plural "you" whom Jesus chides for not believing: "Unless you see signs and wonders you will not believe" (4:48). As the official is returning to Capernaum, he meets his slaves, who tell him that the child is well and that the fever left his son at the same hour that Jesus spoke his words of healing (4:51–53). The narrative is not followed by a discourse, like in the two other healing stories, but ends with the note that the official and his whole house came to faith (4:53).

What are the terms that are used for the child's illness? When first introduced he is just called "sick" (ἠσθένει, 4:46). The verb ἀσθενέω, "to be weak," is a general term often used for illness. As noted in the introduction, weakness and strength are connected with sickness and health in the Greek medical understanding (see §1.5). However, it gradually becomes clear that the boy's illness is quite severe. The boy is described as "at the point of death" (ἤμελλεν γὰρ ἀποθνήσκειν, 4:47), and he has a fever (ὁ πυρετός, 4:52). The boy is about to die, and terms drawing on life and death are repeated throughout the narrative (4:47, 50, 51, 53). There is no such life-and-death urgency in the two other healing narratives. Hence, this narrative seems to have some commonalities with the Lazarus story. Lazarus's illness is also referred to with ἀσθενέω (11:1, 2, 3, 6), and there

---

15. For a discussion of John's use of the term and its convergence with disability, see Koosed and Schumm, "Out of the Darkness," 82–85.

is fear of imminent death and fear that the healing may come too late (11:4).[16]

This is the only healing story that John shares with the Synoptic Gospels (Matt 8:5–13 // Luke 7:1–10). In Matthew and Luke, it is a Roman centurion who approaches Jesus, and it is his slave who is sick.[17] In Matthew the person is paralyzed (παραλυτικός, 8:6), while in Luke he is "ill and close to death" (κακῶς ἔχων ἤμελλεν τελευτᾶν, 7:2). The conversation with Jesus in both these gospels revolves around the command of a legionnaire who has the authority to give orders (Matt 8:9 // Luke 7:8). Jesus, the legionnaire believes, has the power to command the illness, just as he himself has the power to command his soldiers. The notion of commanding reverberates with invasion theories of illness, such as demon possession. It was common in antiquity to understand illness in terms of invasion (see §1.5). Demons, and also fevers, were sometimes understood as foreign bodies or elements entering a person and could thus be expelled by someone more powerful.[18] The references to a legionnaire's authority (ἐξουσία, Matt 8:9; Luke 7:8) in the Matthean and Lukan versions are connected to the invasion paradigm. Luke's version of the healing of Peter's mother-in-law is another synoptic example of understanding fever as demonic. Here Jesus "rebukes" the fever (ἐπετίμησεν, Luke 4:39).[19] John's version of this story is quite different. It is about a caring father who has a child deadly sick with fever. There is no invasion terminology in John's account; the fever is not connected to possession.[20]

The note about the time that the fever left (4:52) rather resembles Hippocratic ideas about fevers and their relation to the crisis of an illness. In

---

16. Jacobus Kok understands the raising of Lazarus as a Johannine "healing narrative" (*New Perspectives on Healing, Restoration and Reconciliation in John's Gospel* [Leiden: Brill, 2016], 44).

17. Luke refers to the slave as δοῦλος (Luke 7:2), whereas Matthew uses the term παῖς (Matt 8:6). There is disagreement in the scholarly literature whether the sick person in Matthew should be understood as a slave or a child. See, e.g., Ulrich Luz, who translates ὁ παῖς μου with "my son," and Elaine M. Wainwright, who refers to "the centurion's servant" (Luz, *Matthew 8–20: A Commentary*, Hermeneia [Minneapolis: Fortress, 2001], 8; Wainwright, *Women Healing/Healing Women*, 144–45). On the use of child language for slaves, see Jennifer A. Glancy, *Slavery in Early Christianity* (Oxford: Oxford University Press, 2002), 24.

18. Martin, *Corinthian Body*, 153–61.

19. Pilch, *Healing in the New Testament*, 126.

20. Pilch, *Healing in the New Testament*, 126; Kok, *New Perspectives on Healing*, 66.

Hippocratic medicine, fever was understood as a disease in itself, not only as a symptom.[21] There are numerous accounts in the Hippocratic treatise *Epidemics* of people suffering from a variety of fevers with different symptoms.[22] Fever was also seen in relation to the so-called critical days or crisis of a disease, when the fate of the patient was decided (see, e.g., *Epid.* 1.3).[23] As the *Prognostic*, another Hippocratic text, explains:

> Those sweats are the best in all acute diseases which occur on the critical days, and completely carry off the fever [τοῦ πυρετοῦ]. Those are favorable, too, which taking place over the whole body, show that the man is bearing the disease better. But those that do not produce this effect are not beneficial. The worst are cold sweats, confined to the head, face, and neck; these in an acute fever prognosticate death. (*Progn.* 6 [Jones])

In terms of the ancient health care systems, it seems that John has a more learned notion of illness than the Synoptics, in which balance rather than invasion is the perspective.

What is this man's social location? In addition to his designation as a royal official, there are other hints about his high status. He has slaves at his command who bring the news of the child's recovery (4:51), and he is in charge of a household, which comes to faith with him at the end of the story (4:53). We may assume that such a wealthy and powerful man would seek the best possible health care for his family. He would have had access to doctors, and his children would also be cared for by slaves and other family members when ill. The man's ethnicity and religious affiliation is not made explicit. Whereas Matthew and Luke clearly designate him as a Roman officer (ἑκατόνταρχος, Matt 8:5; Luke 7:8), it is unclear what kind of "royal official" (βασιλικός, John 4:46) appears in John. He could be a Roman official, and thus most likely not Jewish, or a Jew in the service of Herod Antipas.[24] Francis J. Moloney argues that he is gentile, since the passage concludes a section dedicated to Jesus relating to non-Jews (John 4:1–54).[25]

---

21. Nutton, *Ancient Medicine*, 32.

22. See Hippocrates, *Epidemics*, where most cases include comments on how fever affected the disease.

23. Nutton, *Ancient Medicine*, 92.

24. Ernst Haenchen, *John 1: A Commentary on the Gospel of John Chapters 1–6*, Hermeneia (Philadelphia: Fortress, 1984), 234.

25. Francis J. Moloney, *The Gospel of John*, SP 4 (Collegeville, MN: Liturgical Press, 1998), 160–61.

Jesus's exclamation, "Unless you see signs and wonders you will not believe" (4:48), is not directed toward the official but toward the crowd. The verb is in the second-person plural, so it targets a plural "you." The official is not interested in signs as a persuasion to believe. He already believes Jesus on his word, before he has seen any miracle.[26] No one in this story has really asked for a sign in order to believe. Jesus's expression makes the event into something more than a request for healing between a petitioner and a healer. Ultimately, the healing takes place for the benefit of someone else: the reader of the gospel and their faith.[27] The story has a happy ending in that the entire family comes to faith. In the Lazarus story as well, faith and the confession of faith is a narrative theme.[28] The connection between faith and life is close in the Gospel of John. Faith gives life, as Jesus proclaims: "Indeed, just as the Father raises the dead and gives them life, so also the Son gives life [ζωοποιεῖ] to whomever he wishes" (5:21). The healing story thus undergirds the symbolic theme of life-giving and Jesus as the life-giver in John.[29] This symbolic use of the characters and themes continues in the two other Johannine healing narratives, to which I now turn.

3.3. The Human Being at the Bethesda Pool (John 5:1–15)

John's second healing story follows immediately after the healing of the royal official's son. John 5:1 provides the transition in time and place: "After this there was a festival of the Jews, and Jesus went up to Jerusalem."[30] The event takes place at a pool "called in Hebrew Beth-zatha, which has five porticoes" (5:2). In his description of the place, John creates an image of a group of people with various disabilities who gather around the pool on a daily basis: "In these [the porticoes] lay many invalids [ἀσθενούντων]—blind [τυφλῶν], lame [χωλῶν], paralyzed [ξηρῶν]" (5:4). As noted, ἀσθενέω is here used as an overarching term for disability (see §1.4). The next three terms, *blind*, *lame*, and *paralyzed*, seem to be subcategories of this overarching category. Whereas the term τυφλός, "blind," usually connotes total sightlessness, the term χωλός, "lame," could designate a sliding scale

---

26. Haenchen, *John 1*, 234–35.
27. Kok, *New Perspectives on Healing*, 76.
28. The story ends with Martha's confession of faith (11:27).
29. Kok, *New Perspectives on Healing*, 86–87.
30. Koosed and Schumm, "Out of the Darkness," 82–85.

of mobility impairments, ranging from limping to complete paralysis of the legs.[31] The third category, ξηρός, means "withered, dried out."[32] This label reflects Hippocratic medical ideas. The four humors were associated with the four properties of dry, wet, hot, and cold. To be paralyzed could be understood in terms of the body being dried up and thus unable to move.[33]

The man that Jesus singles out to be healed has a "weakness" (ἀσθένεια, 5:5) that he has had for thirty-eight years. In other words, he is clearly permanently disabled, but he is not designated according to any of the three subcategories mentioned. John's description points toward some sort of mobility impairment. He is described as lying down (κατακείμενον, 5:6), he is unable to get to the pool fast enough when the angels have stirred the water (5:7), and he has a mat to lie on (κράβαττος, 5:8). Jesus asks the man whether he wants to be made well, but the man does not answer with a clear yes or no, saying only that he is alone: "Sir, I have no one to put me into the pool when the water is stirred up; and while I am making my way, someone else steps down ahead of me" (5:7). Jesus heals the man with a simple statement, "Stand up, take your mat and walk" (ἔγειρε ἆρον τὸν κράβαττόν σου καὶ περιπάτει, John 5:8). This healing by word alone is similar to the previous healing story, where the healing at a distance happens at the same time as Jesus says, "Go, your son will live" (John 4:50). The man at Bethesda obeys Jesus's bidding and picks up his mat and takes off. The fact that he is carrying his mat on the Sabbath instigates the following sequence of events. First, "the Jews" accuse him of carrying the mat unlawfully, but the man claims he is only following the instructions of his healer. However, he does not know Jesus's identity when they ask him (5:10–13). Later, they meet again in the temple and Jesus warns him, "Do not sin anymore so that nothing worse happens to you" (5:14). Apparently, the man has learned Jesus's name at this second meeting and goes to tell "the Jews" (5:15). Jesus further provokes "the Jews" by defending his Sabbath healing with an argument that aligns him with God: "My Father is still working, and I also

31. On τυφλός, see Gosbell, "'Poor, the Crippled, the Blind, and the Lame,'" 54–55. LSJ, s.v "χωλός": "lame in the feet, halting, limping." See above, §2.2.

32. LSJ, s.v. "ξηρός": "dry, withered, lean."

33. Aretaeus, *Sign. diut.* 1.7. See above, §2.2. This terminology is also used in the synoptic healing story about the man with a withered hand (Matt 12:10–13 // Mark 3:1–3 // Luke 6:6–10).

am working" (5:17). It is unclear how the reference to sin connects to the man's disability. Some interpreters understand the man's disability to be a result of sin and thus see Jesus's refutation of the link in John 9:2 as applying only to that particular case.[34] Louise A. Gosbell argues that the topic of sin surfaces late in the story and does not seem to be of primary importance for the gospel writer. Nevertheless, it is interesting that the topic surfaces.[35] As I pointed out in the discussion of Mark 2:1–12, stories about disability seem to provoke questions about meaning (see §2.2). Mitchell and Snyder suggest that the search for an explanation is part of the prosthetic narrative scheme.[36]

The way John presents the pool and its surroundings resembles ancient healing sanctuaries.[37] Asclepian temples probably included a spring or pool, since cleansing as well as incubation was part of the ritual.[38] Archeological evidence indicates that there was a double pool with five porticoes at Bethesda.[39] The conversation between Jesus and the man indicates that healing was the purpose for the gathering of disabled people at this site (5:6–7).[40] It is unclear whether the Bethesda sanctuary was Jewish or pagan in the first century.[41] It may be that John is setting up this sanctuary space in contrast to the Jerusalem temple.[42] There are indications in the Hebrew Bible that the lame, the blind, and those with other disability categories, such as skin anomalies, were excluded from entrance to the temple (e.g., Lev 13:45–46; 2 Sam 5:8), but it is unclear whether such exclusion was ever a historical reality.[43] Avalos argues that the temple did not have a petitionary or therapeutic role in the postexilic period, only

---

34. Raymond E. Brown, *The Gospel according to John (I–XII)*, AB 29 (New York: Doubleday, 1966), 208. Haenchen suggests that John has this saying from his source, and that the rejection of illness as retribution of sin in 9:2 is the evangelist's own understanding (*John 1*, 247).

35. Gosbell, "The Poor, the Crippled, the Blind, and the Lame," 294–95.

36. Mitchell and Snyder, *Narrative Prosthesis*, 53.

37. Gosbell, "The Poor, the Crippled, the Blind, and the Lame," 285–86.

38. Edelstein and Edelstein, *Asclepius*, 1:290–91

39. Gosbell, "The Poor, the Crippled, the Blind, and the Lame," 284.

40. 5:3b–4 is not found in the oldest manuscripts. See Haenchen, *John 1*, 244–45.

41. After 135 CE, the pool is associated with the healing gods Asclepius and Serapis. See Gosbell, "The Poor, the Crippled, the Blind, and the Lame," 285–86.

42. Gosbell, "The Poor, the Crippled, the Blind, and the Lame," 286–87.

43. Schipper, *Disability Studies and the Hebrew Bible*, 105 n. 10.

a thanksgiving function.[44] The pool may have met a need for a healing sanctuary space that was not covered by the temple.[45]

The man in this story claims that he has no one to help him (5:7). Why was he in this place? Was he abandoned as a child and had stayed within this sanctuary for most of his life? Or perhaps he was a slave left there by his owners when he was not of use to them any longer, due to his disability? Or did he manage to get there on a daily basis, staying elsewhere overnight? John gives no answer to these questions, but his solitude seems to be what he himself finds to be at the core of his identity. I suggest that this man is presented as the most destitute of the three people Jesus heals in John.[46] The royal official has, as noted above, multiple resources that he can use in his quest for healing for his son. The man born blind, as I will elaborate below, seems to have a family and is also part of a synagogue community, even though he is a beggar (see §3.4). The man by the pool says he has no one to help him, and after his healing, he seems to have nowhere to go. Based on the tradition of abandoning infants and disabled slaves at healing sites, Gosbell suggests that the man may have spent his entire thirty-eight years at Bethesda.[47] After Jesus's instruction to take his mat and walk (περιπάτει, 5:8), the term περιπατέω is repeated several times (5:9, 11, 12). The immobile man has become itinerant: he encounters Jesus in the temple after the healing (5:14), and he goes to "the Jews" to tell them about Jesus's identity (5:15), indicating that he is walking around Jerusalem after the healing. Jesus's instruction to "take your mat and walk" (ἆρον τὸν κράβαττόν σου καὶ περιπάτει) is similar to how Jesus addresses the man with the four helpers in Mark.[48] Yet the paralytic man is instructed to take his mat and "go to [his] home [εἰς τὸν οἶκόν σου]" (Mark 2:11). While the paralytic in Mark 2 has a house to return to, the lame man in John 5 becomes a homeless wanderer.

---

44. Hector Avalos, *Illness and Health Care in the Ancient Near East: The Role of the Temple in Greece, Mesopotamia, and Israel* (Atlanta: Scholars Press, 1995), 357–61.

45. Patricia Bruce, "John 5:1–18 the Healing at the Pool: Some Narrative, Sociohistorical and Ethical Issues," *Neot* 39 (2005): 51

46. Gosbell also notes the man's marginal status (*"The Poor, the Crippled, the Blind, and the Lame,"* 298–99).

47. Gosbell, *"The Poor, the Crippled, the Blind, and the Lame,"* 289.

48. The phrase is identical to the rhetorical question Jesus asks the scribes: "Which is easier, to say to the paralytic, 'Your sins are forgiven,' or to say, 'Stand up and take your mat and walk?'" (ἆρον τὸν κράβαττόν σου καὶ περιπάτει; Mark 2:9).

3.3.1. Weakness as Metaphor

Many commentators on this passage seem to be negative toward the man. The lack of a clearly positive response to Jesus's question ("do you want to be made well," 5:6) is counted against him, as is his perceived lack of gratitude after the healing.[49] He is blamed for not being eager enough to seek healing.[50] R. Alan Culpepper calls him "dull," while Raymond E. Brown labels him an "obtuse and unimaginative paralytic."[51] James M. Howard elaborates: "One gets the impression that the man was somewhat 'dull,' and then once he had more knowledge, he did nothing good with it. There is no mention of gratitude or belief on his part (cf. 9:35–38), only persecution of Jesus as a result of the man's learning who had healed him (5:16)." He continues: "He progressed from being needy, to being indifferent, to denying responsibility for breaking the Sabbath law."[52] It is common to understand the two healing stories in John 5 and 9 as complementing one another and to read the two characters in light of one another so that the "weak" man signifies partial understanding, whereas the blind man represents faith in Jesus.[53]

Sontag's perspectives on the uses of illness imagery may be helpful here. She holds that the metaphorical association of certain illnesses and disabilities with certain moral qualities or societal fears stigmatizes and adds unnecessary suffering to those who are ill.[54] It seems that the interpreters have conflated the man's illness with his personality and understand him as weak in character as well as in body. It is in particular the man's reluctance to seek healing that provokes the commentators. Within the disability

---

49. As Haenchen also notes (*John 1*, 246).

50. Brown, *Gospel according to John (I–XII)*, 209; Jaime Clark-Soles, "John, First-Third John, and Revelation," in Melcher, Parsons, and Yong, *Bible and Disability*, 340; Kerry H. Wynn, "Johannine Healings and the Otherness of Disability," *PRSt* 34 (2007): 66–67.

51. R. Alan Culpepper, *Anatomy of the Fourth Gospel: A Study in Literary Design* (Philadelphia: Fortress, 1987), 138; Raymond E. Brown, *The Gospel according to John (XIII–XXI)*, AB 29A (New York: Doubleday, 1970), 377.

52. James M. Howard, "The Significance of Minor Characters in the Gospel of John," *BSac* 163 (2006): 72, 73.

53. See, e.g., Culpepper, *Anatomy of the Fourth Gospel*, 137–40; Wynn, "Johannine Healings and the Otherness of Disability," 72; Craig S. Keener, *The Gospel of John: A Commentary*, 2 vols. (Peabody, MA: Hendrickson, 2003), 1:639–40.

54. Sontag, *Illness as Metaphor*, 97–99.

movement, it has been pointed out that people with disabilities are often more comfortable with their nonnormative bodies and less interested in cure than able-bodied people tend to assume. It is an ableist assumption, shaped by the medical model, to think that a person who has an impairment necessarily wants to be rid of it. Along these lines, sermons on the healing narratives often present the characters Jesus heals as "symbols of misery."[55] If we look at disability from a social and cultural perspective, rather than a medical one, the problem is instead the attitudes and assumptions of the able-bodied individual. I suggest that such an ableist understanding of disability is part of why many commentators find this character so unlikeable.

Jeffrey L. Staley, who applies a disability optic to this passage, reads the character quite differently from the mainstream commentators. Contrasting his own interpretation to this tradition of casting the man as dull and "weak-kneed," he says, "The sick man … proves to be a daring and risk-taking individual, one who acts unquestioningly upon a stranger's Sabbath-breaking command."[56] Staley sees initiative and daring where others have seen passivity, ingratitude, and lack of understanding. An observation that counters the focus on the negative character of the man is that John actually attributes a variety of labels to him. After initially being designated as "the weak one" (ὁ ἀσθενῶν, 5:7), he is called "the one who had been made well" (τῷ τεθεραπευμένῳ, 5:10) and "the healed one" (ὁ ἰαθεὶς, 5:13), and he is also referred to as ὁ ἄνθρωπος, "the human being," several times (5:5, 7, 15). This variation in terminology is different from the Synoptic Gospels, where the person with a disability is usually designated according to his or her disability and simply called "the lame," "the blind," or "the demon-possessed" throughout the story (see §2.2.). The shorter form of the synoptic healing stories is an obvious reason for this difference. There is simply not enough space to develop the character beyond his or her impairment in the Synoptics. John, however, chooses to make space in his narrative to develop the character and use a variety of designations.

3.4. The Man Born Blind (John 9:1–41)

Jesus's final healing is of a man who had been blind from birth. The story is the longest of John's healing stories and has a complicated sequence of

---

55. See, e.g., Belser and Morrison, "What No Longer Serves Us," 157.

56. Jeffrey L. Staley, "Stumbling in the Dark, Reaching for the Light: Reading Character in John 5 and 9," *Semeia* 53 (1991): 60.

scenes involving Jesus, the disciples, the blind man, his neighbors and parents, the Pharisees, and "the Jews." I will concentrate my observations on the first scene, leading up to and including the healing (John 9:1–8). The scene is initiated by a conversation between the disciples and Jesus. The sight of a blind man causes the disciples to ponder about whose fault it is, and they ask Jesus, "Rabbi, who sinned, this man or his parents, that he was born blind [τυφλὸς γεννηθῇ]?" (9:2). This healing story, too, follows a prosthetic narrative scheme. As Mitchell and Snyder state, "A narrative consolidates the need for its own existence by calling for an explanation of the deviation's origin and formative consequences."[57] Jesus's answer tackles the question of sin and introduces the Johannine symbolic and dualistic framework: "Neither this man nor his parents sinned; he was born blind so that God's works might be revealed in him. We must work the works of him who sent me while it is day; night is coming when no one can work. As long as I am in the world, I am the light of the world" (9:3–5). The correlation between sin and disability is severed by Jesus's answer. Rather than pointing to personal or generational guilt, the man was born blind for revelatory purposes. In these introductory verses, there is also the metaphorical aspect of Mitchell and Snyder's theory of narrative prosthesis. Blindness and seeing, darkness and light are both presented as dualistic categories that represent forces of good and evil and align Jesus with the divine light, which brings revelation.

Some interpreters of this passage attribute the disciples' question to a Jewish understanding that disability is a divine punishment for sin.[58] Jennifer L. Koosed and Darla Schumm caution against this assumption and argue that there were different points of view on this in antiquity. In the Hebrew Bible, the idea that God punishes the children for the sins of the parents is sometimes stated (Exod 20:5; Num 14:18) and other times refuted (Jer 31:29–30; Ezek 18:2–4).[59] Moreover, the idea that the gods could punish wrongdoing through inflicting illness and disability was also held by other peoples and religious systems in the ancient Mediterranean. In a survey article, Nicole Kelley shows that both within Jewish and Greco-Roman sources, congenital disabilities can be attributed to either

---

57. Mitchell and Snyder, *Narrative Prosthesis*, 53.
58. Brown, *Gospel according to John (I–XII)*, 371; Keener, *Gospel of John*, 1:777.
59. Koosed and Schumm, "Out of the Darkness," 83–84.

nondivine or divine causes.[60] This variety in understandings underscores that the notion of a singular premodern moral model, as discussed in the introduction, is not sufficient to describe ancient understandings of the causes of disability (see §1.3).

According to Jesus, the reason for this man's existence and his disabled embodiment is "so that God's works might be revealed in him" (John 9:3). John M. Hull has pointed out that "the man has been born blind in order to provide a sort of photo opportunity for Jesus."[61] Koosed and Schumm argue that John operates with different reasons for why people have disabilities, but God is behind all of them. It is never just an ordinary part of life, never an accident: "And never is the condition seen as a positive gift of God. Rather the disability is always present for some other reason or purpose."[62] Carter warns that these layers of symbolic and spiritualized meaning that are added to the disabled character in fact make the individual invisible. These insights resonate with Sontag's observation that metaphorical thinking and the search for meaning behind illness actually stigmatizes and adds unnecessary suffering.[63]

The man in this story is first designated as "blind from birth" (τυφλὸν ἐκ γενετῆς, 9:1). As already noted, blindness was considered a common disability in antiquity and is a recurring disability in the New Testament (see §1.4). John uses the expression "from birth" (ἐκ γενετῆς) rather than "from the mother's womb" (ἐκ κοιλίας μητρός, Matt 19:12; Luke 1:15; Acts 3:2), which is a more Semitic turn of phrase.[64] The terminology of generation links with John's incarnational theology. According to Moloney, the expression "from birth" is theologically significant for John and makes the

---

60. Nicole Kelley, "The Theological Significance of Physical Deformity in the Pseudo-Clementine Homilies," *PRSt* 34 (2007): 78–80.

61. John M. Hull, *In the Beginning There Was Darkness: A Blind Person's Conversation with the Bible* (London: SCM Press, 2001), 49. John C. Poirier has suggested an alternative reading of this verse, arguing that the punctuation should be placed differently. In Poirier's reading, Jesus does not claim that the man was born blind so that God's healing powers may be revealed; rather, "he said that he must work this healing while it is day, so that others may plainly *see* it." See Poirier, "Another Look at the 'Man Born Blind' in John 9," *JRDH* 14 (2010): 64 (emphasis original).

62. Koosed and Schumm, "Out of the Darkness," 80.

63. Sontag, *Illness as Metaphor*, 93–100.

64. The expression "from my mother's womb," *mibbeten immi*, occurs many times in the Hebrew Bible; see, e.g., Judg 16:17, Ps 22:11, Job 1:21.

healing a new creation.[65] However, the phrase may also reveal some medical insight. It has been shown that John has some knowledge of ancient gynecology and theories of conception.[66] Turid Karlsen Seim has argued that John's genetics eclipses the mother in favor of an omniscient father.[67] In doing so, John draws on Aristotle's theory of *epigenesis*, in which it is claimed that only the father contributes with seed: the man provides form, the woman provides matter. Within this theory the mother contributes to the growth of the fetus with nutriments from her blood; she is the receptacle and nurturer.[68] The theory relies on a hierarchy of bodily fluids in which semen is understood to be blood perfected through a concoction that women cannot achieve due to lack of innate heat. The male semen is infused with spirit, πνεῦμα, and is thus life-giving.[69]

In contrast to the first two healing stories in John, where Jesus heals by his word alone, this story relates a rather complicated process involving mud, spittle, and washing in holy water:

> When he had said this, he spat on the ground and made mud [πηλὸν] with the saliva [τοῦ πτύσματος] and spread the mud on the man's eyes, saying to him, "Go, wash [ὕπαγε νίψαι] in the pool of Siloam" (which means Sent). Then he went and washed and came back able to see [ἦλθεν βλέπων]. (John 9:6–7)

Why such an elaborate process when Jesus has shown that he can heal by words alone? Within ancient folk medicine, it was commonly held that spittle had healing properties. In Mark, Jesus uses a similar healing

---

65. Moloney, *Gospel of John*, 296.

66. See, e.g., Adeline Fehribach, "The 'Birthing' Bridegroom: The Portrayal of Jesus in the Fourth Gospel," in *A Feminist Companion to John*, ed. Amy-Jill Levine with Marianne Blickenstaff, 2 vols. (London: Sheffield Academic, 2003), 2:104–29; Adele Reinhartz, "'And the Word Was Begotten': Divine *Epigenesis* in the Gospel of John," *Semeia* 85 (1999); Deborah Sawyer, "John 19.34: From Crucifixion to Birth, or Creation?," in Levine, *Feminist Companion to John*, 2:130–39.

67. See Turid Karlsen Seim, "Motherhood and the Making of Fathers in Antiquity: Contextualizing Genetics in the Gospel of John," in *Women and Gender in Ancient Religions: Interdisciplinary Approaches*, ed. Stephen P. Ahearne-Kroll, Paul A. Holloway, and James A. Kelhoffer, WUNT 263 (Tübingen: Mohr Siebeck, 2010); Seim, "Descent and Divine Paternity in the Gospel of John: Does the Mother Matter?," *NTS* 51 (2005).

68. Seim, "Descent and Divine Paternity," 362.

69. Solevåg, *Birthing Salvation*, 72.

method, smearing saliva on a deaf and mute man's tongue (7:32–37) and a blind man's eyes (8:22–26). Pliny claims in *Natural History* that ophthalmia may be cured "by using saliva every morning as eye ointment" (28.7 [Jones]). The use of spittle as part of a folk healing ritual may be seen in Tacitus's report on how Vespasian healed a blind man in Alexandria:

> During the months while Vespasian was waiting at Alexandria..., many marvels occurred to mark the favour of heaven and a certain partiality of the gods toward him. One of the common people of Alexandria, well known for his loss of sight, threw himself before Vespasian's knees, praying him with groans to cure his blindness..., and he besought the emperor to deign to moisten his cheeks and his eyes with his spittle. (*Hist.* 4.81 [Moore])[70]

Jesus's behavior toward the blind man is that of a typical ancient folk healer.[71] But to John, Jesus is also something more. The mixing of spittle and clay is significant, because it reveals Jesus in the role of creator, working with the same ingredients as when God created Adam (Gen 2:7). Daniel Frayer-Griggs has argued that there is a creation motif behind John 9:6 by showing that there is an extrabiblical tradition (e.g., in the Dead Sea Scrolls) according to which both spittle and clay played a role in the creation of human beings.[72] John prefaces the entire narrative with Jesus's remark to his disciples that he must "work the works of him who sent me" (9:4). It is Jesus's act of working clay on the Sabbath that provokes the Pharisees (9:15–16), but the act also has christological significance because it reveals Jesus as equal to the creator in bringing light into the world (Gen 1:3; John 9:5). The connection is drawn by the healed man himself in his final confession: "Never since the world began has it been heard that anyone opened the eyes of a person born blind" (John 9:32).

Finally, the healing also includes washing in the dam of Siloam. The waters of Siloam played a significant role in the Feast of Tabernacles, when water was brought from the pool to the altar of the temple. It has also been argued that the pool was the only *miqveh* (pool used for ritual cleansing) in Jerusalem with free-flowing—"living"—water.[73] Again, John adds a

---

70. See also Suetonius, *Vesp.* 7.

71. Pilch, *Healing in the New Testament*, 134.

72. Daniel Frayer-Griggs, "Spittle, Clay and Creation in John 9:6 and Some Dead Sea Scrolls," *JBL* 132 (2013): 667.

73. Gosbell, "*The Poor, the Crippled, the Blind, and the Lame*," 310–11.

symbolic layer of meaning by connecting Jesus, who is the Sent One (9:4; cf. 3:17, 34; 5:36) and the one who has living water (4:10), with this body of water, which also means "sent" (9:7).[74] The complicated healing process is thus overlaid with symbolism that constructs Jesus as divine creator and his healing ritual as more effective and life-giving than the rituals in the Jerusalem temple. Gosbell suggests that seen together, the healing of the man at Bethesda and the man born blind hint at a reversal of the exclusionary tradition of 2 Sam 5:8 ("the blind and the lame shall not come into the house") through Jesus's ministry.[75]

3.4.1. The Social Location of a Blind Beggar

The man is a beggar, doubly designated as such, with both a noun and a verb (προσαίτης, προσαιτῶν, John 9:8). Although it has been claimed that this is typical of disabled characters in the New Testament gospels and Acts, it is only this character and Bartimeus in Mark 10:46 who are designated as blind beggars in the New Testament.[76] Blind beggars were something of a literary stereotype in antiquity, but this does not mean that it was common for blind people to beg. Lisa Trentin and Martha L. Rose both argue that the everyday lives of blind people in antiquity differed from representations of the blind in literature.[77] Many people would lose their eyesight during the course of their lives, due to disease, injury, punishment, or simply old age. Thus, visual impairment did not ban a person a priori from their occupation, and most blind people probably lived fairly ordinary lives.[78]

The man seems to be part of the community in several ways. His parents appear in the story (9:18–23), so he has a family, although it is unclear how involved they are in their son's life. There are neighbors who know him and people who are familiar with him from his usual begging location (9:8). He also belongs to a synagogue community (9:22), from which he is eventually cast out for confessing his faith in Jesus (9:34). This is quite different from the man at the pool of Bethesda, who claims he has no one and never interacts with anyone except Jesus and "the Jews."

---

74. Moloney, *Gospel of John*, 292.

75. Gosbell, "*The Poor, the Crippled, the Blind, and the Lame,*" 318–20.

76. For an example of such a claim, see Bengtsson, "Two-Sided Coin," 4.

77. Trentin, "Exploring Visual Impairment in Roman Antiquity," 92.

78. Rose, *Staff of Oedipus*, 79–80, 90–92.

The man's parents appear on the scene because "the Jews" bring them in for questioning about their son's healing. They answer dismissively when they are asked about the purported miracle: "We know that this is our son, and that he was born blind; but we do not know how it is that now he sees, nor do we know who opened his eyes. Ask him; he is of age. He will speak for himself" (9:20–21). John ascribes their reluctance to speak on their son's behalf to fear of "the Jews" (9:22–23). However, the ability to speak for oneself was crucial in the oral culture of the Roman Empire and closely connected to citizenship and participation. Laes has noted that in Roman civil society the uttering of an oath marked integration as *civis*, that is, Roman citizenship.[79] Deaf-mute people could not hold office, act as guardians or judges, or make a legal will due to this emphasis on oral communication.[80] When the blind man's parents claim that their son can speak for himself, they are insisting that he is a person who can represent himself and does not need anyone else to be a juridical go-between. This legal right was one he would have whether he was blind or seeing. There are a number of references to hearing, listening, and speaking in this part of the story (9:29, 30, 31, 32, 37), thus underscoring an ability this man has had all along.

As with the man at the Bethesda pool, John uses several different designations to refer to the man Jesus heals from blindness. He is referred to as a human being (ἄνθρωπος, 9:1, 24, 30), called by various pronouns, and called by a variety of constructs relating to his new condition: "the man who had formerly been blind (τόν ποτε τυφλόν, 9:13), "the man who had received his sight" (τοῦ ἀναβλέψαντος, 9:18). He is also referred to as a son (9:19–20) and as a beggar. In other words, there are aspects of this narrative that underscores his status as a human being rather than only a disabled person. He is not a one-dimensional character but speaks and acts within a social network of people who relate to him in different roles. Colleen Grant notes that he appears "not only as a broken figure in need of compassion and healing but as a person in his own right. We are able to get to know him as a thoughtful, brave, amusing, but above all, ordinary person."[81]

---

79. Laes, "Silent History?," 153.

80. Laes, "Silent History?," 153.

81. Colleen C. Grant, "Reinterpreting the Healing Narratives," in *Human Disability and the Service of God. Reassessing Religious Practice*, ed. Nancy L. Eiesland and Don E. Salier (Nashville: Abingdon, 1998), 79.

After the healing there is confusion about the man's identity. People who know him do not recognize him after he is healed, and there are some doubts that he really is the same man (9:8–12). In an effort to try and establish his identity, the man exclaims "I am he" (ἐγώ εἰμι, 9:9). Grant argues that "his disability was never his defining characteristic; he knows himself to be the same person, blind or sighted."[82] The phrase ἐγώ εἰμι is a christologically significant phrase in John's Gospel.[83] This is the only time that the phrase is not uttered by Jesus. There is thus an interesting overlap in the identities of Jesus and the man. The confusion around identity is a characteristic that Jesus and the formerly blind man share. Just like with Jesus, people are unclear about the identity of the man, and the phrase ἐγώ εἰμι functions as a "bold revelation in the face of a skeptical crowd."[84] Another similarity between these two characters is that both are called human being through the course of the story (Jesus is called ἄνθρωπος in 9:11, 16, 24). Moreover, both men create a schism with respect to their identity.[85] The narrative ends with Jesus questioning the man, "Do you believe in the Son of Man [τὸν υἱὸν τοῦ ἀνθρῶπου]?" (9:35), and revealing that the Son of Man is the one speaking to him (9:37). It seems, therefore, that the character not only serves as narrative prosthesis, used to reveal Jesus's close connection to the Father, but in some fashion may also func-tion as a christological representative.[86]

3.4.2. Blindness as Metaphor

The symbolic level of blindness is a motif throughout the story. There is a dualistic contrast between day and night (9:4), light and darkness (9:5), faith and disbelief (9:18, 25, 31, 36, 38), blindness and seeing (9:39–41). The healing draws on a metaphorical understanding of blindness and seeing in which ignorance ties in with the former and insight and true faith connects with the latter. This use of blindness was a common liter-ary topos in antiquity. There were several aspects to this topos, sometimes connecting blind characters to helplessness, sometimes to ignorance,

---

82. Grant, "Reinterpreting the Healing Narratives," 81.

83. See, e.g., John 4:26; 6:20, 35; 8:12, 58; 10:7, 11; 18:5.

84. Grant, "Reinterpreting the Healing Narratives," 81. See also Clark-Soles, "John," 348.

85. Moloney, *Gospel of John*, 297.

86. Moloney, *Gospel of John*, 297.

and other times to exceptional insight.[87] The polar opposites mentioned recur throughout the Gospel of John.[88] Thus, the healing story undergirds John's depiction of Jesus as the one who brings light and life, with allusions to the prologue ("the true light, which enlightens everyone," 1:9) as well as to the preceding chapter, where Jesus proclaims himself to be "the light of the world" (ἐγώ εἰμι τὸ φῶς τοῦ κόσμου, 8:12). The passage is thus also connected to one of the ἐγώ εἰμι sayings, which Jesus states in truncated form in the passage: "As long as I am in the world, I am the light of the world [φῶς εἰμι τοῦ κόσμου]" (9:5). Sontag as well as Mitchell and Snyder have pointed to the stigmatizing effects of such metaphorical use of disability. Sontag's observation that certain illnesses (and disabilities, I would add) can take on a particular metaphorical meaning in a culture is helpful in order to understand John's use of blindness. John draws on the culturally assigned place of blindness as a metaphor for ignorance as a key aspect of his dualistic theology. Such metaphors demand that we read people with disabilities "as symbols of brokenness."[89] Although the blind person in the story is good, the association with blindness and ignorance is "unhelpful to actual blind persons trying to function in normate society."[90]

Commentators seem to take more of a liking to the man born blind than to the weak man at Bethesda. Brown draws a sharp contrast between the two characters: "This clever and voluble blind man is quite different from the obtuse and unimaginative paralytic of ch. v."[91] As noted above, these two stories are often understood as complementing each other, and the two characters are read symbolically to signify partial understanding and faith respectively.[92] Colleen Conway has argued against such a symbolic reading of minor characters in John. She claims that the characters are more complicated and that the typical reading flattens John's ambiguity: "Minor characters of the Fourth Gospel do more to complicate the

---

87. Hartsock, *Sight and Blindness in Luke-Acts*, 65–81.

88. Anderson, *Riddles of the Fourth Gospel*, 36–37.

89. Grant, "Reinterpreting the Healing Narratives," 78.

90. Clark-Soles, "John," 353.

91. Brown, *Gospel according to John (I–XII)*, 377. See also Ernst Haenchen, *John 2: A Commentary on the Gospel of John Chapters 7–21*, Hermeneia (Philadelphia: Fortress, 1984, 40).

92. See, e.g., Culpepper, *Anatomy of the Fourth Gospel*, 137–40; Wynn, "Johannine Healings and the Otherness of Disability," 72; Keener, *Gospel of John*, 1:639–40.

clear choice between belief and unbelief than to illustrate it."[93] Conway's suggestion that John's characters may be more ambivalent than straight-forward is useful, as it complements Sontag's observations about the way that metaphor works. Awareness about how disability is used in a narrative is helpful in order both to reveal biases of earlier interpretations and to suggest alternative readings.

3.5. Conclusion: Johannine Paradoxes

In conclusion, the Gospel of John presents a number of paradoxes from a disability perspective. First, there is a paradox when it comes to John's place in the ancient health care system. On the one hand, he shows some knowledge of medical discourse and thus seems to draw on insights from the professional sector of the ancient health care system. I have noted that the attention given to fevers (4:52) and the notion of being "dried up" (5:3) align with Hippocratic ideas. Moreover, I have argued that John draws on Greek gynecological traditions to construct his incarnational theology, which may be glimpsed in the expression "blind from birth" (9:1). Hence John is grounded in a balance etiology rather than an invasion etiology of illness. On the other hand, there are clear folk traditions at work in the healing stories. The setting of the healing of the weak man, the pool of Bethesda, is most likely a healing sanctuary. The elaborate healing process in John 9 likewise draws on folk traditions of healing, with notions of the mystical power of mud and of ritual washing. In John's healing stories, then, we have medical terminology that shows familiarity with the profes-sionalized sector, but the spaces where the healings take place are con-nected to the popular sector.

Another paradox is in the literary representation of the characters. On the one hand, they are more developed in John and thus contribute to more complex identities. The characters do not vanish immediately, like they do in the Synoptics. Both of the longer stories elaborate on what hap-pens after the healing as well as the interactions and relationships of the healed person. Moreover, the common humanity between Christ and the two disabled men is drawn out through the use of the term ἄνθρωπος for both Jesus and these literary characters. They are not stuck with one dis-

---

93. Colleen M. Conway, "Speaking through Ambiguity: Minor Characters in the Fourth Gospel," *BibInt* 10 (2002): 325.

ability label but are designated by various terms through the course of the narrative. On the other hand, the tradition of reading the man at Bethesda as weak in character and John's metaphorical use of blindness as aligned with darkness and misunderstanding are both problematic from a disability studies perspective. As Sontag observed, such metaphorical constructions contribute to the stigmatization of people who are ill or disabled.[94] Nancy L. Eiesland has pointed out that uncritical use of biblical healing stories "reinforce negative stereotypes … and mask the lived realities of people with disabilities."[95]

Finally, as noted in the beginning of this chapter, John casts his healing stories as signs and only narrates three exemplary healings. Of these, only two concern disabilities. The two disabilities may be significant, as lame and blind are two typical categories of disability in antiquity. I concur with Gosbell that the two disabilities are chosen so that they together represent disability as a category. The two stories thus stand in for "all those with physical and sensory impairments who are being healed by Jesus."[96] It should be noted that John does not include any stories about Jesus healing women, although he includes some significant female characters in the gospel (4:4–42; 11:1–53; 12:1–11; 20:11–18). Whereas the Synoptics tell of numerous healings of women, John's three healing narratives, as well as the raising of Lazarus (11:1–43), concern the restoration of male characters. In reducing the miracle stories to only seven, John has chosen these stories for their representative, signifying value. This reflects an understanding of gender in which male is more representative than female.[97]

---

94. Sontag, *Illness as Metaphor*, 97.
95. Eiesland, *Disabled God*, 74.
96. Gosbell, *"The Poor, the Crippled, the Blind, and the Lame,"* 317.
97. As I argue in Solevåg, *"Hysterical Women?,"* 323.

4
Disabling Women in the Acts of Peter

4.1. Introduction: Disability and the Male Gaze

In this chapter, I continue to explore healing narratives as a particular literary space for representations of disability. From examining New Testament examples of this genre, I now turn to the apocryphal Acts of Peter. There are several reasons for the selection of this early Christian text. First, it complicates the picture when it comes to early Christian healing narratives, as it includes several stories of *unhealing*, and even apostolic inflictions of disability. Such unhealings also occur in other early Christian texts (e.g., Acts 5:1–10), but it is a recurring characteristic of the Acts of Peter. Moreover, disability and illness intersect with gender in a number of interesting ways in this work. I will focus on several stories about the un/healing of women, namely, Peter's unnamed daughter, a Christ-believer called Rufina, a group of blind widows, and a female demon. An intersectional approach, viewing gender alongside disability, will provide some new insights into the power relations that operate in the text, I argue.

How a text describes bodies that deviate from the norm can reveal something about the gaze of that text, that is, the viewpoint from which the narrator contemplates the world. This concept was introduced to the study of antiquity from feminist film criticism, which claimed that in modern movie production "the gaze is male." Who is the scrutinizing, gazing subject, and who is the object being looked at in texts from antiquity? Scholars drawing on this theory have convincingly argued that ancient sources

An earlier version of this chapter will appear in a forthcoming anthology and is reworked here by permission. See Anna Rebecca Solevåg, "Apostolic Power to Paralyze: Gender and Disability in the Acts of Peter," in *Marginalised Writings of Early Christianity: Apocryphal Texts and Writings of Female Authorship*, ed. Outi Lehtipuu and Silke Petersen, BW (Atlanta: SBL Press, forthcoming).

objectify women in a number of culturally specific ways.[1] For example, female characters in a number of texts appear nude to the reader, are often mute, are commodified as food, are exposed to the public gaze, and display fear.[2] Whereas female characters are objectified and involuntarily turned into spectacle in ancient texts, the act of looking in itself often asserts authority. Looking and eye contact held cultural significance in the Greco-Roman world, as it manifested and defined status: "Both the right to look and the right to display oneself are part of a definition of status in social interaction. Typically, both rights were denied in Greece to individuals (slaves, boys, women, *kinaidoi*) defined as inferior to free men and forfeited by free men of impaired status."[3] While earlier research was predominantly focused on gendered aspects of the gaze, Sue Blundell and others argue that looking negotiates a more complicated hierarchy of status positions, also involving class, sexuality, and dis/ability.

Within disability studies, too, the act of looking and its stigmatizing and controlling effect has been addressed. Garland-Thomson observes that gender, race, and ability systems intertwine and mutually constitute one another as systems of representation that mark subjugated bodies as other.[4] She posits that staring is a form of nonverbal communication that is used to enforce social hierarchies and regulate access to resources.[5] The male gaze is only one instance of the multiple forms of cultural othering that can take place through looking as an act of domination: "The kind of staring that 'fixes' a person in gender, race, disability, class, or sexuality systems is an attempt to control the other."[6] This chapter uses gaze and

---

1. See, e.g., Amy Richlin, *Pornography and Representation in Greece and Rome* (New York: Oxford University Press, 1992), 107; Richlin, *Arguments with Silence: Writing the History of Roman Women* (Ann Arbor: University of Michigan Press, 2014); Sue Blundell et al., "Introduction," *Helios* 40 (2013); Nancy Sorkin Rabinowitz, "Women as Subject and Object of the Gaze in Tragedy," *Helios* 40 (2013); Marilyn B. Skinner, *Sexuality in Greek and Roman Culture* (Malden, MA: Blackwell, 2005).

2. Amy Richlin, introduction to *Pornography and Representation in Greece and Rome*, xix.

3. Blundell et al., "Introduction," 22.

4. Rosemarie Garland-Thomson, "Integrating Disability, Transforming Feminist Theory," in Davis, *Disability Studies Reader*, 357–59.

5. Rosemarie Garland-Thomson, *Staring: How We Look* (Oxford: Oxford University Press, 2009), 40.

6. Garland-Thomson, *Staring*, 42.

staring as key concepts to scrutinize how women characters and their disabilities are presented in the Acts of Peter.

4.1.1. Women in the Acts of Peter

The Acts of Peter is one of the so-called apocryphal acts.[7] It is not preserved as one coherent whole, and I rely on several different text corpora in three different languages in this chapter: the Coptic Act of Peter from the Berlin Codex (Act Pet.), the Latin Actus Vercellenses (Act. Verc.), and the Greek Martyrdom of Peter (Mart. Pet.).[8] It is likely that all these texts belonged to an original Acts of Peter, but the arguments I make here are not dependent on the original unity of these texts.[9]

The Latin Actus Vercellenses contains the longest portion of text. It starts with Paul's departure from Rome and Peter's subsequent arrival in that city. While the Christ-believers in Rome are without apostolic oversight, they are "seduced" by the Jewish sorcerer Simon Magus and leave their newfound faith. The bulk of the narrative focuses on Peter's contestations with Simon Magus, in a series of miracle competitions, in an effort to win the former believers back. He succeeds, and the tale ends with Peter's

---

7. There are five such acts preserved that date from the second and third centuries. See Hans-Josef Klauck, *The Apocryphal Acts of the Apostles: An Introduction*, trans. Brian McNeil (Waco, TX: Baylor University Press, 2008), 3.

8. For Actus Vercellences and the Martyrdom of Peter, see Constantin von Tischendorf, Max Bonnet, and Richard Adelbert Lipsius, *Acta Apostolorum Apocrypha*, vol. 1 (Darmstadt: Wissenschaftliche Buchgesellschaft, 1959). The Berlin Codex, also referred to as Codex Berolinensis or BG, contains four texts: the Gospel of Mary, the Apocryphon of John, the Wisdom of Jesus Christ, and the Act of Peter. See Douglas M. Parrott, ed., *Nag Hammadi Codices V, 2–5 and VI: With Papyrus Berolinensis 8502* (Leiden: Brill, 1979). For English translations of Actus Vercellences, the Martyrdom of Peter, and the Acts of Peter, see "The Acts of Peter," in *The Apocryphal New Testament*, ed. John K. Elliott (Oxford: Clarendon, 1993), 397–427; Wilhelm Schneemelcher, "The Acts of Peter," in *New Testament Apocrypha*, ed. Wilhelm Schneemelcher and R. McL. Wilson (Cambridge: James Clarke, 1991), 285–317. All English quotations are from Elliott.

9. Jan N. Bremmer dates the Acts of Peter to the last two decades of the second century ("Women, Magic, Place and Date," in Bremmer, *Apocryphal Acts of Peter*, 18). Klauck dates it to ca. 200 CE (*Apocryphal Acts of the Apostles*, 84). As Christine M. Thomas points out, the transmission of this narrative is fluid and the texts multiform, and hence the search for an "original text" is futile (*The Acts of Peter, Gospel Literature, and the Ancient Novel: Rewriting the Past* [Oxford: Oxford University Press, 2003], 39).

martyrdom, including the well-known *quo vadis* scene and the upside-down crucifixion of Peter. The martyrdom is also preserved in the Greek Martyrdom of Peter. It is assumed that the Acts of Peter was originally written in Greek and that Actus Vercellenses is a loose translation of it. It is likely that the original had more material in the beginning than what is preserved in the Actus Vercellenses. The story of how Peter heals and unheals his paralyzed virgin daughter, preserved only in the Coptic Act of Peter, is considered to be part of this otherwise lost first part.[10]

In the Acts of Peter, the apostle's healing activity is an important part of his ministry. Word and deed go hand in hand, and both are signs of his power as an apostle and representative of God. In addition to short comments about Peter's healing ministry (Act Pet. 128:4–7, 10–17; Act. Verc. 29; Mart. Pet. 2), there are several episodes that recount miracles of healing as well as unhealing. Many of these stories include women, and in the following, I focus on four stories concerning the (healing and) unhealing of women.

4.2. Peter's Daughter

The story about Peter's daughter is fascinating and troubling from a disability perspective. At a gathering on the Lord's Day, Peter, who is known for curing many sick people, is asked why he has not healed his own daughter, who is paralyzed and present at the gathering (Act Pet. 128:10–129:8). "God alone knows why her body is sick," says Peter, quickly adding that "God is not unable or powerless" (129:11–15). To prove this point, Peter proceeds to heal his daughter. He asks her to rise and walk toward him, and to the amazement of the crowd, she does so. However, Peter addresses his daughter a second time and says: "Return to your place, sit down there and be helpless again, for it is good for me and you" (131:2–5). The girl walks back to her place and becomes paralyzed again. The crowd laments this turn of events, but Peter assures them again that "this is good for her and for me" (141:14). The reason she is lame, explains Peter, is that when she was ten she became so beautiful that she was a stumbling-block to

---

10. Klauck, *Apocryphal Acts of the Apostles*, 82–83; Thomas, *Acts of Peter*, 18–20. Andrea L. Molinari, however, argues that the Coptic Act of Peter is independent of the Acts of Peter (*"I Never Knew the Man": The Coptic Act of Peter [Papyrus Berolinensis 8502.4], Its Independence from the Apocryphal Acts of Peter, Genre and Legendary Origins* [Leuven: Peeters, 2000], xxxv).

many men. One man in particular, Ptolemy, who had seen her naked when she was bathing, wanted to take her for his wife, but her mother did not consent to the marriage offer. Ptolemy "often sent for her, for he could not wait" (132:18–19), Peter recounts. At this point, there is a lacuna in the papyrus document, and the next two pages of the manuscript are missing. Following the lacuna, Peter and his wife find their daughter paralyzed on the doorstep, left there by Ptolemy. They "found the girl with one side of her body paralysed [sēq] from head to foot and dried up [essosht]" (135:6–9). Apparently, she had become paralyzed at some point during the abduction, and the paralysis seems to be the reason for her safe return to Peter's house.[11] Somehow, the (divine?) disabling of the girl has made her sexually inviolable: "We carried her away, praising the Lord that he had kept his servant from defilement and violation" (135:10–13).

The girl's disability is described as a paralysis of one side of her body from head to foot and also as being "dried up" (essosht). As already noted, paralysis is an illness category that occurs frequently in ancient medical literature as well as in general discourse (see §2.2). The Greek term παράλυσις encompasses a broad range of mobility impairments involving the "disabling of the nerves," ranging from temporary to permanent conditions.[12] Meghan Henning has argued that ancient humoral theory is behind the description of Peter's daughter's illness, pointing to medical writers that posit paralysis as the result of a body deficient in natural heat.[13] She shows how medical texts draw a connection between cold blood, on one side, and sexual dysfunction and infertility, on the other, and she concludes that Ptolemy's rejection of Peter's daughter is because her paralyzed body was read as infertile: "The author of the Coptic fragment could expect his readers to infer that Peter's daughter's paralysis was evidence of any number of problems, from preventing reproduction to precluding sexual activity altogether."[14]

I agree with Henning that humoral theory is behind this description. However, the paradigm of humoral imbalance had two spectrums: hot-cold and wet-dry. It seems more likely to assume that the girl's primary imbalance has to do with humidity, as her condition is explicitly described

---

11. Klauck, *Apocryphal Acts of the Apostles*, 106.

12. Meghan Henning, "Paralysis and Sexualilty in Medical Literature and the Acts of Peter," *JLA* 8 (2015): 311.

13. Henning, "Paralysis and Sexualilty in Medical Literature," 311–13.

14. Henning, "Paralysis and Sexualilty in Medical Literature," 318.

in terms of dryness: she is "paralysed from head to foot and dried up" (Act Pet. 135:6–9). Paralysis could be conceived of in terms of desiccation, as noted in discussions above (§2.2 and §3.3). For a woman to be "dried up" could also signal infertility.[15] According to Hippocratic gynecological treatises, the womb could dry out if it lacked the irrigation of menses and male sperm through intercourse. Such desiccation could cause the womb to dislocate and travel around the body in search of moisture. "The wandering womb" was a condition with symptoms such as suffocation, fever, headache, pains, loss of speech, lethargy, and delirium.[16] Moss has argued that the woman with the flow of blood in Mark 5:26–34 can be understood in light of ancient medical conceptions of women as moist and leaky. Jesus's healing causes a transition from "sickly, effeminate leaker to faith-dried healthy follower."[17] Similarly, Peter's daughter's body may have been read as infertile due to this desiccated state.

In the text, the daughter's dried up, lame body is not a problem; it is a solution, a positive state. This bodily state is possibly also understood as masculinized. The tale of Peter's daughter fits well with the theme of sexual renunciation that is typical of the apocryphal acts. Within this tradition, virginity was regarded as a step in the direction of masculinity and *virtus* and as a way to overcome female passion and passivity.[18] To renounce marriage as part of one's commitment to Christ was conceived of in terms of a gender transition from female to male. Women ascetics were thought of as "becoming male" (e.g., Gos. Thom. 114).[19] A dry, hardened body can from this perspective be seen as a masculinized body.[20] Moss interprets the woman with the flow of blood (Mark 5:21–43) in this light. The healing by Jesus is described as a "drying up" (ἐξηράνθη, 5:29), which may mean that she becomes menopausal as an anticipation of the eschaton.

---

15. Weissenrieder, *Images of Illness in the Gospel of Luke*, 81–84.

16. Nancy Demand, *Birth, Death, and Motherhood in Classical Greece* (Baltimore: Johns Hopkins University Press, 1994), 55.

17. Candida R. Moss, "The Man with the Flow of Power: Porous Bodies in Mark 5:25–34," *JBL* 129 (2010): 515.

18. Solevåg, *Birthing Salvation*, 62–64.

19. See, e.g., Kari Vogt, "'Becoming Male': A Gnostic and Early Christian Metaphor," in *The Image of God and Gender Models in Judaeo-Christian Tradition*, ed. Kari Elisabeth Børresen (Minneapolis: Fortress, 1995); Elizabeth A. Clark, *Reading Renunciation: Asceticism and Scripture in Early Christianity* (Princeton: Princeton University Press, 1999).

20. Moss, "Man with the Flow of Power," 513–14.

Her infertile body is thus a prefiguration of the resurrected body.[21] Like the woman with the flow of blood, she transitions from a moist, female body to a dried-up, masculinized body.[22] The body of Peter's daughter may similarly represent an infertile, masculinized body that prefigures the eschaton. In such a metaphorical use of disability, "lame" and "dried up" signify a more valuable bodily state than being able-bodied.[23]

The impairment is only on one side of the body, from head to foot. A similar description of one-sided paralysis also occurs in the story of Rufina in Actus Vercellenses, and the connection between the two stories will be discussed below. There are accounts of half-paralysis in Greek medical literature. Both Aretaeus and Galen attribute such paralysis to some affection of the spinal cord (Aretaeus, *Sign. diut.* 1.7; Galen, *Loc. aff.* 3.14). This description of the daughter's condition probably has more to do with notions of beauty than medicine. Proportionality and symmetry were important aspects of ancient notions of beauty.[24] It is therefore surprising that the daughter is described as beautiful by Peter's interlocutors: "Why have you not helped your virgin daughter, who has grown up beautiful" (Act Pet. 128:19).[25] The narrative here undercuts the conventional association of beauty with ability and proportionality.[26] The above argued connection between the daughter's disability and her virginity can explain this shift in the understanding of beauty.

4.2.1. Disability as a Good—For Whom?

Peter's claim that the daughter's situation is good for both her and himself reflects Greco-Roman gender values. A young girl was a future bride, and a young, free woman's most important asset was her virginity. Peter's argument also reveals his position as a householder, a male *kyrios*, whose responsibility it was to rule over the household and keep wife, children,

---

21. Moss, "Mark and Matthew," 289, 296.

22. Moss, "Man with the Flow of Power," 515.

23. See Baden and Moss, *Reconceiving Infertility*, 236; Moss, "Mark and Matthew," 292.

24. Alexandre Mitchell, "The Hellenistic Turn in Bodily Representations: Venting Anxiety in Terracotta Figurines," in Laes, *Disability in Antiquity*, 183.

25. Baden and Moss note that this description undercuts the conventional association of beauty with able-bodiedness: "Her condition is not metaphorically disfiguring" (*Reconceiving Infertility*, 195).

26. Baden and Moss, *Reconceiving Infertility*, 195.

and slaves under control. It was shameful for the whole family if a daughter was sexually violated, especially for the head of the household, whose responsibility it was to protect the sexual honor of women in his family. The daughter's disability is framed according to this hierarchy of valued goods. Peter's story suggests that the daughter became paralyzed as a protection against rape or forced marriage. Two different "afflictions" are thus juxtaposed: Which is better, to be lame or to have a violated body? To have a broken leg or a broken hymen? The daughter's disability is held up as the preferred alternative—good both for herself and for her father's honor.

The Roman tradition of abduction marriages may help surmise what happens in the lacuna. Abduction marriages were well known in antiquity. *Raptus*, as it was called, involved the abduction of an unmarried girl by a man who had not made a formal betrothal agreement with her. The assumption that the union had been consummated would then force the consent of the girl's parents to a marriage between the two.[27] The girl would be considered "damaged goods" and hence unmarriageable to anyone but the abductor. Hence, the hoped-for end result was that the abductor would marry his victim. Ptolemy's scheme bears a resemblance to the typical *raptus*.[28] After his marriage offer is repeatedly turned down, Ptolemy becomes impatient and abducts the girl, but something happens to her body during the abduction, and he therefore returns her to her father's home, paralyzed but otherwise unharmed. Ptolemy does not complete the *raptus* scheme of offering to marry the girl. For some reason, she is no longer of interest to him, perhaps, as Henning suggests, because a paralyzed woman would be understood as infertile.[29] It is clear from the narrative that marriage is not an option after the kidnapping, and the daughter remains a virgin in her father's house because of this episode (Act Pet. 128:18).

Exactly how paralysis rescued the daughter from violation is unclear due to the lacuna. There seems to be a logical flaw in the story's argument. It seems more likely that paralysis would make the daughter more vul-

---

27. Judith Evans Grubbs, "Abduction Marriage in Antiquity: A Law of Constantine (CTh. IX. 24. I) and Its Social Context," *JRS* 79 (1989): 61.

28. The fate of Verginia, as told by Livy, has clear likenesses to Peter's daughter. In a desperate attempt to hinder his daughter from being abducted and raped, the statesman Verginius killed his own daughter (Livy, *Urb. cond.* 3.44–48). Molinari also notes the similarities between these two stories ("*I Never Knew the Man,*" 128–56).

29. Henning, "Paralysis and Sexuality in Medical Literature," 309.

nerable to sexual assault.[30] However, the divinely inflicted paralysis functions as an alternative and more honorable explanation for the daughter's unmarried state than sexual violation. The inherent logic of the *raptus* scenario is that the girl does not necessarily have to be raped: her reputation is ruined simply by the possibility that she is no longer a virgin.[31] The narrator glosses over the fact that her reputation is in fact ruined by insisting on her virginity and by focusing on her disability, which likewise renders her unmarriageable.

The combination of householder and apostle that we find in the narrative construction of Peter in this story makes him extremely powerful.[32] As a child, a female, and a disabled person, Peter's daughter is multiply disadvantaged and has no say when her father declares her situation good. Peter has absolute power over his daughter's body, and the benefit seems to be more for the crowd, whose faith is increased, and for Peter, whose honor is preserved, than for the girl herself.[33] The gaze of the reader in this text is in other words male and clearly kyriarchal. What is presented as beneficial and good is from the perspective of a male householder. Although the daughter is at the center of attention, she is not given a name, like her male suitor is. The reader's gaze lingers on the body of Peter's daughter at different moments: she is observed bathing by Ptolemy, her beauty is remarked on by Peter's interlocutors, and she is gazed at as she silently obeys her father's bidding to walk toward him and return to her place. Throughout the narrative she never utters a word but remains silent. The narrative thus displays many of the features typical of the ancient male gaze, drawing on nudity, silence, and public exposure of the female as object.[34]

In the last section of the Act, Peter narrates what happened to Ptolemy in the aftermath of the abduction. According to Peter, Ptolemy regretted

---

30. According to the United Nations (https://www.un.org/development/desa/disabilities/issues/women-and-girls-with-disabilities.html), women and girls with disabilities are particularly vulnerable to gender-based violence and sexual abuse worldwide.

31. Grubbs, "Abduction Marriage in Antiquity," 62.

32. Cornelia B. Horn, "Suffering Children, Parental Authority and the Quest for Liberation?: A Tale of Three Girls in the *Acts of Paul (and Thecla)*, the *Act(s) of Peter*, the *Acts of Nerseus and Achilleus*, and the *Epistle of Pseudo-Titus*," in *A Feminist Companion to the New Testament Apocrypha*, ed. Amy-Jill Levine with Maria Mayo Robbins (London: T&T Clark, 2006), 135.

33. Horn, "Suffering Children," 136.

34. Richlin, "Introduction," xix.

his actions and was contemplating suicide, but then he had a vision: "He saw a great light which illuminated the whole house and he heard a voice saying to him, 'Ptolemy, God has not given the vessels for corruption and shame; it is not right for you, as a believer in me, to violate my virgin, whom you are to know as my sister … go to the house of Peter and you shall see my glory'" (Act Pet. 137:1–9). With the help of his servants, Ptolemy is brought to Peter, who heals him, "and he saw with the eyes of his flesh and with the eyes of his soul" (138:7–10). In a typical metaphorizing move, Ptolemy is given double visionary ability. He regains his eyesight at the same time as he metaphorically sees the light and obtains theological insight. As already noted, this metaphorical use of blindness was a literary topos in antiquity (see §3.4). Here, like in John 9:1–41, this commonplace metaphor connected to a disability is used to develop the text's theology.

Why is Ptolemy granted healing when Peter's daughter is not? Although it is unclear whether or not Ptolemy's blindness is a punishment for sin, it is somehow an effect of his previous sins. If Peter's daughter's beauty was a temptation to Ptolemy, remaining blind could have been a good solution to his bodily weakness. However, the problem of Peter's daughter is bigger than just Ptolemy. As Peter had been told in a vision at the girl's birth: "This daughter will harm many souls, if her body remains well!" (Act Pet. 132:1–4). In this narrative, the woman must carry in her body the problem of male sexual temptation and aggression. The gaze of the text is not only male; it is also disabling: she must be inflicted with disability in order to avoid being a temptation. The narrative turns Peter's daughter into a lesson about what is most beneficial for her father and other men in the Christ-believing community.

4.3. Rufina

The Actus Vercellences begins with the apostle Paul taking leave of the Roman believers to go as an apostle to Spain. Before he leaves, he shares the Eucharist with the Romans for the last time. This scene turns into a confrontation with one of the believers, Rufina:

> Among those present was a woman named Rufina, who wished to receive the eucharist from the hands of Paul. And when she came forward, Paul, filled by the spirit of God, said to her, "Rufina, you do not approach the altar of God as a believer, since you rise from the side not of a husband but of an adulterer, and yet you endeavour to receive God's

eucharist. Behold, Satan will trample down your head and expose you before the eyes of all who believer in the Lord, so that they may see and believe and know that they have believed in the living God, the searcher of hearts…. But if you do not repent while you are still in the body, the devouring fire and the outer darkness will receive you forever." And at once Rufina collapsed, being paralysed on the left side from head to foot [*a sinistra parte a capite usque ad ungues pedum contorminata cecidit*]. Nor could she speak any more, for her tongue was tied [*nec potestas data est loquendi: lingua enim eius obligata est*]. (Act. Verc. 2)

Two different afflictions befall Rufina: she is paralyzed, and she loses her voice. First, like Peter's daughter, Rufina is paralyzed from head to foot. In fact, the Latin is even more specific: she is paralyzed from head to toenails (*ungues pedum*). A comparison of wording is complicated by the fact the story of Peter's daughter is in Coptic, but here, too, nails are specifically mentioned (*eib*, 134:8).[35] In other words, both Peter's daughter and Rufina are described as paralyzed on one side of the whole body. Second, Rufina loses her ability speak. The expression "her tongue was tied" (*lingua obligata est*) should be seen in light of ancient understanding of muteness as some sort impediment to the tongue.[36]

In this passage, there is the same juxtaposition of a powerful, male, able-bodied apostle and a powerless, disabled woman as in the story of Peter's daughter. The gaze of the reader rests on Rufina as she becomes a spectacle: exposed and punished before the eyes of the Christ-believing community at Rome. She is silenced and immobilized through divine interventions, and it is clear that she serves as a lesson for the whole community. When the other believers see her lying there, "they beat their breasts, remembering their former sins" (Act. Verc. 2), and Paul takes the opportunity to give a sermon about repentance and the right way to live as believers. After the sermon, the text never mentions Rufina again, so the reader is left to wonder about her fate. Does she repent her sins? Is she healed? The text provides no answers.

I suggest that the episode with Rufina serves as a preview of what will become of Simon Magus. The two things that happen to her—she becomes mute and paralyzed—also befall Simon through his contests

---

35. Thomas argues that the similarity in wording "from head to (toe)nails" is a strong argument that both texts belong to the same textual tradition (*Acts of Peter*, 20).

36. Christian Laes, "Silent Witnesses: Deaf-Mutes in Graeco-Roman Antuquity," *CW* 104 (2011): 471–72; Weissenrieder, *Images of Illness*, 116.

with Peter. Simon becomes mute in two different episodes. He is ridiculed and silenced by two messengers sent to him by Peter, a dog and a baby (Act. Verc. 11; 15). A man with proper control of his body and his speech should be able to subdue and silence a dog and a child, both of which he is kyriarchically superior to. But the opposite happens; the dog and the baby silence the man: "At once he became speechless, and being constrained he left Rome" (Act. Verc. 15). Simon also becomes paralyzed in the end. In a final contest with Peter he tries to fly to show his superior magic skills. As Simon ascends over Rome, Peter prays that he may fall down and "break his leg in three places" (Mart. Pet. 3), which happens. Simon flees the city and eventually dies from the injury to his leg: "Following an operation Simon, the messenger of the devil, ended his life" (Mart. Pet. 3).

Both of these disabilities, muteness and mobility impairment, are used metaphorically in the narrative. Rufina's loss of speech is juxtaposed to Paul's eloquent talk in the sermon he gives after he exposes her adultery. Whenever Simon's speech is referred to, it is ridiculed. His voice is called shrill (Act. Verc. 4), and the dog calls Simon's voice "weak and useless" (Act. Verc. 12). The baby, on the other hand, speaks with a manly voice (Act. Verc. 15). According to ancient physiognomic treatises, a high-pitched voice was a sign of cowardice. Flaws in vocal control signaled lack of sexual self-control, and this was considered a feminine trait.[37]

When Simon breaks his leg, he is injured on one side of his body, just like Rufina. Rufina, who is caught in adultery, thus prefigures Simon as a seducer of the Roman Christ-believers. As a seducer of the faithful, Simon resembles an adulterous woman. The adulterous woman, often cast as a *foreign* seductress, was a common metaphor for idolatry in the Hebrew Bible that was further developed in early Christianity.[38] Simon, I argue, is cast according to this type. He is called a seducer (*seductor*, 7), and the verb *seduco* is used to describe his actions (Act. Verc. 9, 10).[39] By tying Simon to this literary topos, the text ridicules, disgraces, and effeminizes him. The accusation that Simon is a seducer of the Christ-believers thus plays on the same notions that underlie the references to his inadequate voice: that Simon is an effeminate, weak character. In this interpretation,

---

37. Gleason, *Making Men*, 83.

38. See Gail Corrington Streete, *The Strange Woman: Power and Sex in the Bible* (Louisville: Westminster John Knox, 1997).

39. The Vulgate uses the terms *seduco* and *seductor* about Satan, the Antichrist, and the beast (2 John 1:7; Rev 12:9; 13:14).

Rufina's disability is not only physiognomic, in that it reveals her inner moral character; it is also symbolic, in that it represents the fate of heretics.

4.4. The Blind Widows

The metaphorical potential of blindness is also drawn out in an episode that takes place in the house of Marcellus, where the Roman Christ-believers gather. First, Peter heals a blind widow, saying, "Come here, mother, from this day Jesus gives you his right hand; through him we have light unapproachable which darkness cannot hide. Through me he says to you, 'Open your eyes, see and walk on your own'" (Act. Verc. 20). The woman is healed, and after the healing, Peter gives a sermon on the transfiguration of Jesus. He tells the believers how he, as an eyewitness, thought that he had lost his eyesight when he experienced the brightness as Jesus was transformed. Peter continues to praise Jesus with the following words: "this Great and Small One, this Beautiful and Ugly one, this young man and old man, appearing in time, yet utterly invisible in eternity" (Act. Verc. 20). The healings are used as a starting point to speak metaphorically about sight and blindness, light and darkness, drawing on the literary topos of blindness as lack of insight (see §3.4).

After the sermon, Peter is approached by a whole group of widows who want to be healed. This gives Peter a second opportunity to exploit the metaphorical level of blindness, and he preaches on the different kinds of seeing. "See with the mind what you cannot see with the eyes," he exhorts them (Act. Verc. 21). Seeing with one's eyes, Peter argues, is inferior to seeing with one's mind. He draws attention to the temporality and futility of this sensory ability: "These eyes will be closed again, which see nothing else than men and cattle, and dumb animals and stone and wood; but not all eyes see Jesus Christ" (Act. Verc. 21). Still, he prays for the widows, "that they may see with their eyes" (Act. Verc. 21). A bright light appears, which enters into the widows' eyes and makes them see. The Latin "*et fecit eas uidere*" is translated by Elliot as "and they regained their sight."[40] Perhaps better translated as "he made them see," it is unclear what kind of vision the widows gain and whether the healing lasts. I posit that it is only temporary visionary ability that the widows are granted and that they are not permanently healed from blindness.

---

40. "Acts of Peter," in Elliott, *Apocryphal New Testament*, 415.

During the appearance of the bright light, the widows have visions. Each of the widows sees Christ in different forms, it turns out. One sees a young man, another one sees an old man, and a third sees a boy touching her eyes. The widows are not reported to see anything other than these visions. The widows, it seems, have been granted the superior kind of vision, as they have been given eyes that see Jesus. The widows' visions confirm what Peter preached earlier about the multiform appearance of Christ, and the apostle draws the conclusion that "God is greater than our thoughts, as we have learned from the old widows, how they saw the Lord in different forms" (Act. Verc. 21). The "healings" thus do not heal the widows for their own sake, but they serve as a springboard to empower the community. By gazing at the widows, the community's faith is strengthened. At the same time, this stare also fixes widows in their role as what Garland-Thomson calls "starees"—they are drafted "into a story of the starer's making…, whether they like it or not."[41]

It should be noted that blindness is deployed in the Acts of Peter as a rhetorical device quite different from muteness. The widows are not sexualized, and their faith is not questioned. Whereas blindness is used to elucidate a theological point, muteness is used to stress the power game between Simon and Peter, to ridicule and unman the great apostle's opponent. There is also an ethical component to muteness that is lacking with blindness. Muteness is a bad character trait; it exposes someone as a sinner, like Rufina, or someone connected to the devil, like Simon. Blindness does not have this physiognomic connection. It is not morally bad; rather, it symbolizes insight and wisdom and a connection to the divine. Both Ptolemy and the widows have visions of Jesus in their blind state. These usages draw on the culturally assigned places of blindness and muteness in Greco-Roman society. One aspect of the literary topos of blindness was that this disability sometimes granted other abilities, such as visionary gifts or fortunetelling.[42] Muteness, on the other hand, together with deafness, was aligned with mental disability and stupidity.[43]

---

41. Garland-Thomson, *Staring*, 7–8.

42. Hartsock, *Sight and Blindness in Luke-Acts*, 76–81; Garland, *Eye of the Beholder*, 32–34.

43. Rose, *Staff of Oedipus*, 72, 76–77.

4.5. The Female Demon

In a scene leading up to the final encounter between Peter and Simon, one of the Roman Christ-believers has a vision. Marcellus, a senator and the patron of Peter and Roman believers, has a vision that foretells the violent death of Simon:

> In my sleep I saw you [i.e., Peter] sitting in an elevated place and before you a great multitude and a very ugly woman [*mulierem quendam turpissimam*] in appearance an Ethiopian, not an Egyptian, but very black [*totam nigram*], clad in filthy rags [*sordibus, pannis involutam*], who danced with an iron chain about the neck and a chain on her hands and feet. When you saw her you said to me with a loud voice, "Marcellus, this dancer is the whole power of Simon and of his god; behead her." (Act. Verc. 22)

The female demon is identified as a figuration of Simon. Thus this literary figure serves a similar function to Rufina, who also prefigures the fate of Simon. In the vision, Peter tells Marcellus to behead the demon, but Marcellus hesitates, arguing that he is a senator and has never before killed anyone, not even a sparrow. So Peter calls out to Christ to implement the execution: " 'Come, our true sword, Jesus Christ, and not only cut off the head of this demon, but break all her limbs in the presence of all these whom I have tested in your service.' And at once a man who looked like you, Peter, came with a sword in his hand and cut her into pieces" (Act. Verc. 22).

The demon character, who is mutilated and killed, is described with ethnic, class, and gender characteristics. According to Greco-Roman kyriarchal ideals, she is other and inferior to the Christ/Peter figure in every possible way. Concerning ethnicity, she is identified as an Ethiopian with black skin. It was common in antiquity to describe demons as black.[44] Early Christian writers took over this Greco-Roman trope and often connect blackness in general, and Egyptians and Ethiopians in particular, with demons and the devil.[45] In the Martyrdom of Perpetua and Felici-

---

44. Bremmer, "Women, Magic, Place and Date," 8.

45. Byron, *Symbolic Blackness and Ethnic Difference*, 44–45. Bremmer suggests that the resemblance shows that Perpetua had read the Acts of Peter. In my opinion, the resemblance only reflects the common cultural trope of linking demons with African ethnicity ("Women, Magic, Place and Date," 9).

tas, Perpetua has a similar vision of a fight with the devil. In her vision, Satan is a monstrous Egyptian gladiator. In Actus Vercellences, the female demon is described as "Ethiopian, not Egyptian," which underscores not only that she is black but also that she comes from outside the empire. In Greco-Roman literature, Ethiopia was constructed as the end of the world and thus as barbarian and mythic.[46]

The demon is further described as dirty, scantily clad in filthy rags, chained, and dancing. The figure is, then, also inferior to Marcellus in terms of class. In contrast to the Roman senator, who is powerful, free, and well dressed, this woman is described as a slave figure. To make sure that slaves did not run away, slaves were sometimes tattooed or branded, or they were made to wear metal collars or fetters.[47] Judith Perkins has argued that the Acts reveals "a certain sympathy for the sensibilities of slaves."[48] She points to a scene in which Marcellus's slaves harass Simon and another where Peter argues for the manumission of a senator's slaves after he has raised the senator from death (Act. Verc. 14; 28). The image of the dancing Ethiopian, however, is an image of someone altogether other in race, class, and gender, with no identification or sympathy from the narrator.[49]

Why is the demon dancing? I suggest that she is presented as the lowliest of slaves, the slave prostitute (πόρνη).[50] Prostitutes were commonly associated with dancing and nudity.[51] Among the ethnic stereotypes about Ethiopians and other dark-skinned people was their sexual license, and in early Christian literature, they were used as symbols of sexual vice.[52] The literary trope of the foreign seductress, already introduced through the references to Simon as a seducer and his connection to Rufina, is made even more explicit by tying Simon to this imagery of a foreign slave prostitute. The stereotype of the foreign seductress is also found in Roman lit-

---

46. Byron, *Symbolic Blackness and Ethnic Difference*, 31–34.

47. Glancy, *Slavery in Early Christianity*, 88–89.

48. Perkins, *Suffering Self*, 139.

49. Callon argues against Perkins but does not include the demon passage in her discussion of slaves in the Acts of Peter ("Secondary Characters Furthering Characterization: The Depiction of Slaves in the *Acts of Peter*," *JBL* 131 [2012]: 816–17).

50. Avaren Ipsen, *Sex Working and the Bible*, ed. Philip R. Davies and James G. Crossley, Bible World (London: Equinox, 2009), 126.

51. Elaine Fantham et al., *Women in the Classical World: Image and Text* (New York: Oxford University Press, 1994), 23.

52. Byron, *Symbolic Blackness and Ethnic Difference*, 35.

erature. Shelley P. Haley argues that the representations of foreign women by writers like Vergil and Livy reveal the fear among Roman ruling class men of powerful women and "reinforc[e] the need for patriarchal control of female sexuality, whether domestic or foreign."[53]

The female demon represents Simon "and his god," which is Satan. The text uses physiognomic reasoning to express that an ugly exterior reveals an evil interior. In order to describe the worst evil, Satan, the text conjures an image of a black, Ethiopian slave prostitute. As Garland-Thomson's has observed, gender, race, and ability are often intertwined to form the subjugated other: "Female, disabled, and dark bodies are supposed to be dependent, incomplete, vulnerable, and incompetent bodies. Femininity and race are the performance of disability."[54] The sexual power of the female demon is so dangerous that it needs to be entirely eradicated. The demon figure is tortured and disabled when all her limbs are cut off. The male gaze of the text is yet again directed toward a sexualized and silenced female body, and as with Peter's daughter and Rufina, the male gaze is violent and disabling.

4.6. Conclusion: Spectacles of Female Disablement

In conclusion, I want to make some observations about the disabling function of the male gaze in the Acts of Peter. First, through the male gaze, these women are exposed to the reader. No women are permanently healed. Rather, as their disablement is stared at, the staree, to borrow Garland-Thomson's term, is somehow healed. It has been noted that in the healing and unhealing miracles of the Acts of Peter, it is the community, rather than the individual, that seems to be the main beneficiary. Magda Misset-van de Weg has argued that phrases such as "God cares for his people and prepares for each what is good" (139:9–140:4) and "the Lord always takes care of his own" (Act. Verc. 22) underline this point.[55] In the story about Peter's daughter, Ptolemy is converted, and after his death

---

53. Shelley P. Haley, "Be Not Afraid of the Dark: Critical Race Theory and Classical Studies," in Schüssler Fiorenza and Nasrallah, *Prejudice and Christian Beginnings*, 34.

54. Garland-Thomson, "Integrating Disability, Transforming Feminist Theory," 358.

55. Magda Misset-van de Weg, "'For the Lord Always Takes Care of His Own': The Purpose of the Wondrous Works and Deeds in the *Acts of Peter*," in *The Apoc-

the daughter inherits his fortune, which Peter bequeaths to the poor (139:1–17). Thus, the community benefits both spiritually and materially from the incident. Rufina's disabling likewise becomes an opportunity for the community to repent their sins, and finally the visions of the widows strengthen the believers' faith. The healing of the blind widows is not primarily for the benefit of the women themselves but for the community whose faith is strengthened through their visions of Jesus.

Second, the disabling exposure of the gaze is violent. Todd Penner and Caroline Vander Stichele observe that in the canonical Acts, violence by outsiders is represented as unjustified, whereas insider violence is just.[56] This pattern of violence is gendered, and in the Lukan Acts, both the perpetrators and victims of violence are men.[57] In the Acts of Peter, there is also a gendered narrative strategy of violence, but unlike in Acts, women are the primary victims. Two women, Peter's daughter and Rufina, suffer from an apostle's "just" infliction of disability, and Simon, the third victim, is feminized through his allegorical connections to Rufina and the female demon. In these stories of unhealing, the infliction of disability is a recurring form of narrative violence. Like in Acts, outsider violence is unjustified, but insider violence is just: when Simon injures and kills people, it is unjustified (Act. Verc. 17; 25), but when Peter does the same, it is acceptable, even beneficial.

Third, these stories about disablement are closely tied to sexuality. Rufina is punished for adultery. She brings shame not only upon herself but also upon the congregation through her promiscuous behavior. Peter's daughter has been paralyzed as an act of God to preserve her from being violated by Ptolemy and possibly other men, too. The female demon serves as an allegory of Simon's seductive powers over the Roman Christ-believers. The male gaze is seen in the exposure of these sexualized female bodies as well as in the different valuation of male and female sexual sin (e.g., Ptolemy's healing versus Rufina's unhealing).

---

ryphal Acts of Peter: Magic, Miracles and Gnosticism, ed. Jan N. Bremmer (Leuven: Peeters, 1998), 101.

56. Caroline Vander Stichele and Todd C. Penner, "Gendering Violence: Patterns of Power and Constructs of Masculinity in the Acts of the Apostles," in A Feminist Companion to the Acts of the Apostles, ed. Amy-Jill Levine with Marianne Blickenstaff, FCNTECW (London: T&T Clark, 2004), 198.

57. Stichele and Penner, "Gendering Violence," 199.

Fourth, these stories function to domesticate women. A primary value in the narratives is the kyriarchal preservation of the honor of the family. Through the apostle's actions of preaching, healing, and unhealing, they are put in their place and literally immobilized. Sexual modesty is at the core of Rufina and Peter's daughter's stories, but the aspect of voice is also important. Among these female characters, it is only the widows that speak. Rufina is even explicitly made mute; thus she cannot talk back or oppose the apostle's version of her story. Peter's daughter says nothing but obeys her father silently throughout the story. The women all belong to the semi-private space of the Christian community. They are inside patrons' houses or attending worship services.

It should be noted that speech, vision, and mobility have very different connotations in the Acts of Peter. As noted, muteness is connected to sin and draws on gendered notions of silence and voice through a physiognomic, moralizing move. The story about the blind widows, however, primarily draws on the trope of seeing as understanding, recognition, and faith through a symbolic move. Mobility serves a third function. In each of the three female characters—the paralyzed adulteress, the lame virgin, and the mutilated slave prostitute—there is a connection between sexuality and lameness. All three women are paralyzed to reduce their sexual power. Peter's daughter is an involuntary seductress. She cannot help it, but her beauty drives men to extremes, and her disability rescues her from the consequences—the (revelation of the) loss of her virginity. Rufina is exposed and humbled before the Christian community after her sexual transgression, and the dancing Ethiopian is mutilated and killed to subdue the demonic power of her sexuality. Lameness seems to occupy a gendered space that has to do with limitation of sexualized power. Women, who either succumb to such vices or through their beauty awaken lust in men, may be disabled for the benefit of the community.

5

THE RHETORIC OF MADNESS AND DEMON POSSESSION

5.1. Introduction: Stigma and the Normate

In the three preceding chapters, I looked at various aspects of early Christian healing narratives. I now turn to other representations of disability in early Christian literature, looking at how disability is used rhetorically and functions as a label in polemical discussions. Ancient rhetoric was "a man's world," in which deportment and proper display of manliness in speech was important.[1] As noted in the introduction, discourses on disability and masculinity overlapped, as the norms of masculinity entailed a fully functioning, intact body (see §1.6). This chapter focuses on the intersection of disability and masculinity discourses and shows how accusations about deviant bodies were used as invective in order to vilify opponents. I will study two cases: accusations against Jesus in the gospels that he was possessed (Matt 12:22–32; Mark 3:19b–30; Luke 11:14–23; 7:28; 8:48–52; 10:20–21) and Paul's self-defense against accusations of madness and bodily weakness in the Corinthian correspondence (e.g., 1 Cor 2:3–5; 2 Cor 5:13; 11:16–30).

In this chapter, I use Erving Goffman's notion of stigma and the way it has been developed within disability studies. *Stigma* is a Greek term that originates in antiquity, and Goffman uses it in order to look at how physical marks can be used to socially ostracize. As he notes, in antiquity, slaves and criminals were physically marked "to expose something unusual and bad about the moral status of the signifier. The signs were cut or burnt into the body and advertised that the bearer was ... a blemished person."[2] Goff-

---

1. Gleason, *Making Men*, 72–73.
2. Erving Goffman, *Stigma: Notes on the Management of Spoiled Identity* (Harmondsworth: Penguin, 1968), 11.

man uses the term stigma to refer to "an attribute that is deeply discrediting," and he argues that "the normals" need the stigmatized as a category against which to define their own normality.[3] Goffman notes that physical deformities are often stigmatized but observes that cultural attributions of difference also include other aspects, such as race, religion, and nationality.[4] The set of norms that modern society has set up has the effect of disqualifying many people: "There is only one complete unblushing male in America: a young, married, white, urban, northern, heterosexual, Protestant, father, of college education, fully employed, of good complexion, weight, and height, and a recent record in sports."[5] Garland-Thomson argues that the process of stigmatization legitimates the status quo and naturalizes attributions of inherent inferiority and superiority. Stigma theory is useful because it resituates the "problem" of disability from the body of the disabled person to the social framing of that body.[6]

Lerita M. Coleman Brown argues that stigma is a response to the dilemma of difference. She notes that it is not only socially constructed but also quite arbitrary: "The infinite variety of human attributes suggests that what is undesired or stigmatized is heavily dependent on the social context and to some extent arbitrarily defined."[7] She also observes that the stigmatizing process allows some individuals to feel superior to others: "In order for one person to feel superior, there must be another person who is perceived to be or who actually feels inferior. Stigmatized people are needed in order for the many nonstigmatized people to feel good about themselves."[8] Garland-Thomson also exposes this dependent relationship between the nonstigmatized and the stigmatized. She argues that the normate and the disabled figure mutually constitute one another: the cultural other and the cultural self operate together as opposing twin figures that legitimate a system of social, economic, and political empowerment justified by physiological differences."[9] Stigma theory provides a means to trace the production of cultural others and reveal how particular traits

---

3. Goffman, *Stigma*, 13–17.

4. Goffman, *Stigma*, 14–15.

5. Goffman, *Stigma*, 153.

6. Thomson, *Extraordinary Bodies*, 31–32.

7. Lerita M. Coleman Brown, "Stigma: An Enigma Demystified," in Davis, *Disability Studies Reader*, 180.

8. Brown, "Stigma," 181.

9. Thomson, *Extraordinary Bodies*, 8.

are deemed not only different but deviant.[10] Although the kinds of bodies that are stigmatized may vary in different cultures and different historical times, the phenomenon of stigmatization seems to have a place in most societies.[11] Stigma theory is useful because it examines the interrelationships between social identities rather than relying on dichotomies such as male/female or able-bodied/disabled. Moreover, it resituates the problem of disability in the social construction of bodies rather than in the individual bodies of disabled persons.[12] I will use the notion of stigma and the hegemonic construction of the normate to explore how nonnormative bodies were stigmatized in ancient rhetoric.

5.1.1. Madness and Demon Possession as Competing Illness Paradigms

Whereas demon possession belonged to the popular health care sector and was based on an invasion etiology, madness was a more sophisticated label, connected with professional medicine, philosophy, and the Greek literary tradition.[13] From the Hippocratics onward, madness was an important topic in the medical literature. The medical writers agreed that the causes of madness were to be found in the body, and they developed various theories of mental illness based on the humoral theory and the Hippocratic notion of balance.[14] Within this discourse we find a distinct vocabulary connected to madness, with terms such as παράνοια, ἄγνοια, μανία, μαίνομαι, ἄφρων, and ἐξίσταμαι.[15] Although there were a variety

---

10. Thomson, *Extraordinary Bodies*, 31.

11. Brown, "Stigma," 179–84.

12. Thomson, *Extraordinary Bodies*, 8, 32.

13. On demon possession, see §1.4. On madness, see the various articles in William V. Harris, *Mental Disorders in the Classical World* (Leiden: Brill, 2013), e.g., Philip J. van der Eijk, "Cure and (In)curability of Mental Disorders in Ancient Medical and Philosophical Thought," in Harris, *Mental Disorders*, 311; Chiara Thumiger, "The Early Greek Medical Vocabulary of Insanity," in Harris, *Medical Disorders*, 72. See also Martin, *Corinthian Body*, 146–59.

14. Jacques Jouanna, "The Typology and Aetiology of Madness in Ancient Greek Medical and Philosophical Writing," in Harris, *Mental Disorders*, 98–102; Chris F. Goodey and Martha Lynn Rose, "Mental States, Bodily Dispositions and Table Manners: A Guide to Reading 'Intellectual' Disability from Homer to Late Antiquity," in Laes, Goodey, and Rose, *Disabilities in Roman Antiquity*, 17–18; Chiara Thumiger, "Mental Disability? Galen on Mental Health," in Laes, *Disability in Antiquity*, 268.

15. Thumiger, "Early Greek Medical Vocabulary of Insanity."

of theories, the vocabulary used to define and describe mental illnesses shows a remarkable coherence throughout antiquity.[16]

In the Hippocratic treatise *The Sacred Disease*, the author discusses the illness that is called sacred (τῆς ἱερῆς νούσου, *Morb. sacr.* 1). This illness is described with symptoms such as sudden seizures, rigid limbs, and frothing around the mouth, which modern interpreters have often understood as a description of epilepsy.[17] I am wary of such retrospective diagnosis and more interested in understanding the disease within its own medical framework.[18] The author of *The Sacred Disease* argues that this illness has become known as sacred only because people do not understand its causes and have thus thought it must come from the gods. He calls those who try to treat the illness by means of purifications and incantations charlatans and quacks who do so for their personal gain and without any real understanding of the illness (*Morb. sacr.* 2). The writer then goes on to explain the cause of the illness by way of humoral theory. It is caused by excess phlegm that blocks the flow of air to the brain (*Morb. sacr.* 5–10). The illness has a physical cause and is thus like all other:

> This disease styled sacred comes from the same causes as others, from the things that come and go from the body, from cold, sun, and from the changing restlessness of winds…. Whoever knows how to cause in men by regimen moist or dry, hot or cold, he can cure this disease also, if he distinguish the seasons for useful treatment, without having recourse to purifications and magic. (*Morb. sacr.* 21 [Jones])

In this treatise, the writer attacks proponents of an invasion etiology of illness at the same time as he develops his own views about the physical causes of illness according to a paradigm of imbalance. Treatment of the

---

16. According to Joanna, the semiotics of insanity is fairly constant throughout the period, although the etiology differs among the different writers and develops over time ("Typology and Aetiology of Madness," 97, 117–18; see also Thumiger, "Early Greek Medical Vocabulary of Insanity," 72).

17. Nicole Kelley, "'The Punishment of the Devil Was Apparent in the Torment of the Human Body': Epilepsy in Ancient Christianity," in Moss and Schipper, *Disability Studies and Biblical Literature*.

18. For a discussion of retrospective diagnosis, see Lutz Alexander Graumann, "Monstrous Births and Retrospective Diagnosis," in Laes, Goodey, and Rose, *Disabilities in Roman Antiquity*. See also Marx-Wolf and Upson-Saia, "State of the Question," 267.

illness depends on restoring the proper balance between moist and dry, hot and cold in the body of the afflicted person. In the same text, the writer also comments on madness, which he argues likewise derives from imbalances in the brain:

> It is the same thing [the brain] which makes us mad or delirious [μαινόμεθα καὶ παραφρονέομεν], inspires us with dread or with fear.... These things that we suffer all come from the brain [τοῦ ἐγκεφάλου], when it is not healthy, but becomes abnormally hot, cold, moist or dry, or suffers any other unnatural affection to which it is not accustomed. Madness comes from its moistness. When the brain is abnormally moist, of necessity it moves.... But all the time the brain is still the man is intelligent [φρονεῖ]. (*Morb. sacr.* 17)

The author's argument is that physiological and external factors, such as heat, cold, and moisture, each in its own way, can affect a person's brain, causing different types of madness.

It is important to note that ancient Mediterranean constructions of the body, and the mind's place within it, were significantly different from the modern understanding. Since Descartes, we have in the Western world distinguished sharply between body and soul. According to Descartes, although it is a substance, the soul or the "I" is not corporeal and can have no participation in the physical, material, or natural realm.[19] The premodern understanding is very different. Among the Hippocratic writers, many do not make a categorical distinction between mind and body. They present mental affections as being of a physical nature and having a physical cause.[20] In *The Sacred Disease*, for example, madness and the so-called sacred disease are both illnesses caused by different obstructions in flows of air to the brain. Even those writers who speak about the soul as distinct from the body, like Plato, still conceive of the soul as something physical.[21] To strictly differentiate between physical and mental illness in antiquity is therefore anachronistic and untrue to the ancient sources.

The above presentation shows that demon possession and madness may be understood as belonging within competing illness paradigms and different sectors of the ancient health care system (see §1.5). The terminol-

---

19. Martin, *Corinthian Body*, 5.
20. Van der Eijk, *Medicine and Philosophy in Classical Antiquity*, 26–27.
21. Van der Eijk, *Medicine and Philosophy in Classical Antiquity*, 27.

ogy of madness and insanity belongs to the professional health care sector and its etiology of imbalance, and it is constructed over against folk healers belonging to an invasion paradigm. This distinction may be helpful in order to understand the use of demon possession and madness as invective against Jesus and Paul.

5.1.2. Sanity and the Manly Self-Presentations of Jesus and Paul

"Are you crazy?" "You must be out of your mind!" "Have you gone mad?" In antiquity, much like today, exclamations such as these were easily tossed at adversaries. One example of such an accusation comes from Acts. During Paul's trial, the Roman governor Festus hears Paul's defense and exclaims, "You are out of your mind [μαίνῃ], Paul! Too much learning is driving you insane [εἰς μανίαν περιτρέπει]!" (Acts 26:24). Paul denies the accusations and claims that he is speaking the truth. By throwing such accusations, one did not claim to make any real medical judgment. These were rhetorical attacks meant to question a person's behavior or utterances. Nevertheless, the label of madness categorized a person as deviant, specifically concerning his or her health—it was a label that had to do with illness and/or disability. Such accusations may be called *disability invective* and understood as a rhetorical strategy of drawing attention to someone's nonnormative body as part of an attempt to vilify that person.

According to ancient protocols of masculinity, manliness and virtue were closely tied to the ability to control oneself and one's own body.[22] The idea that elite males had superior control of their own bodies and minds justified the kyriarchal structure of society, in which such men ruled over women, clients, slaves, and children. The ancient medical writers held some gendered assumptions about madness in alignment with this understanding of masculinity. Their writings construct women as closer to the irrational than men.[23] It was their particular sexual organs that rendered them vulnerable to madness. One such female affliction was "the wandering womb," which was a condition understood to be caused by the womb being too dry (see §4.2). Unless the womb was regularly irrigated with sperm through intercourse and anchored through pregnancy, it might wander in search of moisture and cause madness and a feeling of suffoca-

---

22. Smit, "Masculinity and the Bible," 50–52.

23. Lesley Dean-Jones, *Women's Bodies in Classical Greek Science* (Oxford: Clarendon, 1994), 115.

tion, ὑστερικός πνίξ.[24] Despite the "medical fact" that women were physically prone to weakness in general and madness in particular, men had to constantly prove that they were not slipping into effeminacy. Gleason has shown how proper speech was an important part of male comportment and self-fashioning. Rhetorical practices were a means by which a man could display his rational mind. At the same time, rhetoric was an arena in which an opponent's speech and bodily appearance could be attacked with the charge of effeminacy, weakness, and evil.[25]

In the Synoptics, demon possession is a recurring phenomenon. If we look more closely at how demon possession manifests itself in the Synoptics, we see that there is a range of symptoms. While some of the demon-possessed are silent, even explicitly mute (Mark 9:17; Luke 11:14), others are loud, either screaming and shouting or even crying out the truth (Mark 2:23–24; 5:6–10). While some of the demon-possessed are said to have been afflicted continually for many years (e.g., the Gerasene demoniac in Mark 5:3–5), others seem to have fits of temporary affliction (Mark 9:18–22). Sometimes the one afflicted is said to behave wildly and pose a danger to her- or himself and to others (Mark 5:5; 9:22). In other stories, demon possession seems to be accompanied by or only manifested through physical disabilities like deafness and blindness (Matt 12:22; Luke 11:14). Some but not all of these descriptions involve some sort of erratic or violent behavior and out-of-place speech. This means that to cross the boundaries of socially accepted behavior could categorize a person as demon-possessed, but the category is not exhausted by this factor.

In Paul's letters, on the other hand, there are no references to demon possession. He speaks about the existence of demons once, in 1 Cor 10:20–21, but he does not mention the possibility that people can become possessed by them, nor does he refer to exorcisms. He exhibits, I will argue, a familiarity with Greek medical ideas and terminology, and in the Corinthian correspondence he invokes a number of terms related to madness, as we shall see. Paul was an educated man, and he took pains to show his knowledge through his rhetoric and his vocabulary. John seems to occupy a space between the Synoptics and Paul, drawing on terms relating both to madness (10:20) and to demon possession (7:20; 8:48–49; 10:20–21). In

---

24. Dean-Jones, *Women's Bodies in Classical Greek Science*, 11. For ancient medical discussions of the wandering womb, see, e.g., Hippocrates, *Mul.* 1.2; *Epid.* 3.253–78; Soranus, *Gyn.* 2.26; Galen, *Meth. med.* 1.15.

25. Gleason, *Making Men*, 7.

this gospel, Jesus is accused of being demon-possessed but never performs any exorcisms himself.

Judging from these accusations against Jesus and Paul, demon possession seems to have been used rhetorically in a similar fashion to madness accusations: as a label used to vilify a person's utterances and behavior. The central notion of demon possession in first-century Palestine was that a foreign force entered a person's body and took control of their behavior as well as their speech.[26] Such an invasion would be understood as emasculating for a hegemonic male, as the core of one's masculinity was tied to self-control. By looking at two key figures in the New Testament, Jesus and Paul, I try to show how these texts negotiate accusations that are simultaneously attacks on a man's masculinity and his health.

5.2. "Possessed by Beelzebul": Accusations against Jesus

All the Synoptics have parallel reports that Jesus was accused of being possessed by Beelzebul, the prince of demons. I quote Mark's version:

> Then he went home; and the crowd came together again, so that they could not even eat. When his family [οἱ παρ᾽ αὐτοῦ] heard it, they went out to restrain him, for people were saying, "He has gone out of his mind" [ἔλεγον γὰρ ὅτι ἐξέστη]. And the scribes who came down from Jerusalem said, "He has Beelzebul [Βεελζεβοὺλ ἔχει], and by the ruler of the demons he casts out demons." And he called them to him, and spoke to them in parables, "How can Satan cast out Satan? If a kingdom is divided against itself, that kingdom cannot stand. And if a house is divided against itself, that house will not be able to stand. And if Satan has risen up against himself and is divided, he cannot stand, but his end has come. But no one can enter a strong man's house and plunder his property without first tying up the strong man; then indeed the house can be plundered. Truly I tell you, people will be forgiven for their sins and whatever blasphemies they utter; but whoever blasphemes against the Holy Spirit can never have forgiveness, but is guilty of an eternal sin"—for they had said, "He has an unclean spirit [πνεῦμα ἀκάθαρτον]." (3:19b–30)

This incident occurs immediately after the appointment of the apostles. As noted, Mark foregrounds healing stories at the beginning of his gospel and puts Jesus's healing ministry forth as the reason for his large follow-

---

26. Sorensen, *Possession and Exorcism*, 118–24.

ing (see §2.4). While some say Jesus is "out of his mind" (3:21), the scribes claim he has Beelzebul (3:22). The references to Beelzebul as the ruler of demons suggest that the demonic world was understood as hierarchical. Both Jewish and other sources from this time period refer to demons as relatively stronger or weaker than other demons and as holding different powers. The term Beelzebul occurs in several writings from Second Temple Judaism as a demonic name, probably deriving from Baal Zabul.[27] In the Testament of Solomon, Beelzebul also appears as the name of the "ruler of demons" (T. Sol. 2:8; 3:1).[28] The ruler of demons was, then, the most powerful of the demonic world but was less powerful than God, who belongs to a realm above the demonic.

Matthew relates two instances of accusations against Jesus, both in close connection with exorcisms performed by Jesus. In the first, Jesus has just healed "a demoniac who was mute" (ἄνθρωπον κωφὸν δαιμονιζόμενον, 9:32). The Pharisees claim that the exorcism is performed because Jesus is affiliated with demons: "By the ruler of the demons [ἄρχοντι τῶν δαιμονίων], he casts out the demons" (9:34). In the second pericope, Jesus heals "a demoniac who was blind and mute" (δαιμονιζόμενος τυφλὸς καὶ κωφός, 12:22). Here, too, it is the Pharisees who claim that Jesus's power derives from demonic affiliation: "It is only by Beelzebul, the ruler of the demons [Βεελζεβοὺλ ἄρχοντι τῶν δαιμονίων], that this fellow casts out the demons" (12:24). In the second instance, the accusation elicits a lengthy response from Jesus in fairly similar wording to Mark (12:25–29).

In Luke's version, it is someone in the crowd who throws these accusations at Jesus (11:15). Rather than the crass judgment of blasphemy against the Holy Spirit as an unforgiveable sin, which is Jesus's retort in Matthew and Mark, the Lukan Jesus elaborates on the image of the strong man:

> When a strong man, fully armed, guards his castle, his property is safe. But when one stronger than he attacks him and overpowers him, he takes away his armor in which he trusted and divides his plunder. Whoever is not with me is against me, and whoever does not gather with me scatters. (11:21–23)

In all these versions, it is suggested by the accusers that Jesus himself is demon-possessed and that it is this possession that gives him the abil-

---

27. Collins, *Mark*, 229–31.
28. Collins, *Mark*, 230–31.

ity to cast out demons. The claim is an attack on Jesus's authority. He is given a stigmatizing label that singles him out from the normate group. Although Jesus does not explicitly deny the charge in any of the versions, the lengthy response and the strong wording is clearly meant to refute any such accusations.

In Jesus's reply in each of these versions, he conjures the image of the "strong man" (ὁ ἰσχυρός, Matt 12:29; Mark 3:27; Luke 11:21). In Matthew and Mark, the hierarchy of the demonic and heavenly worlds is described in kyriarchal metaphors, in terms of conflict within a kingdom or a household. Kingdom and household need one strong ruler in order to avoid internal conflict and protect the property within (Matt 12:25; Mark 3:24–25). In Luke, however, the notion of a strong householder (11:17) is combined with images from warfare, with references to fighting, armor, and spoils of war (11:21–23). Both these sets of metaphors draw on ideas about masculinity in terms of control and protection of land and property. Representations of Jesus as exorcist undergird notions of masculinity by presenting Jesus as powerful, as a householder expelling what does not belong, and as a military leader defeating defeats his enemy by sheer physical force.

In the Gospel of John, Jesus is accused of being demon-possessed in three different episodes (7:20; 8:48–52; 10:20). The accusations arise in reaction to Jesus's teaching, not his healing activity. In the first episode, it is people in the crowd who make the accusation, while in the latter two, it is "the Jews" who voice the charge (8:48; 10:19–20). These episodes form part of the recurring Johannine theme of controversy with "the Jews" who do not accept or understand who Jesus is. In the final instance, "the Jews" are split concerning Jesus's enigmatic teaching: "Many of them were saying, 'He has a demon [δαιμόνιον ἔχει] and is out of his mind [μαίνεται]. Why listen to him?' Others were saying, 'These are not the words of one who has a demon. Can a demon open the eyes of the blind?'" (10:20–21). Μαίνομαι is one of the terms for madness that we find in the Greek medical writings.[29] In this passage the distinction made above between an invasion etiology of demon possession and an imbalance etiology of madness is blurred, and the labels of madness and demon possession are combined. In the previous chapter, I argued that John, to a larger extent than the Synoptics, draws on professional medical language and insights. The refer-

---

29. Thumiger, "Early Greek Medical Vocabulary of Insanity," 65.

ence to madness here, and the fact that Jesus never performs exorcisms in John, fits with this observation that John draws primarily on an etiology of balance.[30] At the same time, I also noted that John frames Jesus as a folk healer and places his healing miracles in spaces connected with folk healing. The blurring of terminology in John 10:20–21 follows this pattern of paradoxical overlap between folk and professional sectors in the ancient health care system. Jesus's preaching is found to be so strange by some of the listeners that they explain it in terms of madness *and* demon possession, while others dismiss the notion altogether. What is most important for all the gospel writers, though, is that the charge is refuted. Jesus is neither mad nor possessed.

5.2.1. Negotiating the Stigmatizing Demon Label

The accusations in the gospels that Jesus was demon-possessed are not only attacks on Jesus's masculinity; they are simultaneously disability invective. It is a rhetorical claim suggesting a nonnormative bodily state that is stigmatizing in the social environment.

The gospels go to great lengths to show that Jesus is *not* a weak man, and they dismiss the notion that he is demon-possessed. In other words, the main line of defense against accusations of demon possession is to show that Jesus is manly, that he conforms to protocols of masculinity. In the Synoptic Gospels, Jesus rejects the notion with imagery suggesting that he is a strong man who cannot be invaded by demonic forces. In John, the masculinity of Jesus is closely tied to his relationship to the Father, from whom comes his power and authority to speak the truth and perform the signs.[31] What I want to focus on in this section is the interesting combination of both demon possession and madness labels in Mark 3:21–22 and John 10:20–21. I argue that these passages reflect a discussion about different understandings about illness and that the stigmatizing label of demon possession is negotiated not only through display of hegemonic masculinity but also through a negotiation of illness labels.

In the Markan passage, it is claimed both that "he has gone out of his mind" (3:21) and that "he has Beelzebul" (3:22). The term used here, ἐξίστημι, is one that the Greek medical writers use as a terms for madness.[32]

---

30. Martin, *Corinthian Body*, 165.
31. Conway, *Behold the Man*, 144–45, 50–51.
32. Thumiger, "Early Greek Medical Vocabulary of Insanity," 77.

As I will come back to below, Paul also uses this term to denote madness (2 Cor 5:13). Whereas the scribes from Jerusalem offer the explanation of demon possession for Jesus's powerful but out-of-place behavior, Jesus's family (οἱ παρ' αὐτοῦ, 3:21) claim that he is out of his mind. According to Collins, οἱ παρ' αὐτοῦ denotes someone who is intimately connected, like family or relatives, and the group mentioned here is further defined in 3:31 as his mother and his brothers.[33] It seems, then, that what some saw as demon possession, which could be cured by exorcism, others may have ascribed to insanity.

What would be the cure if madness was the diagnosis? The Greek medical paradigm put an emphasis on environmental factors such as weather (heat, cold, moisture, and dryness), exertion, and diet as the physical causes of illness. Treatment involved restoring the proper balance in the body by providing whatever was lacking or reducing whatever was in excess. In the professional medical literature, diet and rest were important parts of the doctor's treatment.[34] At the beginning of the passage, Mark indicates that Jesus went home, but the crowd followed him so that he could not even eat (3:19b–20). This introduction to the encounter suggests that exertion and lack of food were things Jesus experienced. When Jesus's family comes "to restrain him," perhaps they want to provide treatment for temporary madness by giving him food and rest. It should be noted that it is Jesus's family that says he is out of his mind, while it is Jesus's adversaries, the scribes, who call him possessed. The ascription of madness can be understood as less stigmatizing because it did not align Jesus with evil forces. In this story from Mark, the medical categories of madness and demon possession are used rhetorically to negotiate the understanding of Jesus. In this particular case, I argue, demon possession works as a negative charge and (temporary) madness works as a defense on the part of Jesus's family. Nonetheless, Jesus does not relent to his family; he shows them away (Mark 3:31–35). Although the accusations of demon possession receive a strong rhetorical refutation, his family is also dismissed and replaced with the metaphorical family of followers in Jesus's reply: "Whoever does the will of God is my brother and sister and mother" (Mark 3:35).

---

33. Collins, *Mark*, 226–27.

34. See, e.g., Hippocrates's *Regimen in Acute Diseases*, which is wholly devoted to the treatment of the patient, primarily in terms of proper administration of food, drink, and rest.

In John 10:20, it is a group among "the Jews" who claim that Jesus is both demon-possessed and mad: "He has a demon and is out of his mind." In this passage, both madness and possession are grouped together as invective against Jesus without distinction. As Jesus's main adversaries, "the Jews" have no authority in this gospel, so the reader knows the accusations are not to be trusted. The voice of the implied reader can be heard in the counterargument that concludes the episode: "These are not the words of one who has a demon. Can a demon open the eyes of the blind?" (10:21). In the dismissal, both Jesus's words and his healing activity are counted as signs of a sound mind rather than madness and possession. Conway has argued that the Johannine Jesus exhibits masculinity through a strong display of control, even over his own death.[35] To be in control of oneself is not compatible with demon possession. Jesus's eloquent discourses and his power through signs have established him as a man in control of himself and one with legitimate power, as the only begotten son of the heavenly Father.[36]

In summary, all the stories where Jesus is charged with demon possession refute the charges. Matthew and Luke seem concerned only with demon possession, while in Mark and John both demon possession and madness appear in the same passage. In Mark, different groups have different opinions: while his opponents charge Jesus with demon possessions, his family claims that he is out of his mind. In John, the two categories are combined, and Jesus is accused of being both possessed and out of his mind. While Matthew and Luke negotiate the accusations by reassuring the readers about Jesus's masculinity, Mark and John also seem to negotiate the categories of illness. In the next section, I look at the correlation between madness and demon possession in Paul's letters to Corinth.

5.3. Rhetoric, Weakness, and Cognitive Dis/abilities in the Corinthian Correspondence

Paul's Corinthian correspondence is particularly rife with references to disability and illness, compared to his other letters.[37] My interest here is

---

35. Colleen M. Conway, "'Behold the Man!' Masculine Christology and the Fourth Gospel," in *New Testament Masculinites*, ed. Stephen D. Moore and Janice Capel Anderson, SemeiaSt 45 (Atlanta: Society of Biblical Literature, 2003), 174.

36. Conway, "'Behold the Man!,'" 170.

37. For interpretations of the Pauline letters from a disability perspective see, e.g., Candida R. Moss, "Christly Possession and Weakened Bodies: Reconsideration of the

in how Paul negotiates accusations of madness and bodily weakness, and how he uses madness vocabulary strategically in his discourse. I start with the so-called fool's speech in 2 Cor 11, as this is the central passage in which madness vocabulary is invoked. This passage connects with other passages from 1 and 2 Corinthians that I regard as part of Paul's rhetorical "mad talk." In 2 Corinthians, Paul's authority as an apostle is an important theme.[38] In chapter 11, Paul is defending himself against certain adversaries at Corinth, the so-called super-apostles (τῶν ὑπερλίαν ἀποστόλων, 11:5). Paul asks the Corinthians to bear with his madness (ἀφροσύνη, 11:1) as he embarks upon his defense, and in this section of the letter, he engages a number of different terms and phrases that have to do with insanity and lack of mental capacity, such as ἄφρων (11:16 [2x], 19; 12:6, 11), ἀφροσύνη (11:1, 17, 21), and παραφρονέω (11:23).[39] The madness terminology is particularly dense in his so-called fool's speech:

> I repeat, let no one think that I am a fool [ἄφρονα]; but if you do, then accept me as a fool [ἄφρονα], so that I too may boast a little. What I am saying in regard to this boastful confidence, I am saying not with the Lord's authority, but as a fool [ἐν ἀφροσύνῃ]; since many boast according to human standards, I will also boast. For you gladly put up with fools [τῶν ἀφρόνων], being wise yourselves! For you put up with it when someone makes slaves of you, or preys upon you, or takes advantage of you, or puts on airs, or gives you a slap in the face. To my shame, I must say, we were too weak [ἠσθενήκαμεν] for that! But whatever anyone dares to boast of—I am speaking as a fool [ἐν ἀφροσύνῃ]—I also dare to boast of that. Are they Hebrews? So am I. Are they Israelites? So am I. Are they

---

Function of Paul's Thorn in the Flesh (2 Cor 12:7–10)," *JRDH* 16 (2012); Adela Yarbro Collins, "Paul's Disability: The Thorn in His Flesh," in Moss and Schipper, *Disability Studies and Biblical Literature*; Martin Albl, "'For Whenever I Am Weak, Then I Am Strong': Disability in Paul's Epistles," in Avalos, Melcher, and Schipper, *This Abled Body*; Arthur J. Dewey and Anna C. Miller, "Paul," in Melcher, Parsons, and Yong, *Bible and Disability*; Amos Yong, *The Bible, Disability, and the Church: A New Vision of the People of God* (Grand Rapids: Eerdmans, 2011), 82–117.

38. Victor Paul Furnish, *II Corinthians*, AB 32A (Garden City, NY: Doubleday, 1984), 37. The unity of this letter is contested, and it is common to assume that 2 Cor 1–9 was originally a separate letter from 2 Cor 10–13 (Furnish, *II Corinthians*, 35–41). The arguments I make here are not dependent on any particular composition hypothesis.

39. LSJ, s.v. "ἄφρων": "senseless, silly, foolish"; s.v. "ἀφροσύνη": "folly, thoughtlessness"; s.v. "παραφρονέω": "to be beside oneself, deranged."

descendants of Abraham? So am I. Are they ministers of Christ? I am talking like a madman [παραφρονῶν]—I am a better one: with far greater labors, far more imprisonments, with countless floggings, and often near death. (11:16–23)

In this passage, Paul is denying that he is a fool (11:16), but he is also admitting that he is speaking like a fool (11:21). Moreover, he admits that he is weak and even boasts of physical beatings (11:23–27). At the end of this section of the letter, he declares himself the winner of the weakness contest: "Who is weak and I am not weak [οὐκ ἀσθενῶ]? Who is made to stumble and I am not indignant? If I must boast, I will boast of the things that show my weakness [ἀσθενείας μου καυχήσομαι]" (11:29–30).

The terms Paul uses (μωρία, ἐξίστημι, μαίνομαι, ἄφρων, ἀφροσύνη, παραφροσύνη, and σωφροσύνη) are the same terms that the Greek medical writers use when writing about madness.[40] Paul also invokes such madness terminology earlier in the letter. In 2 Cor 5:13 Paul says: "For if we are beside ourselves [ἐξέσταμεν], it is for God; if we are in our right mind [σωφρονοῦμεν], it is for you." This exclamation, too, is part of Paul's effort to defend himself against accusations from rivals for the leadership of the Corinthian congregation.[41] It seems like he is accused of being mad, or at least is in disagreement with his opponents about what constitutes madness and what constitutes sanity. In his response, he allows for the possibility when he says, "*If* we are beside ourselves it is for God." To cross over the boundaries of acceptable behavior and acquire the label "insane" when it is for the cause of spreading the gospel is for Paul acceptable. The gospel in itself has changed the rules, and Christ's death and resurrection reinterpret what madness, as well as weakness, means (1 Cor 1:18–2:5).[42]

Terms relating to madness also appear in 1 Corinthians. Paul opens the letter with a defense of the gospel as madness or foolishness, μωρία (1:18, 21, 23; 2:14; 3:19). Paul's first topic in this letter is an attack on the divisions in the Christ-believing community in Corinth (1:10). Without going into a discussion of the nature of the divisions and parties, I just want to note the language of wisdom versus madness, as well as weakness versus strength. This language is deeply embedded in a discourse on masculinity, but it also draws on ideas about health and illness. In his

---

40. Thumiger, "Early Greek Medical Vocabulary of Insanity," 61.
41. Furnish, *II Corinthians*, 321.
42. Yong, *Bible, Disability, and the Church*, 100–103.

argument, Paul clearly aligns with the weak and foolish, attributes that he connects with the core of his message:

> But God chose what is foolish [τὰ μωρὰ] in the world to shame the wise [τοὺς σοφούς]; God chose what is weak [τὰ ἀσθενῆ] in the world to shame the strong [τὰ ἰσχυρά]; God chose what is low and despised in the world, things that are not, to reduce to nothing things that are, so that no one might boast in the presence of God. He is the source of your life in Christ Jesus, who became for us wisdom from God [σοφία ἡμῖν ἀπὸ θεοῦ], and righteousness and sanctification and redemption. (1:27–30)

Mad talk also comes up in an argument about orderly behavior during worship. In 1 Cor 14, Paul warns the Corinthians about behavior and speech that may lead to charges of insanity. People may think that the Christ-believers are mad if they all speak in tongues at the same time: "If, therefore, the whole church comes together and all speak in tongues, and outsiders or unbelievers enter, will they not say that you are out of your mind [μαίνεσθε]?" (14:23). Glossolalia should be practiced with care to avoid that people about town accuse the Christ-believers of being crazy. This reference shows that madness is a label that Paul is not above pinning on others, and although he tries to subvert its meaning, it is not an entirely positive designation, even for Paul.

What is Paul being accused of and defending himself against in 2 Corinthians? Is he accused of being foolish and stupid, or of being mentally ill? We only have Paul's side of the story. What is important to note is that these terms do have connotations to medical madness vocabulary, so the frame of reference can include accusations of insanity, not just foolishness. These accusations should be seen in light of the broader picture Paul paints of his adversaries at Corinth. In 2 Cor 10, Paul refers to something his opponents are saying about him: "For they say, 'His letters are weighty and strong, but his bodily presence [ἡ παρουσία τοῦ σώματος] is weak [ἀσθενὴς], and his speech contemptible [ὁ λόγος ἐξουθενημένος]" (10:10). He may be referring to the same claim when, a few verses prior, he gives a similar statement about his appearance: "I myself, Paul, appeal to you by the meekness and gentleness of Christ—I who am humble when face to face with you, but bold toward you when I am away!" (10:1). In 1 Corinthians, Paul seems to be saying something similar about the weakness of his own appearance:

> And I came to you in weakness [ἐν ἀσθενείᾳ] and in fear and in much trembling. My speech [ὁ λόγος μου] and my proclamation [τὸ κήρυγμά

μου] were not with plausible words of wisdom, but with a demonstration of the Spirit and of power, so that your faith might rest not on human wisdom but on the power of God. (2:3–5)

Paul here admits to a bodily presence that is weak and a manner of speech that does not meet the expectations of eloquent wisdom. He seems to be admitting to a lack of masculinity. His speech and bodily comportment do not conform to the expectations of a public speaker and rhetorician.[43]

These statements about bodily weakness may be understood in connection with what Paul says about his flogged and beaten body (2 Cor 11:23–25) and his "thorn in the flesh" (12:7–10).[44] Over and over again he admits that his body is weak (11:29; 12:9–10). In Galatians as well, Paul mentions an illness or infirmity:

You know that it was because of a physical infirmity [ἀσθένειαν τῆς σαρκὸς] that I first announced the gospel to you; though my condition put you to the test, you did not scorn or despise [ἐξεπτύσατε] me, but welcomed me as an angel of God, as Christ Jesus. What has become of the goodwill you felt? For I testify that, had it been possible, you would have torn out your eyes and given them to me. (4:13–15)

The term ἀσθένεια could mean simply an illness or a disability, or it could refer to weakness more generally (see §1.4). The weakness Paul mentions here is echoed in a remark in the ending of his letter to the Galatians, where he says that he carries "the marks of Jesus [τὰ στίγματα τοῦ Ἰησοῦ] branded on my body" (6:17). Taken together, these references from Galatians and the Corinthian letters have led some scholars to ask if Paul was disabled. Amos Yong argues that he is "the first disabled theologian." He suggests that he had an eye condition, since the Galatians were willing to give up their eyes for him (Gal 4:15), and Acts claims that he was temporarily blinded around the time of his conversion (Acts 9:8–18).[45] Collins reviews the history of interpretation concerning Paul's thorn in the flesh and concludes that the most likely diagnosis is epilepsy. The so-called sacred disease was often connected to demonic possession, and she reads the verb ἐκπτύω, to "spit out" (Gal 4:13), in light of an ancient tradition

---

43. Gleason, *Making Men*, 103–30.

44. Jennifer A. Glancy, *Corporal Knowledge* (Oxford: Oxford Univerisy Press, 2010), 24–47.

45. Yong, *Bible, Disability, and the Church*, 83–85.

that one would spit upon meeting an epileptic person as a charm to ward off the disease.[46]

In my opinion, it is impossible—and perhaps not so interesting—to diagnose Paul by pinpointing a particular disability or illness that he may have had. I do, however, find it plausible that throughout his life he may very well have acquired some bodily weaknesses, some sort of disability, and that his body appeared as nonnormative. The references to a weak and marked body should not be dismissed as purely figurative speech.[47] Martin Albl holds that Paul had a "personal experience of disability" and that there was a social stigma attached to the appearance of his body.[48] In the Corinthian correspondence, his bodily deviation is used by his opponents to vilify him, and Paul has to defend himself against accusations that such bodily signs should be read as demeaning his character. Glancy has argued that Paul's beaten body is the corporal problem that the Corinthian adversaries despise and that Paul needs to reinterpret as a positive corporal knowledge, one that has branded him as a slave of Christ.[49]

The many references to madness in the Corinthian correspondence, and particularly in 2 Cor 11–12, indicate that whatever the accusations concerning Paul's weak body were, they are somehow connected with his manner of speech and concomitant mental illness. J. Albert Harrill argues that the accusations Paul is referring to in 2 Cor 10:10 are rhetorical invective that conforms to physiognomic conventions.[50] The invective against Paul uses physiognomic reasoning to claim that Paul's weak body and unreasoned speech reveal that he is unmanly and hence morally inferior: "By questioning the legitimacy of Paul's body and logos, the rival apostles tried to get the Corinthians to think of Paul not as an individual but in terms of his alleged group affiliation with slavish men generally … unfit to rule either family or community."[51] According to Harrill, Paul's opponents argue that his body is "slavish."[52] However, in the kyriarchal framework of antiquity, the relation between slave and free was only one of many hierar-

---

46. Collins, "Paul's Disability," 172–74.

47. For an overview of the various interpretations, see Furnish, *II Corinthians*, 547–50.

48. Albl, "Disability in Paul's Epistles," 152–53.

49. Glancy, *Corporal Knowledge*, 45–46.

50. Harrill, "Invective Against Paul," 190–91.

51. Harrill, "Invective Against Paul," 209.

52. Harrill, "Invective Against Paul," 191.

chical relations. The free, able-bodied male was the normate and not only slaves but women, children, and people with disabilities were conceived of as relatively weaker, as cultural other. In my opinion, the rhetorical feud between Paul and his opponents in Corinth is focused on the stigma of madness and somatic ideas about weak bodies, rather than strictly on the class-related notion of slavery. However, these ideas interacted and overlapped. Kartzow's insight about "asking the other question" is relevant here. When accusations about madness and a weak body are invoked, what does that reveal about gender and class? Within the kyriarchal framework of ancient Mediterranean society, an accusation about Paul's mental instability would infer both slavishness and effeminacy.

5.3.1. Paul's Strategic Disabilities

How does Paul defend himself against these accusations of madness and a weak bodily presence? He not only chooses to boast about his weak body but also enlists madness as another strategic disability in his counterattack. I argue that Paul uses a double strategy of simultaneously admitting and defending himself against these accusations. On one level, Paul tries to invert the meaning of madness and weakness by aligning it to Christ and the gospel. He argues that both weakness and madness connect him deeply with Christ. His weakness shows that he suffers with Christ (2 Cor 1:4; 12:10) and that he bears Christ's marks on his body (Gal 6:17). His madness aligns him with the gospel, which is likewise foolishness (1 Cor 1:18–31). In his line of defense, Paul uses disabilities strategically to his advantage. He reinterprets bodily signs of weakness and disability as Christlike and thus ultimately representing strength.[53] In this way he subverts the social stigmatization of weakness and negates the physiognomic connection between a weak bodily presence and a morally reprehensible character.[54] He claims that he has the moral authority to be a leader not despite his weak bodily presence but because of it (2 Cor 11:23, 30; 12:10).

However, Paul does not completely invert the meaning of weak bodies and mental incapacity. His admissions are only to a certain degree. He is mad, but just a little bit (2 Cor 11:1, 16). He is weak, but his weakness has been honorably earned through his work for the gospel (2 Cor 11:24–29).

---

53. Glancy, *Corporal Knowledge*, 46–47.
54. Harrill, "Invective Against Paul," 210–11.

This makes it more acceptable according to protocols of masculinity.[55] Paul walks a fine line when he boasts about his weaknesses. Boasting was considered unmanly, unless one followed the parameters within which self-praise was justified.[56] When Paul is boasting about himself, he follows the rules Plutarch sets up in the treatise *On Praising Oneself Inoffensively* (*De laude* 1–22 [539b–547f]).[57] In this essay, Plutarch discusses the circumstances in which self-praise is acceptable and shows how it should be presented to be palatable to the reader. Among these circumstances, he lists situations in which the speaker needs to defend himself from accusations, has suffered ill fortune, or is victim of injustice (*De laude* 4–6 [540c–541e]). Paul appeals to exactly these circumstances: he refers to his opponents, who accuse him (2 Cor 10:10–11); he points to the many hardships he has suffered (11:23–29); and he presents himself as a victim of unjust treatment (10:1–2; 11:6).

The mode in which self-praise should be carried out is also of importance to Plutarch. It is commendable to praise others whose merits are similar to one's own achievements, to credit chance or God for one's achievements, to mix self-praise with confessions of shortcomings, and to appeal to the hardships endured (*De laude* 7–13 [541e–544c]). Paul applies many of these aspects: he extols his triumphs by comparing his own achievements to that of his opponents (2 Cor 11:21–23), he credits God (11:31; 12:1, 3, 9), and he mixes self-praise with short-comings (12:7). Thus, Paul's fool's speech negotiates masculinity: he does not unman himself through unseemly boasting but keeps within the acceptable frame. As Arthur J. Dewey and Anna C. Miller have noted, Paul constructs himself as a servant leader and frames his authority as the community's founder and father, both appropriate male roles. He associates his opponents with the wrong kind of wisdom and appropriates God's power and divine wisdom for himself (1 Cor 2:5).[58]

In summary, 1 and 2 Corinthians reveal an interesting discursive negotiation between Paul and his opponents in the Corinthian community. Paul is accused of being mad and of having a weak bodily presence. In his defense, Paul uses a strategy of almost, but not quite, admitting to madness. At the same time as he agrees to bodily weakness and mental

---

55. Glancy, *Corporal Knowledge*, 24–37.
56. Gleason, *Making Men*, 9.
57. See, e.g., Furnish, *II Corinthians*, 498; Glancy, *Corporal Knowledge*, 38–39.
58. Dewey and Miller, "Paul," 395.

incapacity, these afflictions are recast as not emasculating. His weak body has been won through courage in his servitude to Christ and aligns him with God's power and wisdom. Moreover, Paul makes an effort to keep within the culturally accepted norms of masculinity when he boasts about his weakness and insanity.

5.4. Conclusion: Stigmatic Accusations

In this chapter, I have argued that both demon possession and madness were stigmatizing labels that could be used as disability invective in order to attack an adversary. Masculinity was perceived in terms of control over one's own body and mind. An elite male had to constantly prove his superior intellect through self-comportment. Thus, poise and speech were important measures of masculinity: the ancient conception of the normate was an eloquent, self-composed man. Jesus and Paul were attacked by opponents who tried to stigmatize them by accusing them of madness and demon possession. Madness and demon possession were thus disability-related labels that stigmatized men in particular, as they went against expectations of how a man should behave. It is clear from the vehement defense that the texts display that these accusations carried with them stigma.

I have argued that the gospels, on the one side, and Paul's Corinthian correspondence, on the other, reveal a difference in the understanding of illness. Within the popular sector of health care, demon possession was an important explanatory model based on the invasion paradigm, while within the professional sector, physical explanations drawing on the Hippocratic paradigm of humoral balance were used. We find traces of both these discourses in the New Testament. The Synoptic Gospels rely heavily on the popular notion of demon possession. Yet Mark and John show traces of both discourses, as terms related to madness and terms related to demon possession surface in the same narratives. When Paul writes about madness in the abovementioned passages of the Corinthian correspondence, he uses many the same terms that we find in the medical writers; thus I argue that he draws on an etiology of balance rather than invasion.[59] Demon possession does not seem to be part of the picture at all. Paul

---

59. Martin argues that Paul draws on notions of invasion and pollution (*Corinthian Body*, 173–74).

does not engage with these categories, and his adversaries probably did not either. He exhibits a familiarity with medical knowledge and medical terminology. He does not deny that demons exist, but demon possession does not seem to be part of his understanding of illness and health, as he chooses to speak in a more educated, sophisticated way, using the medical vocabulary of madness. As already noted, in daily life these ideas would cross each other's paths, as they seem to do in Mark and John.

In the texts I have presented in this chapter, negotiations of stigmatizing labels have been the focus. Stigma theory reveals that attributions of difference are socially constructed and quite arbitrary. The rhetorical strategies of the gospel authors and Paul show that such cultural constrictions can be harsh and devastating but also that negotiation is possible. There is a possibility to "talk back." Goffman's theory of stigma exposed societal mechanisms of stigmatization but offered little in terms of constructive critique of categories of deviance.[60] Garland-Thomson, however, situates the cultural self and the cultural other as interdependent and culturally malleable and thus as dependent on historical conceptions of deviance.[61] By exposing the veiled subject position of the normate, as well as the disabled as a figure of otherness, hopefully new and diverse subject positions may emerge.

---

60. Goffman, *Stigma*, 167–74.
61. Thomson, *Extraordinary Bodies*, 39–40.

6

JUDAS THE MONSTER:
POLICING THE BORDERS OF THE HUMAN

6.1. Introduction: Monster Theory

In this chapter, I continue to examine disability in relation to masculinity and ancient rhetoric. I will look at a particularly harsh example of disability invective: the church father Papias's description of the death of Judas, the disciple who betrayed Jesus.[1] Using the framework of monster theory, I argue that medical and physiognomic ideas are combined in this text fragment in order to construct a body that is altogether other. Exposed as grotesquely disabled and effeminate, Judas is portrayed in monstrous terms in order to reveal his depraved soul, and his painful illness and death underline the divine punishment for his betrayal.

The monster is a figure in the cultural imagination that can be understood as an embodiment of fears. Jeffrey Jerome Cohen argues that the monster is "an embodiment of difference, a breaker of category, and a resistant Other known only through process and movement."[2] Since every culture has its own anxieties and preoccupations, monsters are culturally determined. They are constructed over against a community's definitions

---

An earlier version of this chapter appeared in *Patristica Nordica Annuaria* and is reworked here by permission. See Anna Rebecca Solevåg, "Monsteret Judas: Papias beskrivelse av Judas' død," *PNA* 31 (2016): 59–68.

1. The fragment (Papias, *Frag.* 4) is found in a quotation by Appolinaris of Laodicea. See *Epistle of Barnabas; Papias and Quadratus;Epistle to Diognetus; The Shepherd of Hermas*, ed. and trans. Bart D. Ehrman, vol. 2 of *The Apostolic Fathers*, LCL (Cambridge: Harvard University Press, 2003), 104–7.

2. Jeffrey Jerome Cohen, "Preface: In a Time of Monsters," in *Monster Theory: Reading Culture*, ed. Jeffrey Jerome Cohen (Minneapolis: University of Minnesota Press, 1996), x.

of what is good, acceptable, and natural.[3] In other words, looking at a culture's monsters can give us insights into its fears and repressions. Monster theory is a "means of understanding and describing the tools used to abject, to reject and exclude people."[4] It is a method that reads culture through the monsters they create.[5]

Monsters are category defying, according to Catherine Atherton: "As anomalies by definition, [monsters] are prime bearers of 'taxonomic perversity,' thronging the spaces between categories."[6] The monstrous creates a sense of vertigo because it reveals the inadequacies in our systems of categorization.[7] However, at the same time as it disrupts categories, the monster also defines them; by pointing to the fuzzy borders, it simultaneously defines the center, what is considered normal. Judith Halberstam argues that the Gothic novels contributed to the modern production of normativity in such a way: "Monsters have to be everything the human is not and, in producing the negative of human, these novels make way for the invention of human as white, male, middle class, and heterosexual."[8] In this chapter, I argue that the production of early Christian monsters contributed to the creation of the normate Christ-believer in a similar fashion.

For the Greeks and the Romans, monsters represented the opposite of the ordered, rational society.[9] Both the Greek term τέρας and the Latin *monstrum* denote a physically unnatural being, something that is "not clearly human or animal but rather in-between, a disturbing hybrid mixture."[10] Greek mythological monsters have certain traits in common: they are huge, have morphological oddities (usually loathsome), and are

---

3. Catherine Atherton, introduction to *Monsters and Monstrosity in Greek and Roman Culture*, ed. Catherine Atherton (Bari: Levante, 1998), x.

4. Asa Simon Mittman, "Introduction: The Impact of Monsters and Monster Studies," in *The Ashgate Research Companion to Monsters and the Monstrous*, ed. Asa Simon Mittman and Peter J. Dendle (Farnham: Ashgate, 2012), 8.

5. Jeffrey Jerome Cohen, "Monster Culture (Seven Theses)," in Cohen, *Monster Theory*, 4.

6. Atherton, introduction, xiv.

7. Mittman, "Introduction," 8.

8. Judith Halberstam, *Skin Shows: Gothic Horror and the Technology of Monsters* (Durham, NC: Duke University Press, 1995), 22.

9. D. Felton, "Rejecting and Embracing the Monstrous in Ancient Greece and Rome," in Mittman and Dendle, *Ashgate Research Companion to Monsters*, 114.

10. Felton, "Rejecting and Embracing the Monstrous," 114.

evil.[11] It should also be noted that a large proportion of Greek mythological monsters are female, revealing men's fear of women's destructive potential and male fantasy of conquering and controlling the female.[12] Hydra, Medusa, and the Sphinx are female monsters in Greek mythology that are less rational and more enigmatic and emotional than the younger male generation of heroes who overthrow them.[13]

However, monsters did not only inhabit the mythic world of gods and heroes. The geographical borders of the inhabited human world were perceived to be populated by monstrous races. Travel literature and ethnographies like Herodotus's *Histories* and the Alexander Romance provided tales of dog-headed and goat-footed races, headless men with eyes in their breasts, and one-legged as well as one-eyed creatures in the furthest regions of the earth.[14] But even closer to home, the monstrous could be found. In *On the Generation of Animals*, Aristotle comments on monstrous births. Monsters are those who "do not take after a human being at all in their appearance, but have gone so far that they resemble a monstrosity [τέρατι]" (*Gen. an.* 767b [Peck]). It is hard to ascertain what Aristotle considers the parameters to be. Rose is cautious and argues that in Classical Greece not all physical oddities in a newborn were considered monstrous. Defined standards of normalcy did not exist, and thus deformed babies were not necessarily seen as inferior, unattractive, or in need of medical care. Rather the monstrous would be extreme aberrations such as the ethnographers' tales of animal heads on human bodies or humans with extra heads.[15] However, individuals who were considered to be anomalous could be called monsters, *monstra*, by the Romans. Such monsters would include deformed babies, ugly people, and castrated slaves.[16] Monsters were sometimes thought of as omens and could also serve as scapegoats in times of crisis.[17] Monsters were feared, but they also held a titillating

---

11. Felton, "Rejecting and Embracing the Monstrous," 114.

12. Felton, "Rejecting and Embracing the Monstrous," 115.

13. Felton, "Rejecting and Embracing the Monstrous," 126–28.

14. Felton, "Rejecting and Embracing the Monstrous," 132–35.

15. Rose, *Staff of Oedipus*, 7, 36.

16. Bert Gevaert and Christian Laes, "What's in a Monster? Pliny the Elder, Teratology and Bodily Disability," in Laes, Goodey, and Rose, *Disabilities in Roman Antiquity*, 213.

17. Garland, *Eye of the Beholder*, 23–26. There are some variations in the understanding of the monstrous within the ancient Mediterranean according to time and place. For example, there is a shift in the perception of hermaphrodites, from *prodigii*

attraction. Plutarch describes the "monster's market" in Rome, where deformed slaves could be bought (*Curios.* 10 [520c]). Such slaves, used as entertainment at dinner parties and serving as *deliciae*, pets, were popular among wealthy Romans and were staples of the imperial household.[18] Hunchbacks and dwarfs held a particular attraction, and they were often portrayed in miniature figurines know as grotesques. These terracotta artifacts were understood to have talismanic qualities as averters of evil.[19]

A physiognomic logic underlies the construction of monstrous figures in antiquity.[20] The repulsive exterior of the monster speaks the hidden truth about its evil, menacing inside. In relation to disability, monster studies highlight the visual aspects as well as the moral qualities often ascribed to nonnormative bodies. It shows how ideas about beauty are intricately connected with ideas about disability. Moreover, it underscores how nonnormative bodies often evoke anxiety, fear, and repugnance. I will argue that the depiction of Judas in Papias's fragment verges on the monstrous, drawing on insights from monster theory to show how this perspective may shed some light on the text and its early Christian context.

6.2. Disability and Physiognomic Reasoning in Papias's Fragment

Papias (ca. 60–130), bishop of Hierapolis in Phrygia (Asia Minor), was a contemporary of Polycarp, and he wrote a five-volume work, now lost, called *Expositions of the Sayings of the Lord.*[21] His writings have been preserved only in citations of later church fathers. Papias's fragments shed light on the sequence and compilation of the Synoptic Gospels, but they also give some insight into the polemics and fractions of second-century Christianity.[22]

(fearful signs) during the Roman Republic to *delicii* (entertaining curiousites) in the Roman Empire (Graumann, "Monstrous Births and Retrospective Diagnosis," 190–91).

18. Garland, *Eye of the Beholder*, 45–46. See also Carlin A. Barton, *The Sorrows of the Ancient Romans: The Gladiator and the Monster* (Princeton: Princeton University Press, 1993), 107–8.

19. Garland, *Eye of the Beholder*, 104.

20. Garland, *Eye of the Beholder*, 87.

21. Ehrman, *Epistle of Barnabas*, 86–87.

22. For recent studies on Papias, see, e.g., Charles E. Hill, "Papias of Hierapolis," *ExpTim* 117 (2006); Christopher B. Zeichmann, "Papias as Rhetorician: Exphrasis in the Bishop's Account of Judas' Death," *NTS* 56 (2010); Jesse E. Robertson, *The Death*

A recent study by Jesse E. Robertson compares the early Christian accounts of Judas's death in Matt 27:3–5, Acts 1:18–20, and Papias, *Frag.* 4.2–3. Robertson argues that the death account was a genre used in antiquity to reveal the true character of a person. Ancient authors found appropriate justice in the horrid heaths of notorious figures, as their deaths were considered punitive.[23] The focus in this chapter will be on how physiognomic reasoning is intertwined with ideas about illness and disability in the Papias fragment.[24] Underlying both of these discourses—the medical and the physiognomic—are notions of gender and dis/ability. It is the combination of effeminate and disabled characteristics that in my opinion are used to denigrate Judas in the text. In the previous chapter I argued that Jesus and Paul are defending themselves against *disability invective* in the gospels and in 1 and 2 Corinthians, respectively. Such disability invective only works if the physiognomic link between outside and inside is part of the basic assumption. But the trajectory from outer appearance to inner morality can also be reverted. What one presumes about a person's inside can also shape the reading of the outside and even *construct* that outside in the text. The body of Judas, as described by Papias, is a vilifying physiognomic construction made to fit the presumed bad moral character of the person who betrayed Jesus.

The following is Papias's version of the death of Judas:

> Judas was a terrible, walking example of ungodliness [μέγα δὲ ἀσεβείας ὑπόδειγμα] in this world, his flesh so bloated [πρησθεὶς ἐπὶ τοσοῦτον τὴν σάρκα] that he was unable to pass [μηδὲ ... δύνασθαι διελθεῖν] through a place where a wagon passes easily, not even his bloated head by itself [τὸν τῆς κεφαλῆς ὄγκον αὐτοῦ]. For his eyelids, they say, were so swollen [βλέφαρα τῶν ὀφθαλμῶν αὐτοῦ φασὶ τοσοῦτον ἐξοιδῆσαι] that he could not see the light [το φῶς μὴ βλέπειν] at all, and his eyes could not be seen, even by a doctor using an optical instrument, so far had they sunk below the outer surface [τοσοῦτον βάθος εἶχον ἀπο τῆς ἔξωθεν ἐπιφανείας]. His genitals [τὸ δὲ αἰδοῖον αὐτοῦ] appeared more loathsome and larger [ἀηδέστερον καὶ μεῖζον] than anyone else's, and when he relieved himself there passed through it pus and worms [ἰχῶράς τε καὶ σκύληκας] from every part of his body, much to his shame. After much agony and punishment, they say, he

---

of Judas: The Characterization of Judas Iscariot in Three Early Christian Accounts of His Death, New Testament Monographs (Sheffield: Sheffield Phoenix, 2012), 117–40.

23. Robertson, *Death of Judas*, 13, 32.

24. As Robertson also argues (*Death of Judas*, 127–35).

finally died in his own place, and because of the stench the area is deserted and uninhabitable even now; in fact, to this day no one can pass that place unless they hold their nose, so great was the discharge from his body and so far did it spread over the ground [διὰ τῆς σαρκὸς αὐτοῦ καὶ ἐπὶ τῆς γῆς ἔκρυσις]. (*Frag.* 4.2–3 [Ehrman])

Judas is described as extremely large, bloated, and swollen. In the description, special attention is given to his eyes, his head, and his genitals, which are all described as overly large and ugly.[25] His intestines are infested with worms and pus, and he dies a painful and prolonged death. Finally, the effects that his dead body had on the property are noted. The description of his body follows the tradition of ancient diagnostic handbooks of starting with the head and working top-down, *a capite ad calcem*—from head to foot.[26] The introductory statement that Judas was an example of ungodliness cautions the reader that this death account is an indicator of the divine judgment of his character.[27]

6.2.1. Unmanly Obesity

Extreme swelling is the most significant characteristic of Judas's body. Papias uses a number of different terms to describe the bloated condition of various body parts (πίμπρημι, ὄγκος, ἐξοιδέω) and creates the vivid image of a monstrously huge body that cannot even pass through a gate fit for a wagon.[28] Judas's size is thus described as a mobility issue: he is not able to move (μηδὲ ... δύνασθαι διελθεῖν, *Frag.* 4.2). In other words, he is disabled. The fragment gives the impression that Judas's mobility is restricted to his own land, on which he eventually dies from this condition.

Judas's obesity is not only a question of restricted mobility. Obesity was considered unmanly in Greco-Roman culture. Self-restraint, σωφροσύνη,

---

25. Zeichman argues that this is a typical *ekphrasis*, a rhetorical device known from the *progymnasmata*, which systematically elaborates the description of a subject ("Papias as Rhetorician," 428).

26. Christian Laes, Chris F. Goodey, and M. Lynn Rose, "Approaching Disabilities *a Capite ad Calcem*: Hidden Themes in Roman Antiquity," in Laes, Goodey, and Rose, *Disabilities in Roman Antiquity*, 2.

27. Robertson, *Death of Judas*, 139.

28. The gate may be a reference to Jesus's logion about the camel passing through a needle's eye (Matt 19:24 // Mark 10:25 // Luke 18:25). If so, his inability to move through the gate is a metaphor for his inability to enter the kingdom of God.

was a key masculine virtue, and overindulgence in food and drink, as well as in sexual activity, was a sign of poor self-restraint. Women, in contrast to men, were considered to be less capable of controlling their emotions and urges.[29] Signs in a man that he lacked self-control was thus seen as a slip toward effeminacy. In the physiognomic handbooks, obesity is referred to as a sign of gluttony, fornication, and excessive drink, but it could also signal greed and lack of intelligence.[30] Polemon asserts that "largeness of the stomach and great fleshiness, especially if it has softness and droop, indicates much movement, drunkenness, and love of sexual intercourse. If it is very fleshy and strong, that indicates wickedness of deeds, malice, deceit, cunning, and lack of intellect."[31]

The references to Judas's bulk and swollen condition not only draw on a physiognomic discourse but also link to medical ideas. In ancient medicine, a swollen body was the typical symptom of dropsy, known in ancient Greek medical literature as ὕδρωψ. This illness was a condition in which water was retained in the body, causing extreme swelling and acute pain and often leading to death.[32] Although dropsy is not specifically mentioned in the text, Papias's description corresponds to the symptoms of dropsy as described by the medical writers.[33] The terms Papias uses to describe Judas's swelling, πρῆσθης and ὄγκος, are terms used by the medical writer Aretaeus when discussing the symptoms of dropsy (*Sign. diut.* 2.1). Aretaeus describes it in dire terms, as an illness incurable by doctors: "Dropsy is indeed an affection unseemly to behold and difficult to endure; for very few escape from it, and they more by fortune and the gods, than by art; for all the greater ills the gods only can remedy" (*Sign. diut.* 1.13 [Adams]). Some of the other symptoms mentioned by Papias, such as misshapen genitals; pus; smelly, putrefied excrements; and extreme discharges from the body, are also mentioned by Aretaeus in his discussions of dropsy (*Sign. diut.* 2.1). According to a Hippocratic treatise, dropsy could be treated by draining the excess liquid through some kind of cut, although the operation was not always a success: "Whenever cases of empyema or dropsy are treated by the knife of cautery, if the pus or water flow away all at once, a fatal result is certain" (*Aph.* 6.27 [Jones]).

---

29. Conway, *Behold the Man*, 22–25, 27–28.
30. Swain, *Seeing the Face, Seeing the Soul*, 404–5.
31. Swain, *Seeing the Face, Seeing the Soul*, 405.
32. See, e.g., Hippocrates, *Flat.* 12; *Epid.* 7.20–21; Aretaeus, *Sign. diut.* 1.13; 2.1.
33. Robertson, *Death of Judas*, 130.

The physiognomers' negative attitude toward obesity has a parallel in the doctors' understanding of dropsy. Dropsy was not a morally neutral illness but was considered a result of bad habits. According to Aretaeus, dropsy is caused by καχεξία, that is, "bad habits of the body," such as over-eating and inactivity (*Sign. diut.* 1.13; 2.1).[34] He also notes that intemperance is among the causes of dropsy. Outside of medical literature, dropsy had become a trope for overindulgence in food and drink and thus an illness that revealed a person lacking in self-control. Aristotle likens dropsy to vice in *Nicomachean Ethics* (1150b), and according to Horace, "By indulgence the dreadful dropsy grows apace" (*Od.* 2.2 [Rudd]).[35] Chad Hartsock argues that "the dropsy metaphor" is connected with greed and love of money in particular in rhetorical writings.[36] The vice of greed fits the gospels' construction of Judas as driven by money (Matt 26:15; Mark 14:10; Luke 22:4; John 12:4–6) and may also underlie the physiognomic description here.[37] However, the fragment does not have any clear references to Judas's vice as greed. In my opinion, the bloated, dropsical body represents a more general bad moral character that also includes insinuations of overindulgence in bodily pleasures. The description of Judas as large and swollen both disables and feminizes the character. The references to his inability to move are disabling, whereas the connection to an illness and bodily shape that suggests lack of self-control is effeminizing.

6.2.2. Invisible Eyes

From the swelling of the entire body and head, Papias moves on to describe Judas's eyes. His eyelids are swollen, making Judas unable to see (μὴ βλέπειν, *Frag.* 4.2) and making anyone else unable to see his eyes. The eyes were important in physiognomic literature and were thought to be particularly revealing of moral character (see §1.7). As the "gateway to the heart," the eyes would give the physiognomer "the truest information … about good and bad."[38] Most of Polemon's examples concerning eyes

---

34. LSJ, s.v. "καχεξία."

35. See also Horace, *Ep.* 1.2.34: *Si noles sanus, curres hydropicus*, "If you won't take up running in health, you'll have to do it when dropsical" (trans. Fairclough).

36. Chad Hartsock, "The Healing of the Man with Dropsy (Luke 14:1–6) and the Lukan Landscape," *BibInt* 21 (2013): 342.

37. Robertson, *Death of Judas*, 130–31.

38. Swain, *Seeing the Face, Seeing the Soul*, 341.

reveal various negative traits in their owners.[39] Swollen eyelids, according to Polemon, signified love of women and love of sleep: "I will mention to you something of swollen eyes. If you find that the lower eyelids of this eye are coarse and thick, judge for them love of women. If the upper ones are like that, judge for them love of sleep. If this is found in the lower and the upper together [judge likewise]."[40] He also notes that heavy eyelids are a sure sign of evil: "Know that he is suspected of evil and is contemplating it, so judge for him treachery and faithlessness."[41] Judas's swollen eyes are thus indicative of moral depravity and evil intentions.

The reference to a doctor with an optical instrument draws attention to the medical aspect of Judas's condition: that he is in fact blind.[42] It shows that Papias was familiar with doctors and their treatments and instruments, just like the insinuations about dropsy do. However, in the text, both the condition of dropsy and Judas's blindness are exploited physiognomically; they are used as a narrative prosthesis to draw out Judas's bad moral character. According to Papias, it is literally swollen flesh that obscures his eyes and makes him unable to see. Papias is here drawing on the ancient literary topos of blindness as lack of insight.[43] As noted, this topos is found in the Gospel of John and the Acts of Peter (see §3.4, §4.2, and §4.4). If the eyes are the gateway of the soul, Judas's soul is completely and entirely dark. Judas cannot see the light, neither literally nor figuratively. In the text, Judas is rhetorically disabled; he is made blind in order to draw out his lack of insight and his spiritual darkness.

6.2.3. Unsightly Private Parts

From the eyes, Papias moves on to describe Judas's genitals and his infested intestines. Just like his body in general, his forehead, his eyes, and his eyelids, Judas's genitals are oversized. They are "more loathsome and larger" (ἀσχημοσύνης ἀηδέστερον καὶ μεῖζον, *Frag.* 4.2) than anyone else's. The physiognomic literature has little to say about genitals, but

---

39. Hartsock, *Sight and Blindness in Luke-Acts*, 59.

40. Swain, *Seeing the Face, Seeing the Soul*, 381.

41. Swain, *Seeing the Face, Seeing the Soul*, 345.

42. The instrument referred to, διόπτρα, is not medical but astronomical (LSJ, s.v. "optical instrument; aperture-sight"). The term occurs mainly in mathematical and astronomical works, and never in the medical literature of antiquity.

43. Hartsock, *Sight and Blindness in Luke-Acts*, 65–81.

swollen and distorted genitals are among the symptoms of dropsy (e.g., *Epid.* 7.20). The attention devoted to bowel movements in Papias is also reminiscent of the medical literature. In many Hippocratic treatises, stools and urine are described in minute detail, as they were thought to hold prognostic significance (Hippocrates, *Epid.* 1.23).[44] In one case from *Epidemics*, the doctor comments on the stools and urine of sufferers of a summer fever in the region: "For the bowels were in most cases quite easy, and hurt to no appreciable extent. Urine in most cases of good colour and clear, but thin, and after a time near the crisis it grew concocted" (*Epid.* 1.1.3 [Jones]). Such details and interest shows that it was expected that the medical doctor had intimate access to the body of the sick person.

The fluids of the body were important in Hippocratic medical theory. The fluids of Judas's body are pus and worms rather than the healthy combination of the four Hippocratic humors, blood, phlegm, black bile, and yellow bile. This is, of course, not only a symptom of illness but, again, a metaphor for his rotten soul. If one were to believe ancient writers, death by worms often afflicted the evil king or emperor. Pausanias describes a death by dropsy and worms for the terrible ruler Cassander: "He was filled with dropsy, and from the dropsy came worms [εὐλαί] while he was yet alive" (*Descr.* 9.7.2 [Jones]). Josephus recounts the death of Herod the Great in a similar way, with worms, excruciating pain, and a bloated body:

> But Herod's illness became more and more acute, for God was inflicting punishment upon him for his lawless deeds.... He also had a terrible desire to scratch himself because of this, for it was impossible not to seek relief. There was an ulceration of the bowels and intestinal pains that were particularly terrible.... And he suffered similarly from an abdominal ailment, as well as from gangrene of his privy parts that produces worms.... Accordingly it was said by the men of God ... that all this was the penalty that God was exacting of the king for his great impiety (*Ant.* 17.168–171 [Marcus])

Josephus's description has several resemblances to Papias, such as excruciating pain and worm-infested genitals. The underlying causes also seem to

---

44. Nutton, *Ancient Medicine*, 90. For examples, see the descriptions of individual cases in *Epidemics* and *Prognostics*.

be the same, stemming from lack of self-restraint and general impiety. Robertson has argued that Papias follows a literary trope for descriptions of the death of bad rulers, one that indicates that they suffer divine retribution.[45]

6.3. Body and Land as Topographies of Evil

Voice and gait were among the signs that the physiognomic handbooks deciphered (see §1.7). Judas never speaks in Papias's fragment, but his lack of voice might in itself denote effeminacy. In some of the medical descriptions of dropsy, loss of voice is among the symptoms (Hippocrates, *Epid.* 6.20–21). Judas's movement is commented upon. Although not gait per se, aspects of Judas mobility, and lack thereof, runs through the fragment like a red thread: he is a "walking example of ungodliness," he is unable to pass through a door, worms and puss pass through his body, and the discharge from his dead body spreads over the ground. In the initial designation of Judas as a "walking example of ungodliness" (ἀσεβείας ὑπόδειγμα ... περιπάτησεν, *Frag.* 4.2), the verb περιπατέω is used. This term was used to designate walking while teaching and discoursing and was the trademark of Aristotle's Peripatetic school of philosophers.[46] Judas, in contrast, is an antiphilosopher and an exemplar of ungodliness rather than of the good life.

Despite his lack of mobility, worms and puss pass through his body, and after his death, his disintegrating body spreads across his land. Papias describes his body as a stinking heap of flesh (σάρξ, *Frag.* 4.3) covering the ground. The land thus seems to be an extension of his body. It has the same properties of rot, decay, and stench. Through the lingering smell, Judas haunts the land where he died. His memory will not go away, as "even to this day no one can pass by the place without holding his nose" (*Frag.* 4.3). Even after his death he polices the borders and serves as a warning to the living.

The reference to Judas's land echoes the two New Testament references to the death of Judas. Both Matthew and Acts connect the field to the blood money, the thirty pieces of silver Judas got from the high priests in order to betray Jesus. According to Matthew, the chief priests buy a field for the thirty pieces of silver after Judas has committed suicide. It is

---

45. Robertson, *Death of Judas*, 135–39.
46. LSJ, s.vv. "περιπατέω," "περιπατετικός."

designated as a place to bury foreigners and called the Field of Blood (Matt 27:5–8). According to Acts, Judas himself acquires a field from the money he received. He dies there, leaving the land desolate: "falling headlong, he burst open in the middle, and all his bowels gushed out" (Acts 1:18–20). This connection likely lies behind Papias's linkage of man and land, although there is no reference to the field of blood or how it was acquired. Papias's version is closer to Acts, where Judas does not commit suicide but somehow dies on his property, and his body disintegrates there, leaving the land desolate.[47] In fact, the introduction to the fragment asserts that Judas did not "die by hanging" (*Frag.* 4.1) and quotes Acts 1:18 as proof.

6.3.1. Judas the Monster

The figure of the monster may prove helpful in understanding the cultural meaning of Papias's tale of Judas. The way Judas is described is monstrous in several respects. First, immense body size is one of the characteristics of the monsters of ancient Greece. The Titans, the Cyclops, and the Gorgons are examples of giant monsters from the Greek tradition. Like the classical monsters of Greek mythology, Judas is huge, ugly, and malign.[48] The particular mention of Judas's "bloated head" (τὸν τῆς κεφαλῆς ὄγκον) underscores this monstrous aspect of his body, as does the comment that he could not pass through a gate fit for a wagon. Judas's body is beyond human scale. Second, monsters were hybrid creatures that exhibited unnatural physical characteristics. The description of Judas's misshapen genitals and the pus and worms that flow from his body are details that enhance the repugnance and also push Judas beyond what is human. Third, as noted above, monsters were thought to inhabit desolate, remote spaces. Judas's land is constructed in this fragment as just such a remote, monstrous space in which the stench of his rotting body still haunts.

I argue that the connection between Judas and his land underscores his monstrous characteristics and, at the same time, also contributes to his feminization. In the fragment, Judas is said to have died on his land, which is still "desolate and uninhabited because of the stench" (*Frag.* 4.3). In the fragment, Judas never interacts with other human beings, except, perhaps, for hypothetically being inspected by a doctor with an optical

---

47. Robertson, *Death of Judas*, 135.
48. Felton, "Rejecting and Embracing the Monstrous," 114.

instrument. He is constricted to the piece of land on which he eventually dies. In antiquity, free men were associated with the public spaces of the city, which signaled activity and social and political dominance.[49] Male space within the household was that of the father, son, brother, and husband.[50] By disconnecting Judas from these male spaces and relationships that can define him in a masculine role, Judas is feminized. The space he is associated with is his land (ἡ γῆ, *Frag.* 4.3). Earth was conceived of as feminine. Like women, the earth was "fertile soil," which passively received and nurtured the male seed.[51] In chapter 5, I argued that the depiction of women in the Acts of Peter has features typical of the ancient male gaze. Women are exposed as vulnerable, naked, and mute.[52] The figure of Judas has some of the same features as the female objects of the male gaze. He is voiceless, and his private parts are exposed. However, although his body is vulnerable, it is not attractive. Judas's nakedness is repulsive rather than titillating.

The porousness and disintegration of Judas's body can be read as an allegory of borders and containment, inside and outside. Julia Kristeva's notion of abjection compliments monster theory, as it explains psychologically the human need to define the intolerable and disgusting as outside the self. She defines the abject in similar terms as the monstrous in monster theory, as having to do with disturbance of taxonomy: "It is thus not lack of cleanliness or health that causes abjection but what disturbs identity, system, order. What does not respect borders, positions, rules. The in-between, the ambiguous, the composite."[53] The rejection and repulsion of everything within that threatens or disturbs order is palpable in the description of Judas's death.

Monster theory is helpful in order to understand what lies behind the grotesque description of Judas's body. Monsters embody the fears of a culture and haunt the borders between defined categories. As Cohen notes, "the monster's body quite literally incorporates fear, desire, anxiety, and

---

49. Smit, "Masculinity and the Bible," 52.

50. Halvor Moxnes, *Putting Jesus in His Place: A Radical Vision of Household and Kingdom* (Louisville: Westminster John Knox, 2003), 72–73.

51. Økland, *Women in Their Place*, 42–43.

52. Richlin, introduction, xix.

53. Julia Kristeva, *Powers of Horror: An Essay on Abjection* (New York: Columbia University Press, 1982), 4.

fantasy."[54] Behind Papias's construction of Judas lies the question of how an insider, a disciple, could betray Jesus. The figure of Judas polices the borders of what it means to be "one of us." Judas is created as altogether other, a monster, not one like us. Judas's monstrous body signals the magnitude of his evildoing. At a time when Christians were persecuted for their faith, the fear of betrayal from an insider is an important undercurrent in the story. The terrible torments he experiences are also a warning of the terrors awaiting those who are willing to betray their fellow believers for a handful of silver coins. It is important to note that it is categories of disability and gender that construct Judas the monster. Through his monstrous construction, Papias thus confirms and reappropriates the position of women and people with disabilities as on the margins of society—and on the borders of the human.

6.4. Conclusion: The Monster as Border Police

In conclusion, Papias is making use of medical categories as well as drawing on physiognomic tradition in his description of Judas's body and his death. The text disables Judas in order to demonstrate his sinfulness. In reference to both Judas's size and his eyes, his lack of abilities are pointed out: "He was unable to pass" ($\mu\eta\delta\grave{\epsilon}$ ... $\delta\acute{\upsilon}\nu\alpha\sigma\theta\alpha\iota$ $\delta\iota\epsilon\lambda\theta\epsilon\tilde{\iota}\nu$), "He could not see" ($\mu\grave{\eta}$ $\beta\lambda\acute{\epsilon}\pi\epsilon\iota\nu$, *Frag.* 4.2). Judas's impairments, which simultaneously cast him as effeminate, are constructed as bodily signs of a depraved soul. The combined effect of this description, with its extreme exaggeration and repetitious insistence, pushes Judas toward the borders of what can be called human; he is not a man, he is a monster. By creating Judas as other, Papias tries to come to terms with the anxiety that looms in the knowledge that an insider was the betrayer of Jesus. Monsters can reveal which categories and borders a community struggles to uphold.[55] In this text, there is a taxonomic effort to place Judas beyond, to categorize him as deviant and monstrous. In this need to assert difference, Judas is inscribed with the alterity of gender deviance and disability.

While most of Papias's writings have been lost, this text has been preserved through its citation by other early Christian writers. Halberstam's insight about why Victorians consumed Gothic novels in vast quantities is

---

54. Cohen, "Monster Culture," 4.
55. Cohen, "Monster Culture," 3.

helpful in order to understand why Christ-believers would read and distribute at text like this:

> Gothic gave readers the thrill of reading about so-called perverse activities while identifying aberrant sexuality as a condition of otherness and as an essential trait of foreign bodies. The monster, of course, marks the distance between the perverse and the supposedly disciplined sexuality of the reader. Also, the signifiers of "normal" sexuality maintain a kind of hegemonic power by remaining invisible.[56]

As a monster, Judas polices the border of Christian identity. The monster Judas also simultaneously constructs the normate Christ-believer as everything that Judas is not. This subject position is that of the healthy, fully masculine man, with self-restraint and insight, situated within the male space of the Christ-believing community.

---

56. Halberstam, *Skin Shows*, 13.

7
Eunuchs in/and the Kingdom of God

7.1. Introduction: Crip Theory

The term eunuch (εὐνοῦχος) occurs in only two passages in the New Testament (Matt 19:12; Acts 8:26–40). In this chapter I explore the bodily signs of the eunuch and their meaning in these passages. How was a eunuch marked, and what were the social consequences of his bodily marks? I will argue that the eunuch figure can be understood as a disabled character—a crip figure. Within the disability community, the term *crip* represents a reclaiming of the derogatory term *cripple*. It is used as an inclusive term that expresses identity within disability culture and a resistance to regimes of normalcy.[1] The usage has similarities to how the term *queer* has been reappropriated by the LGBT+ community. Like queer, crip is not only a defiant term but also one that questions identity categories and simple binaries, for example, the boundary between able-bodied and disabled. The term reveals the impossible standard of the "normal body" and shows how the idea of normal is dependent on its binary opposite, the abnormal.[2] *Cripping* may be understood as a process of critique, disruption, and reimagining that aims to "spin main-

---

An earlier version of this chapter appeared in *Biblical Interpretation* and is reworked here by permission. See Anna Rebecca Solevåg, "No Nuts? No Problem! Disability, Stigma, and the Baptized Eunuch in Acts 8:26–30," *BibInt* 24 (2016): 81–99.

1. Carrie Sandahl, "Queering the Crip or Cripping the Queer? Intersections of Queer and Crip Identities in Solo Autobiographical Performance," *GLQ* 9 (2003): 26–27.

2. Davis, *Bending over Backwards*, 38–39. See also Sharon L. Snyder and David T. Mitchell's video documentary, *Vital Signs: Crip Culture Talks Back*, www.youtube .com/watch?v=r5rWHA0KcFc.

stream representations or practices to reveal able-bodied assumptions and exclusionary effects."[3]

Robert McRuer uses the term crip more specifically for the convergence of queerness and disability. He argues that the cultural constructions of disability and homosexuality are dependent on one another and reinforce one another. Despite ideals of tolerance and diversity in postmodern culture, there is an undergirding idea of normalcy as the preferred state, according to McRuer. Although able-bodiedness and heterosexuality lack definitional clarity, the opposites they construct, disability and homosexuality, serve the purpose of being contrasts to the "normal," which is the preferred subject position.[4]

As noted in the introduction, I have selected texts for this study that represent variety in disability categories and themes (see §§1.1 and 1.8). The eunuch figure represents what may be called a reproductive disability.[5] Like barren women, eunuchs as a category were defined by their inability to reproduce.[6] I first give an overview of the eunuch figure in Greco-Roman discourse and the Hebrew Bible and then discuss the two New Testament texts. Drawing on crip perspectives and McRuer's theory, I suggest that the eunuch can be understood as a crip figure with the potential to destabilize established categories.[7]

7.1.1. The Eunuch Figure in Greco-Roman Discourse

In Hellenistic and Roman culture a eunuch (Greek: εὐνοῦχος, σπάδων; Latin: eunuchus, spado) was a castrated male or a person born with non-

---

3. Sandahl, "Queering the Crip or Cripping the Queer?," 37.

4. Robert McRuer, *Crip Theory: Cultural Signs of Queerness and Disability* (New York: New York University Press, 2006), 7–10.

5. For a comprehensive study of infertility in the Bible informed by disability studies, see Baden and Moss, *Reconceiving Infertility*.

6. J. Blake Couey, "Prophets," in Melcher, Parsons, and Yong, *Bible and Disability*, 239.

7. Burke similarly argues for the eunuch's destabilizing, queering potential but does not employ the categories of disability and *crip* in his analysis. See Sean D. Burke, "Queering Early Christian Discourse," in *Bible Trouble: Queer Reading at the Boundaries of Biblical Scholarship*, ed. Teresa J. Hornsby and Ken Stone, SemeiaSt 67 (Atlanta: Society of Biblical Literature, 2011); see also Marianne Bjelland Kartzow and Halvor Moxnes, "Complex Identities: Ethnicity, Gender and Religion in the Story of the Ethiopian Eunuch (Acts 8:26–40)," *R&T* 17 (2010): 184–204.

normative genitalia. Whereas the Hebrew term *saris* could simply denote a court official, and is sometimes used about a noncastrated person connected to a ruler's court, this is not usually the case in Roman and Greek literature.[8] It is possible to distinguish between three main eunuch categories for the Greco-Roman world: manmade eunuchs (i.e., enslaved eunuchs), self-made eunuchs and congenitally ascribed eunuchs. The jurist Ulpian, for example, describes three categories of eunuchs, although his third category is rather vague: "those who are eunuchs by nature, those who are made eunuchs, and any other kind of eunuchs" (*Dig.* 50.16.128 [Watson]).[9]

Of all the eunuchs within the Roman Empire, slave eunuchs—persons who according to Ulpian's taxonomy had been made eunuchs by others—were the most common. The tradition of keeping eunuchs as court officials goes back centuries before the Hellenistic period, to the Assyrian and Persian Empires.[10] Sean D. Burke offers several reasons why ancient rulers found castrated slaves to be dependable servants.[11] First, they could not establish rival dynasties. They were doubly dependent on their masters, as they were both removed from their family of origin and physically incapable of establishing a family through procreation. Second, they were generally despised by other people and thus dependent on their masters for protection. Finally, as castrated males, they functioned as intermediaries between male and female spaces. In other words, they served as surrogates for and extensions of the ruler's person in spaces he would not or could not enter. Since eunuchs could not marry and reproduce, the place of the eunuch was perceived as one outside household and family.[12]

According to Suetonius (*Dom.* 7), castration of another person was forbidden by law during the reign of Domitian (81–96 CE). It continued to be a subject of legislation in the centuries that followed.[13] Yet import of castrated slaves was legal and became increasingly common in the first

---

8. On its use for a noncastrated person connected to a ruler's court, see Sean D. Burke, *Queering the Ethiopian Eunuch: Strategies of Ambiguity in Acts* (Minneapolis: Fortress, 2013), 22–26.

9. "Spadonum generalis appellatio est: quo nomine tam hi, qui natura spadones sunt, item thlibiae thlasiae, sed et si quod aliud spadonum est, continentur."

10. J. David Hester, "Queers on Account of the Kingdom of Heaven: Rhetorical Constructions of the Eunuch Body," *Scr* 90 (2005): 812.

11. Burke, *Queering the Ethiopian Eunuch*, 101–2.

12. Moxnes, *Putting Jesus in His Place*, 78–80.

13. See Ra'anan Abusch, "Circumcision and Castration under Roman Law," in *The*

centuries of the common era.[14] Moreover, eunuchism was a widespread practice despite the ban, and eunuch slaves were sought after for their presumed loyalty but also as luxury articles and sexual partners.[15] The medical procedure to make someone a eunuch could be performed in several ways: by amputation of the penis (with or without the testicles), by tying up the scrotum, or by crushing the testicles.[16] The latter two procedures would sterilize the person but leave the appearance of the genitals more or less indistinguishable from other men's. These were also the safest and simplest procedures and hence more common than penis amputation.[17] If castrated before puberty, a eunuch would retain the appearance of sexual immaturity, lacking masculine secondary sex characteristics such as facial hair, body hair, and a deep voice.[18] Slaves were usually castrated before puberty, as this would heighten their value on the slave market.[19] The primary purpose of castration was to render the eunuch incapable of procreation, *not* to make him incapable of engaging in sexual relations.[20]

Men born with nonnormative genitalia or whose genitals did not develop at puberty were also categorized as eunuchs (Ulpian's category of eunuchs by nature).[21] A third category of eunuch, although not specifically mentioned by Ulpian, was the self-made eunuch. Some men castrated themselves as a religious commitment. In Asia Minor, there were self-castrated men connected to the fertility cults of Cybele and Dea Syria. These so-called *galli* were not priests but itinerant musicians and singers

---

Covenant of Circumcision: New Perspectives on an Ancient Jewish Rite, ed. Elizabeth Wyner Mark (Hanover, NH: Brandeis University Press, 2003).

14. Mathew Kuefler, *The Manly Eunuch: Masculinity, Gender Ambiguity, and Christian Ideology in Late Antiquity* (Chicago: University of Chicago Press, 2001), 62–63.

15. Hester, "Queers on Account of the Kingdom of Heaven," 5–6. Eunuchism remained widespread even within the empire, according to Burke (*Queering the Ethiopian Eunuch*, 102–3).

16. Kuefler, *Manly Eunuch*, 33.

17. Burke, *Queering the Ethiopian Eunuch*, 97.

18. Kuefler, *Manly Eunuch*, 34.

19. Abusch, "Circumcision and Castration under Roman Law," 77.

20. Burke, *Queering the Ethiopian Eunuch*, 97.

21. Kuefler, *Manly Eunuch*, 33. Note, however, that intersex individuals suffered a harsher fate. While the Greeks considered *hermaphrodites* "an unusual but essentially routine part of nature," the Romans considered such births an evil omen and treated intersex individuals as abhorrent and accursed (Garland, *Eye of the Beholder*, 3).

with special functions at festivals.[22] Roman writers such as Lucian, Catullus, and Ovid scorned self-made eunuchs for their uncontrolled religious fervor. The act was cast as un-Roman, and linked to Eastern, and thus foreign, religious rites (e.g., Lucian, *Syr. d.* 51; Catullus, *Carm.* 63; Ovid, *Fasti* 4.183–186, 351–366. Lucian describes the castration ceremony of the Cybele worshipers thus:

> On these days men become galli. While others are piping and performing the rituals, a madness communicates itself, and many who have come as spectators behave in the following manner. The young man for whom this fate lies in store casts aside his garments and comes to the center with a great cry, seizing up a sword.… Seizing it he castrates himself, then runs through the city carrying in his hands the objects he has excised. He receives female clothing and ornament from whatever house he throws them into. (*Syr. d.* 51 [Lightfoot])

The act of castration is depicted as an ecstatic and out-of-control act that removes the indicators of male status.[23] In several respects, eunuchs were ambiguous figures that challenged the kyriarchal boundaries of society.[24] They exposed the potential fluidity of gender categories but also frustrated binaries concerning status and ethnicity. A eunuch did not always have visible bodily features that could single him out as such. He could be bearded or smooth-skinned; his voice could be deep or it could be high-pitched, depending on his age at castration. Moreover, the eunuch's genitalia could have a variety of forms, according to the manner of his castration or his congenital impairment. The eunuch was the quintessential effeminate man.[25] A eunuch's sexuality was also surrounded by uncertainty and ambiguity: Did he experience desire? Was he able to perform sexually as a man, that is, could he perform penetrative acts?[26] These were questions that could have different answers.

Eunuchs thus challenged ancient notions of male and female. There probably existed several competing gender systems in antiquity, including

---

22. Moxnes, *Putting Jesus in His Place*, 79.

23. Kartzow, *Destabilizing the Margins*, 51.

24. For a thorough investigation of the many ambiguities of the eunuch figure, see Burke, *Queering the Ethiopian Eunuch*.

25. Hester, "Queers on Account of the Kingdom of Heaven," 815.

26. All these uncertainties are voiced in Lucian's *The Eunuch*; see esp. 10–13 (Kuefler, *Manly Eunuch*, 34–35).

the so-called one-sex model.[27] What is common for these ancient gender systems is that the male was the ideal, the norm, and the female, whether conceived of as opposite to the male or treacherously similar, fell short of this ideal.[28] In such a phallocentric economy, masculinity was connected to virtue. As discussed in previous chapters, masculinity tied in with a man's ability to penetrate and dominate, and, conversely, to be penetrated (and beaten) was considered effeminate and slavish.[29] Eunuchs, although men, did not meet this masculine ideal, and the ancients therefore struggled with how to categorize them. Eunuchs were sometimes described as a third gender, or something in between male and female.[30] In *The Eunuch*, Lucian ascribes to one of his characters the opinion that "a eunuch was neither man nor woman but something composite, hybrid, and monstrous, alien to human nature" (6 [Harmon]). In other words, the gender of the eunuch was ambiguous and thus represented the threat of effeminacy.

In Greco-Roman discourse, both slave eunuchs and *galli* were constructed as slavish and foreign.[31] There was a literary fascination with the court eunuch figure serving in the women's quarters of a foreign royal

---

27. Thomas Laqueur has argued that the ancients thought of gender as a scale on which male and female were different versions of the same sex (*Making Sex: Body and Gender from the Greeks to Freud* [Cambridge: Harvard University Press, 1992], 3–8). This model has been contested by scholars who instead hold that ancient gender discourse is occupied with sexual difference and the absolute divide between male and female. See, e.g., Helen King, *Hippocrates' Woman: Reading the Female Body in Ancient Greece* (London: Routledge, 1998), 11; Kuefler, *Manly Eunuch*, 19–26.

28. Solevåg, *Birthing Salvation*, 70–72; Økland, *Women in Their Place*, 40.

29. See, e.g., Jonathan Walters, "Invading the Roman Body: Manliness and Impenetrability in Roman Thought," in *Roman Sexualities*, ed. Judith P. Hallett and Marilyn B. Skinner (Princeton: Princeton University Press, 1997); Glancy, *Slavery in Early Christianity*, 25–29; see discussion in §§1.6 and 5.1.

30. According to the anonymous Historia Augusta, Severus (r. 225–235) removed eunuchs from service at the imperial court except for the care of the women's baths: "For he used to say that eunuchs were a third sex of the human race [*tertius genus hominum*], one not to be seen or employed by men and scarcely even by women of noble birth" (Hist. Aug., Sev. 23.7 [Magie]). Eunuchs were constituted as a third gender during the Byzantine Age (Kathryn M. Ringrose, *The Perfect Servant: Eunuchs and the Social Construction of Gender in Byzantium* [Chicago: University of Chicago Press, 2003], 4–7). Catullus uses both male and female pronouns in his description of Attis, the self-castrated Cybele devotee (*Carm.* 63). Apuleius refers to eunuchs as "half-men" (*semiviri*, *Metam.* 8.28).

31. Burke, *Queering the Ethiopian Eunuch*, 106.

court.[32] Slave eunuchs were connected with this "barbarian" tradition, and, similarly, the self-made eunuchs were presented as followers of foreign religious traditions and slaves to their Eastern gods in their uncontrolled ecstasy, as noted above. Despite these constructions, which clearly reveal a eunuch stigma, the class status of eunuchs was ambiguous. Self-made eunuchs were not necessarily slaves, and slave eunuchs could have prominent and trusted positions within powerful households.[33]

7.1.2. The Eunuch in the Hebrew Bible

In Deuteronomy, eunuchs are prohibited from participating in the worshiping assembly: "No one whose testicles are crushed or whose penis is cut off shall be admitted to the assembly of the LORD" (Deut 23:2). Crushed testicles and cut-off penises are considered defects.[34] *Defect* (*mum*) is an important category of classification in the legal material of the Hebrew Bible. In Lev 21:17–23, God forbids anyone with a defect to serve as priests. Among the defects listed are blindness, lameness, skin rashes, and crushed testicles. According to Leviticus, a eunuch was therefore excluded from serving as a priest. Leviticus 22:24–25 likewise prohibits the offering of animals with damaged genitals. Genital impairments caused by castration are also here categorized as defects. David Tabb Stewart argues that anxieties about reproduction and concern for proper gender boundaries lie behind the strong reaction against castration and congenital genital anomalies in biblical law.[35]

The socially constructed nature of genital defects comes into sharp relief when compared to the Hebrew custom of male circumcision. Saul M. Olyan has noted that circumcision, as an alteration of the body, is not unlike other imposed alterations, such as castration, which the same body of texts labels as defects.[36] In Roman law, castration and circumcision are in fact compared and at times even identified.[37] Circumcision,

---

32. See, e.g., Polybius, *Hist.* 22.22; Plutarch, *Art.* 16.1; Chariton, *Chaer.* 5.9; Esth 1:10–15; 2:14.

33. Kartzow, *Destabilizing the Margins*, 48–52.

34. David Tabb Stewart, "Sexual Disabilities in the Hebrew Bible," in Moss and Schipper, *Disability Studies and Biblical Literature*, 73.

35. Stewart, "Sexual Disabilities in the Hebrew Bible," 78–80.

36. Olyan, *Disability in the Hebrew Bible*, 36.

37. Abusch, "Circumcision and Castration under Roman Law," 84–86.

like castration, was viewed in terms of masculinity, and the ideal, male body had a penis with an intact foreskin.[38] In the Hebrew Bible, however, circumcision is cast as socially and ritually *enabling* rather than disabling.[39] The stories of covenant are sealed by the ritual of circumcision (e.g., Gen 17:9–14; Exod 12:43–49), and a number of texts speak about circumcision and uncircumcision metaphorically, associating circumcision with positive, enabling characteristics such as eloquent speech and the capacity to listen (e.g., Exod 6:12; Deut 10:16; Jer 6:10).[40] All these texts construct the normate male body in the Hebrew Bible as circumcised. In the biblical context, circumcision becomes physically normative, Olyan argues, "as if the foreskin were itself a kind of 'defect.'"[41] In other words, circumcision becomes a sign that socially constructs ability based on a biological deficit.[42]

The liturgical exclusion of eunuchs in Deut 23:2–9 is contested within the Hebrew Bible. Isaiah gives an eschatological promise about the inclusion of eunuchs into the community of worship when he speaks of the foreigner who will be included into God's people and the eunuch who will receive a name in the house of the Lord:

> Do not let the foreigner joined to the LORD say,
> "The LORD will surely separate me from his people";
> and do not let the eunuch say, "I am just a dry tree."
> For thus says the LORD: To the eunuchs who keep my sabbaths,
> who choose the things that please me and hold fast my covenant,
> I will give, in my house and within my walls,
> a monument [*yād*] and a name better than sons and daughters;
> I will give them an everlasting name that shall not be cut off. (Isa 56:3–7)

The eschatological vision of this passage is that eunuchs, excluded from the assembly of worship according to Deut 23:2–9, will be assured a place

---

38. Matthew R. Anderson and Karin B. Neutel, "The First Cut Is the Deepest: Masculinity and Circumcision in the First Century," in *Biblical Masculinities Foregrounded*, ed. Ovidiu Creanga and Peter-Ben Smit (Sheffield: Sheffield University Press, 2014), 229–30.

39. Olyan, *Disability in the Hebrew Bible*, 36; Jeremy Schipper, "Joshua–Second Kings," in Melcher, Parsons, and Yong, *Bible and Disability*, 97.

40. Olyan, *Disability in the Hebrew Bible*, 37.

41. Olyan, *Disability in the Hebrew Bible*, 37.

42. Stewart, "Sexual Disabilities in the Hebrew Bible," 72.

in the Lord's house if they are pious.[43] The lament of the eunuch, that he is a "dried tree," recalls a common Isaianic comparison between barren landscapes and disabled bodies, according to J. Blake Couey.[44] There is no direct promise that the eunuch's reproductive capabilities will be restored, although there is perhaps a pun on this possibility if *yād*, which literally means "hand," is taken as a euphemism for "penis" (see, e.g., Isa 57:8, 10; Song 5:4). Rather than through children, the eunuch's name will be remembered within the sanctuary, Couey argues.[45] In other words, the eunuch experiences a restoration of honor without any change in his body. He is included without being healed.

7.2. Becoming a Eunuch for the Kingdom of Heaven (Matt 19:12)

In the Gospel of Matthew, Jesus is questioned about a man's right to divorce his wife. It is in the context of this discussion that Jesus introduces eunuchs as a paradigm for the kingdom of heaven:

> There are eunuchs who have been so from birth [ἐκ κοιλίας μητρὸς], and there are eunuchs who have been made eunuchs by others [εὐνουχίσθησαν ὑπὸ τῶν ἀνθρώπων], and there are eunuchs who have made themselves eunuchs [εὐνούχισαν ἑαυτοὺς] for the sake of the kingdom of heaven. (Matt 19:12)

Jesus's words about eunuchs in Matt 19:12 testify to the three different ways of becoming a eunuch mentioned above. The third category, the self-made eunuchs, may be understood in light of the *galli* tradition. Like the *galli*, the Christ-believer who makes himself a eunuch "for the sake of the kingdom" does so as part of a religious commitment. Ulrich Luz surmises that the background of the logion is that hostile opponents may have compared Jesus and his disciples to the *galli* due to their unmarried, itinerant lifestyle.[46] Halvor Moxnes likewise sees the saying as a response to slander that tried to frame the Jesus movement's ascetic way of life as unmanly. He understands the logion as a "call to leave male space" and "a challenge to

---

43. Olyan, *Disability in the Hebrew Bible*, 11.
44. Couey, "Prophets," 239.
45. Couey, "Prophets," 239.
46. Luz, *Matthew 8–20*, 501–2.

the standards of masculinity in antiquity."[47] Moxnes likens this subversive use of a despised term to designate a positive identity to the modern use of the term queer. Like eunuch in antiquity, queer defies categorization and is a protest against categorization, he suggests: "Therefore, 'queer' is the most useful term to apply when we try to make sense of Jesus's eunuch saying from a modern perspective."[48]

I suggest that the term crip, similarly to queer, shares the subversive and category-defying qualities of the term eunuch. Crip, in McRuer's conception, challenges assumptions about normative bodies and normative sexualities, and the eunuch logion may be understood to do the same. The logion subverts the attempt to stigmatize by calling on people to crip themselves: to enter into the despised category and devote themselves to a eunuch lifestyle. The logion crips the Jesus movement. Does it also crip Jesus? Jesus's appropriation of the term eunuch allows us to question ancient and modern assumptions about the body of Jesus. What if Jesus was a eunuch? As Moxnes notes: "Since the masculinity of Jesus has been taken for granted, it has been impossible even to contemplate that Jesus might be a eunuch in the physical sense, that is, castrated."[49] Whether Jesus was castrated or not, the eunuch logion encourages the follower to "perform disability" by making oneself a eunuch and/or live as a eunuch.[50] The logion destabilizes categories of ability and disability by reinterpreting eunuch as a preferred state, an insider position, rather than a despised category.

With the reference to the kingdom of heaven, the body of the eunuch is also connected to the ideal, eschatological body. In the resurrection, infertility is no longer a disability, since Jesus has dismissed the idea of marriage in heaven: "For in the resurrection they neither marry, nor are given in marriage, but are as the angels of God in heaven" (Matt 22:30; see §4.2). Statements like these and Jesus's blessing of barren women (Luke 23:29) underscore the apocalyptic backdrop of the Jesus movement, but as Moxnes notes, they might also have a prescriptive function: "Such statements might signal a reversal of status already, here and now."[51] The

---

47. Moxnes, *Putting Jesus in His Place*, 73–75, quote on 73.
48. Moxnes, *Putting Jesus in His Place*, 89–90.
49. Moxnes, *Putting Jesus in His Place*, 89.
50. Moss, "Mark and Matthew," 283.
51. Moxnes, *Putting Jesus in His Place*, 94.

eunuch logion crips Jesus and his movement by appropriating the despised category of eunuch and subverting its meaning.

7.2.1. Castration as an Early Christian Bodily Practice

Jesus's words about making oneself a eunuch for the kingdom of heaven were taken literally by some Christ-believers in the first centuries. Justin Martyr (100–165 CE) describes how a fellow Christian in the city

> presented to Felix the governor in Alexandria a petition, craving that permission might be given to a surgeon to make him an eunuch.... And when Felix absolutely refused to sign such a permission, the youth remained single, and was satisfied with his own approving conscience, and the approval of those who thought as he did. (*1 Apol.* 29 [Schaff])

According to Eusebius, Origen (ca. 184–253 CE) castrated himself as part of his commitment to Christ:

> At this time while Origen was conducting catechetical instruction at Alexandria, a deed was done by him which evidenced an immature and youthful mind, but at the same time gave the highest proof of faith and continence. For he took the words, "There are eunuchs who have made themselves eunuchs for the kingdom of heaven's sake," in too literal and extreme a sense. And in order to fulfill the Saviour's word, and at the same time to take away from the unbelievers all opportunity for scandal,—for, although young, he met for the study of divine things with women as well as men,—he carried out in action the word of the Saviour. (*Hist. eccl.* 6.8.1 [Oulton])

It is unclear how widespread the practice was. Most of the sources on this practice are critical of it, such as Justin and Eusebius in the quotations above. Moxnes notes that early Christian writers were educated men who shared Roman masculine ideals, including a critical attitude toward eunuchs, and that they took pains to distance themselves from the perceived excesses of the Eastern cults and their *galli*.[52] However, the fact that self-castrated eunuchs were banned from the priesthood at the Council of Nicea shows that it must have been a palpable problem in many Christian

---

52. Moxnes, *Putting Jesus in His Place*, 80.

communities.[53] Luz notes that there was a certain reserve in the use of Matt 19:12 in the ancient church due to the "exaggerated ascetic tendencies" that the text occasioned.[54]

A spectacular rather than historic tale of Christian self-castration can be found in the Acts of John. The theme of sexual renunciation frames many of the episodes in the apocryphal Acts (see §4.2). In one such episode, a young man kills his father because the father had advised him to end an adulterous relationship. John raises the slain father from the dead; the young man repents, converts, and takes action to rid himself of his uncontrollable lust:

> He took the sickle and cut off his genitals. And running into the house where he kept his adulteress, he flung them at her saying, "On your account I became a parricide and should also become a murderer both of you two and myself. Here is the cause of all." (53 [Elliott])

Interestingly, the tale of self-mutilation from Acts of John is very similar to Lucian's description of how the *galli* castrated themselves, quoted above. The genitals are cut off with a sharp instrument and then flung into the house of a woman in both accounts. The text does not clearly condemn the young man's action. Moreover, the apostle John does not heal the man, even though he performs many miracles in the narrative. The words by Jesus and the early Christian practice that followed show how a cultural inscription on the body can serve as a sign of adherence and ascribe insider status. The use of bodily signs such as circumcision and castration in defining insider status will be further explored as I look at the Ethiopian eunuch in Acts.

7.3. The Ethiopian Eunuch (Acts 8:26–40)

The eunuch in Acts 8 is described initially as "an Ethiopian man, a eunuch, a court official of Candace, queen of the Ethiopians" (ἀνὴρ Αἰθίοψ εὐνοῦχος δυνάστης Κανδάκης βασιλίσσης Αἰθιόπων, Acts 8:27 [my trans.]). The description in Acts 8:27 employs two different terms to designate the man—he is a eunuch (εὐνοῦχος) and a court official (δυνάστης). As the

53. Hester, "Queers on Account of the Kingdom of Heaven," 14; Moxnes, *Putting Jesus in His Place*, 81.

54. Luz, *Matthew 8–20*, 497.

story unfolds, however, he is consequently referred to as "the eunuch" (ὁ εὐνοῦχος, 8:34, 36, 38, 39). Although the text does not describe his bodily signs, it is clear from this designation that the author of Acts constructs the figure of a castrated male in this story.[55] The character's status as a eunuch is his most important—indeed, his identifying—trait.

The dense description of the Ethiopian eunuch in Acts 8:27–28 plays on many of the stereotypical aspects of the eunuch figure. He is cast as the typical court eunuch, which means that he is a slave who has been made a eunuch by others. The ambiguities noted about the eunuch figure can be seen in the Lukan figure.[56] As a slave he is a surrogate body, representing the queen in her absence.[57] He is a person completely dependent on his mistress's goodwill and deprived of family connections and the ability to reproduce. His connection to a female owner, and thus to female space, further reduces his claim to masculinity. Yet he is initially called man (ἀνήρ). Although he is a slave, the Ethiopian traveler holds a position high up in the slave hierarchy. He is a court official (δυνάστης) and guardian of Candace's treasury. When the reader encounters him, he sits in a carriage and he reads from a scroll, both of which are symbols of power and status (8:28). He must have been taught to read and has the means to own a book scroll. Although invisible in the text, the reader can assume that the eunuch is in command of an entourage, probably consisting of slaves under his command.[58]

These ambiguities in gender and class have been noted by many scholars.[59] However, the social location of the eunuch is also connected to a

---

55. As many commentators have concluded; see, e.g., Luke Timothy Johnson, *The Acts of the Apostles*, SP 5 (Collegeville, MN: Liturgical Press, 1992), 155; Richard I. Pervo, *Acts: A Commentary*, Hermeneia (Minneapolis: Fortress, 2009), 224; Scott Shauf, "Locating the Eunuch: Characterization and Narrative Context in Acts 8:26–40," *CBQ* 71 (2009): 764; Parsons, *Body and Character in Luke and Acts*, 133.

56. I consider Acts to be written by the same anonymous author as the Gospel of Luke; see Pervo, *Acts*, 5, 19.

57. For slaves as surrogate bodies, see Glancy, *Slavery in Early Christianity*, esp. 12–29.

58. Pervo notes that although the chariot must have had a driver, "the narrator exhibits no interest in this person, an example of Acts' characteristic social snobbery" (*Acts*, 225).

59. See, e.g., Kartzow, *Destabilizing the Margins*, 46–58; Burke, *Queering the Ethiopian Eunuch*, 15–16. Kartzow describes the Ethiopian eunuch as a "borderline identity." Shauf, however, argues that there is no ambiguity: "There is no evidence in the

bodily impairment. Few have considered the eunuch as a character with a disability. Although it is impossible to map the outline of the Ethiopian eunuch's body, the eunuch's social status has something to do with his marked body. The eunuch has a bodily inscription, a stigma, "an attribute that makes him different," in Goffman's words.[60] His body tells a story about being inflicted with pain and deformity. Castration is a procedure meant to disable; it constructs a person with an inability to procreate and sometimes a reduced ability or inability to perform sexually. The Ethiopian eunuch can thus be characterized as disabled. It is his crushed genitals, his broken body, that renders him a "third sex." It is also his procreative disability that makes him an entrusted slave in Candace's administration. Both power and stigma are ascribed to the eunuch by his castration.

Luke's desert traveler is reading from Isaiah when the apostle Philip approaches him. The suffering servant passage is the starting point for the conversation between the two:

> Like a sheep he was led to the slaughter,
> and like a lamb silent before its shearer,
> so he does not open his mouth.
> In his humiliation justice was denied him.
> Who can describe his generation?
> For his life is taken away from the earth.
> The eunuch asked Philip, "About whom, may I ask you, does the prophet
> say this, about himself or about someone else?" (Acts 8:32–34)

The eunuch is reading about a person being slaughtered and sheared, about remaining silent when afflicted with pain and about being humiliated. Perhaps the eunuch identifies with the suffering servant? Jeremy Schipper argues that "Acts hints at a connection between the eunuch and the servant's respective social experiences of disability."[61] Philip gives a christological interpretation of the servant's identity, proclaiming "the good news about Jesus" to the eunuch (8:35). But this text describes experiences familiar to a eunuch: of being cut and humiliated and of being excluded from a family. Like the servant, the eunuch is doubly cut off:

---

text that the eunuch—this eunuch, at least—occupies a despised place in the world" ("Locating the Eunuch," 772).

60. Goffman, *Stigma*, 12.

61. Schipper, *Disability and Isaiah's Suffering Servant*, 77.

sheared of his genitalia and cut off from the possibility of reproduction.[62] As the eunuch reads his own experience into the passage, he underscores the physical experience of the suffering servant. Schipper has noted the tendency throughout the interpretive history of this passage of disregarding that Isaiah describes the servant's disability as a social and political experience.[63] It is this common experience of social and political exclusion that the eunuch picks up on in his reading.

According to Luke, the eunuch had come to Jerusalem to worship and was on his way home when he encounters Philip (8:28), but the narrator is unclear about whether he had accomplished his mission.[64] It is uncertain if a eunuch would have been allowed to worship in the temple during the Second Temple period.[65] As noted above, Deut 23:1 excludes eunuchs from worship in the assembly of the Lord. Sarah J. Melcher argues that by the first century CE the Pentateuch had reached canonical status and that Acts 8:26–40 is an attempt to counter the exclusionary ideology of Deut 23:1–6 and Lev 21:17–23.[66] The historical reality may not play such an important role in Luke's narrative. Rather, the reference to Jerusalem serves as a hint to the exclusion of eunuchs in the Mosaic law. This exclusionary practice becomes the backdrop for the inclusion of the Ethiopian eunuch through the baptism that takes place in the narrative. As Richard I. Pervo notes, traveling away from the temple and toward the prophets is for Luke a move in the right direction.[67]

As noted above, Isa 56:3–7 grants an eschatological opening through which eunuchs may become part of the worshiping community. These verses from Isaiah come only a few chapters after the verses the eunuch is reading. If we imagine that the eunuch continued reading scripture after

---

62. In the Hebrew of the Isaiah passage, this twofold "cutting" is more obvious, as the two verbs for cutting that are used have similar sounds, *gozezeha* (Isa 53:7, from the verb *gazaz*, to shear, cut) and *nighzar* (Isa 53:8, from the verb *gazar*, "to cut," "cut off"). Luke, of course, relied on LXX in his quotation.

63. Schipper, *Disability and Isaiah's Suffering Servant*, 2.

64. Pervo, *Acts*, 224.

65. See discussions in Olyan, *Disability in the Hebrew Bible*, 32–33; Saul M. Olyan, "'Anyone Blind or Lame Shall Not Enter the House': On the Interpretation of Samuel 5:8b," *CBQ* 60 (1998): 218–27. Olyan argues that "a ban on worshipers with at least some physical defects was in force in Jerusalem at some point in time" (227).

66. Sarah J. Melcher, "A Tale of Two Eunuchs: Isaiah 56:1–8 and Acts 8:26–40," in Moss and Schipper, *Disability Studies and Biblical Literature*, 124.

67. Pervo, *Acts*, 224.

his baptism, he might have come across these words.[68] It may well have been Luke's intention that this passage should echo in his story about the Ethiopian. The eschatological prophecy of Isaiah is, after all, realized in Acts, when Philip baptizes the eunuch on the Gaza road. Although Isa 56:3–7 is not quoted, it is alluded to, I contend, through a number of likenesses between the Ethiopian eunuch of Luke and the pious eunuchs of Isaiah.[69] In Isaiah, inclusion is promised to eunuchs who "keep my sabbaths, who choose the things that please me and hold fast my covenant" (56:4). The Ethiopian is a foreigner (56:3) as well as a eunuch, and by reading scripture and going to Jerusalem to worship, he is certainly among the eunuchs who "keep the sabbath" and "hold fast to the covenant." He receives "a monument and a name" when he is included into the Christian believing community through baptism and thus ensures for himself a blessing "better than sons and daughters" as well as "an everlasting name" (56:5).[70] The story thus reinterprets the eunuch as someone included rather than excluded. Although his genitals are "cut off," he is no longer cut off from the house of God. Through baptism, his body is transformed. His physical impairment is given a new meaning; his stigmata no longer signify exclusion. By giving a new meaning to a nonnormative, stigmatized category, I suggest that the story crips the eunuch category. In the healing stories of the gospels and Acts, healing is aligned with conversion and faith. In contrast, the eunuch's conversion takes place here without any prevenient healing. It is the interpretation of the category that has changed, and thus no transformation of the body is needed.

7.3.1. Constructing Another Other

From a disability perspective, the story of the Ethiopian eunuch is interesting because it disrupts the above-noted connection between healing and faith and shows that there is a diversity of disability representations within New Testament texts. But each story also has multiple layers of

---

68. Pervo, *Acts*, 222; Mona West, "The Story of the Ethiopian Eunuch," in *The Queer Bible Commentary*, ed. Deryn Guest et al. (London: SCM, 2006), 573–74.

69. See also Melcher, "Tale of Two Eunuchs," 126.

70. The everlasting name is, in fact, doubly secured, *both* through the promise of redemption and salvation that lies in baptism (see Acts 2:38–40) *and* through his remembrance in the text of Acts.

meaning. I will now consider the function of the Ethiopian eunuch within the larger literary context of Acts. The eunuch disappears as abruptly as he appeared from the pages of Acts. After his baptism, "he went on his way rejoicing [χαίρων]" (Acts 8:37). What is the purpose of this story? How does it function in the literary structure of Acts? I argue that the passage is significant in Luke's project of drawing new boundaries, of defining new in-groups and out-groups. The baptism of the Ethiopian eunuch is an important step in Luke's universalizing project, in which the meeting in Jerusalem (Acts 15:1–35) is the pivotal point.[71] What is particularly interesting for my concerns here is the reinterpretation of bodily signs that accompanies this project. Castration is not the only genital alteration that is resignified in the book of Acts. Luke also gives new meaning to another practice, namely, circumcision (see Acts 10:45; 11:2–3, 15:1–29). The story about Cornelius serves as a prooftext showing that God has opened up the community of worship also for the uncircumcised. This story concludes with the Holy Spirit descending on everyone who heard Peter preach, and Peter asking rhetorically, "Can anyone withhold the water for baptizing these people who have received the Holy Spirit just as we have?" (Acts 10:45–47). Peter's question here echoes the eunuch's in Acts 8:36: "What is to prevent me from being baptized?" The question is, in both instances, about the limits of inclusion: Who can be included into the people of God through baptism? Eunuchs? Yes! Uncircumcised gentiles? Yes! The meeting in Jerusalem seals the deal when it is decided that no one uncircumcised needs to become circumcised after his conversion (Acts 15:29–21).

As noted above, these two imposed alterations of the male genitalia, circumcision and castration, are constructed within the Hebrew Bible as more or less opposites. In Acts, however, both these bodily signs are given new meaning. The stories about the Ethiopian eunuch and Cornelius reflect early Christian negotiation over and reinterpretations of the meaning of such bodily signs as circumcision and castration. Rather than important signifiers that include or exclude, circumcision and castration are seemingly rendered irrelevant. According to Acts, the Christ-believers adopted an inclusive practice whereby these bodily signs were eclipsed by the symbolic act of baptism. Acts 8:26–40 is the story of the obliteration of

---

71. I concur with Schauf that "Luke's description of the eunuch, as well as other details in the story, functions specifically to make the story fit in the broader scheme of the expansion of the Christian mission in Acts" ("Locating the Eunuch," 763).

castration as a sign of religious exclusion, just as the stories about Cornelius and the Jerusalem meeting are about the obliteration of uncircumcision as sign of religious exclusion.

This reinterpretation of bodily signs is not, however, driven by a genuine concern for eunuchs but by an identity conflict within Judaism that is under negotiation in Acts. The passage constructs the Ethiopian eunuch as an alien other, different from us in race, class, gender, and physical/sexual ability, for a specific purpose.[72] The Ethiopian eunuch is a literary figure created to serve as an example of inclusive Christ-believing practices in contrast to traditional Jewish practices and to show that it is in the Christ-believing community that the biblical prophecies have their fulfillment. The story of the Ethiopian eunuch exhibits, according to Pervo, "Lukan theology in a nutshell."[73] The outsider is included, but in the process, circumcised Jews become the new other.[74]

In Acts 8:26–40, the eunuch's disability is overcome through baptism. In terms of Mitchell and Snyder's theory of narrative prosthesis, the solution to the problem of deviance is not through cure but through rescue from social censure and revaluation of modes of being.[75] Although he is not healed, his physical impairment is dispensed with as a problem of access to the divine. The passage functions in the larger narrative structure of Acts as a bridge, a prosthesis, to prop up the message of the ever widening circle of the power of the Holy Spirit from Jerusalem to Rome. As the story ends, the Ethiopian travels happily off and is never seen again (8:39). He has served his purpose and is of no further use for Luke. The question is whether the story really challenges the category of eunuch. There is no "serious contemplation of the difference that disability makes as a socially negotiated identity."[76] Rather, the text contributes to a cementing of the category of eunuch and to the continued stigmatization of eunuchs. The aftermath of Matt 19:12 in the early Christian

---

72. Parsons, however, praises Luke's "subversive reading" (*Body and Character in Luke and Acts*, 131). See also Yong, who follows Parsons's interpretation (*Bible, Disability, and the Church*, 68–69).

73. Pervo, *Acts*, 219.

74. Mitzi J. Smith argues that the Jews are one of the groups that identity is constructed over against in Acts (Smith, *The Literary Construction of the Other in the Acts of the Apostles: Charismatics, the Jews, and Women* [Eugene, OR: Pickwick, 2011]).

75. Mitchell and Snyder, *Narrative Prosthesis*, 53–54.

76. Mitchell and Snyder, *Narrative Prosthesis*, 10.

practice of castration shows, however, that Luke's interpretation was not universal. Other Christ-believers wanted signs and chose castration as a new signifier of insider status.

7.4. Conclusion: Cripping the Eunuch—Cripping Christ

This chapter has looked at the ancient eunuch figure as a category of reproductive disability. I have analyzed the two New Testament occurrences of the term εὐνοῦχος in Matt 19:12 and Acts 8:26–40 and shown how this ambiguous category challenged kyriarchal notions of gender, sexuality, class, and ethnicity. I argued that the notion of crip identity and cripping as a process of critique, disruption, and reimagination reverberates with the ancient eunuch category. The eunuch logion in Matthew subverts the designation of eunuch as a despised category by appropriating the term as a signifier of insider status and aligning the body of the eunuch with the eschatological bodies of the kingdom of heaven. The story of the Ethiopian eunuch, although I have argued that it was not written out of concern for eunuchs, destabilizes the connection between conversion and healing, and reveals the cultural and arbitrary nature of stigmatizing categories. The Ethiopian eunuch is included into the Christ-believing community through a resignification of the social category, rather than an alteration of his body.

The two eunuch passages in the New Testament may also destabilize a normate understanding of Jesus. The experiences of the suffering servant in Isa 53 (Acts 8:32–33) reverberates with the experiences of a eunuch as well as the experiences of Jesus's suffering. Crucifixion was a painful and degrading form of capital punishment. In 1 Pet 2:22–24, drawing on the same passage from Isaiah as Acts 8:32–33, Jesus is also presented as a bodily crushed, suffering servant who defies codes of masculinity by not asserting his rights or talking back.[77] The experiences of Jesus and of the Ethiopian eunuch clearly overlap: Jesus may be read as a eunuch with a broken body, excluded from his family, silent as he was being cut. Matthew 19:12, moreover, singles out eunuchs as special representatives of the kingdom of heaven and thus aligns eunuchs with Christ in a special way. In these passages, Christ emerges as a crip figure, as one who defies both norms of

---

77. For a discussion of the likeness between Christ and slaves in this passage, see Glancy, *Slavery in Early Christianity*, 148–51.

masculinity and norms of ability.[78] By embracing the term eunuch, and by succumbing to passive suffering and inflictions of violence, Christ is crip. The two New Testament eunuch passages thus have the potential to locate the queer, broken, disabled body at the center of Christianity, as aligned with the crip body of Christ.

---

78. McRuer, *Crip Theory*, 2.

8

CONCLUSION: POLYPHONIC VOICES

8.1. Introduction

In this book I have looked at a variety of representations of disability in early Christian texts. When I selected the case studies, diversity was my main criterion. Thus, the preceding chapters discuss different disabilities, a variation of genres, characters from diverse social locations, and multiple theoretical concepts. Nevertheless, there are some recurring motifs and themes across these representations that I want to point out. First, I want to stress that the intersectional variation that can be seen in the texts is an important insight in itself. This study shows that the understanding and conceptualization of disability is intricately connected with gender, class, ethnicity, age, and other social factors. Both the lived experience of disability and its representation in the texts vary. For example, the man at the Bethesda pool (John 5:1–15) says he has no one to help him and seems to be quite destitute, while the man with the four helpers (Mark 2:1–12) is probably a householder carried by slaves. Several of the case studies show that disability is used as one among several markers of otherness (e.g., Judas in Papias's fragment, the Ethiopian eunuch in Acts 8:26–40, and the female demon in the Acts of Peter).

Second, the textual representations of disability in this study reveal something about the negotiation of difference: deviating bodies serve a social function; they are used to think with; at the same time as they are seen as problematic, a *problem* that requires a solution. All the case studies I have presented have one or more aspects of what Mitchell and Snyder call narrative prosthesis. Thus, Mitchell and Snyder's theory is useful in order to reveal the cultural work that disability does. I have argued that it might be helpful to differentiate more clearly between the narrative and the metaphorical uses that Mitchell and Snyder include in their description of narrative prosthesis (see §2.1 and §2.4). I have used the phrase *prosthetic narrative scheme* to describe the typical narrative features of the concept. Even within this storytelling aspect of narrative prosthesis, there is variation in how narrative prosthesis is used as a storytelling device in these case studies: as an impetus, whereby the story expresses a need to explain a nonnormative body (e.g., Peter's daughter in the Acts of Peter), or as a crutch, whereby disability is needed to prop up and magnify the protagonist (e.g., in the Markan healing stories). When it comes to the metaphorical aspect of narrative prosthesis, I find it helpful to distinguish between a physiognomic move, from outer appearance to inner morality, and a symbolic move, in which disability or a disabled character becomes representative of a group or a wider category. The description of Judas by Papias (ugly appearance reveals evil soul) is an example of the physiognomic move, while the Syro-Phoenician daughter in Mark (girl's illness represents the animality of her ethnic group) is an example of the symbolic move. This aspect of narrative prosthesis is not restricted to narrative genres but is used as a stigmatizing disability invective across genres, as I have argued in chapters 5 and 6.

This study has also shown that the various metaphorical uses of disability categories rely on cultural tropes that connect certain disabilities to particular vices or weaknesses. I have used Sontag's insights about illness and metaphor to tease out the metaphorical uses of blindness as lack of insight (e.g., John 9:1–41, the Acts of Peter, Papias, *Fragments*), demon possession as animality and racial otherness (Mark 7:24–40), dropsy as bad moral character (Papias, *Fragments*), and the combination of muteness and lameness as sign of sexual sin or temptation (the Acts of Peter).

8.2. The Familiar and the Strange

To a modern reader, the early Christian representations of disability I have presented are sometimes quite strange but sometimes also surprisingly familiar. In 2015, Microsoft had a Super Bowl commercial that featured Braylon, a boy with leg prostheses that incorporate Microsoft technology. According to Microsoft's own presentation, Braylon "lives his life without limits and inspires others to do the same."[1] There are two features of this ad that I find to have echoes of early Christian texts.

---

1. Microsoft, "Braylon O'Neill: Making Strides," https://www.microsoft.com/en-us/empowering/?story=braylon.

First, this ad resembles the New Testament genre of healing narratives. As I have argued, the healing stories follow a prosthetic narrative scheme: A character is identified and named according to his or her disability. Jesus or a Christian apostle, martyr, or saint enters the scene, and healing is sought or at least expected by the surrounding crowd. After overcoming some sort of obstacle, the character with the disability is healed and disappears from the story; she or he is dispensable. Several of the healing stories in the gospels involve characters with some sort of mobility impairment. "Stand up and walk" is Jesus's characteristic pronouncement (e.g., Matt 9:5; Mark 2:11; John 5:8; Acts 3:6), and the healed character does so, becoming a spectacle before the crowd.

The Microsoft ad follows the plot of such early Christian healing narratives. The story about Braylon is a healing story in which Microsoft has taken the place of Jesus and miraculous deeds are traded for technology. The bulk of the commercial features Braylon doing sports activities with the help of his prostheses. All we really know about him is that now he can "stand up and walk," thanks to Microsoft. The ad depends on the same trope as the New Testament healing stories: a disabled character is used to reveal the protagonist as good and powerful. Although Braylon is the cinematic focus of the commercial, he disappears toward the end, as a clip of Braylon zooms out and turns out to be only a pixel in one of the panes of Microsoft's window logo. Microsoft is the real hero of the story, just like Jesus is in the gospels. I have argued that the healing narratives support the writers' claims about Jesus's divinity and the divinely sanctioned power of the apostle. The disabled characters function as narrative prostheses to prop up the divine healer's authority and power and support the narrative's truth claims.[2] Likewise, Microsoft depends upon Braylon's disability to communicate the message that it is a company that does good and makes the world a better place. But, like a prosthesis, Braylon, too, is dispensable in the end. The message is not about Braylon but about Microsoft "empowering us all."[3]

The second echo of early Christian thought is the notion of a "life without limits." The ad takes for granted that a life without limits is something everybody wants and also something that should be within reach. The idea of and drive toward living lives without limits are deeply

---

2. Mitchell and Snyder, *Narrative Prosthesis*, 49.
3. Microsoft, "Braylon O'Neill."

engrained in contemporary culture. Narratives of progress and development have been pervasive since the Enlightenment, and with the biotechnology available today, the drive toward perfecting our bodies and deselecting the nonnormative is stronger than ever. There is a strong current in contemporary discourse that a life with disability is a life that no one wants. Disability, Alison Kafer argues, "plays a huge, but seemingly uncontested, role in how contemporary Americans envision the future. Utopian visions are founded on the elimination of disability, while dystopic, negative visions of the future are based on its proliferation."[4] Kafer unveils and challenges these ableist notions of the future and their increasingly eugenicist drive.

However, notions about a limitless future of bodily perfection can also be found in early Christianity. One of the core beliefs of early Christianity was the belief in the resurrection of the body.[5] Christ's resurrection after three days in the grave was seen as a sign that all believers would rise at the end of time and live forever in heaven. In contrast to contemporaneous Greek and Roman thought, most Christians were clear that the *body* would rise, in contrast to ideas about the immortality of the soul.[6] Hence, early Christian thinkers debated what this resurrection body would look like.[7] Most early Christian thinkers, however, were in agreement that the resurrection body would be free of blemishes and impairments.[8] Opponents attacked early Christian belief in the resurrection body by pointing to the issue of disability. If there is a bodily resurrection, what about those who died with a disability? Would they rise again as lame, deaf, or blind? In a pseudepigraphical treatise from the second century, a Christian writer tries to answer these questions:

> Well, they say, if then the flesh rise, it must rise the same as it falls; so that if it die with one eye, it must rise one-eyed; if lame, lame; if defective in any part of the body, in this part the man must rise deficient. How

---

4. Alison Kafer, *Feminist, Queer, Crip* (Bloomington: Indiana University Press), 2.

5. See, e.g., Caroline Walker Bynum, *The Resurrection of the Body in Western Christianity, 200–1336* (New York: Columbia University Press, 1995).

6. Candida R. Moss, "Heavenly Healing: Eschatological Cleansing and the Resurrection of the Dead in the Early Church," *JAAR* 79 (2011): 996–1001.

7. Kristi Upson-Saia, "Resurrecting Deformity: Augustine on Wounded and Scarred Bodies in the Heavenly Realm," in Schumm and Stoltzfus, *Disability in Judaism, Christianity, and Islam*, 95–99.

8. Moss, "Heavenly Healing"; Upson-Saia, "Resurrecting Deformity."

truly blinded are they in the eyes of their hearts! For they have not seen on the earth blind men seeing again, and the lame walking by His [i.e., Jesus's] word.... For if on earth He healed the sicknesses of the flesh, and made the body whole, much more will He do this in the resurrection, so that the flesh shall rise perfect and entire. (Pseudo-Justin, *Res.* 4 [*ANF* 1:295])

When Pseudo-Justin argues for the resurrection of perfected bodies, he draws on the gospels' healing narratives as his prooftexts. Jesus's ability to heal in his lifetime on earth parallels his power to raise perfected bodies into the afterlife. This shows how closely linked the idea of able-bodiedness and resurrection as "life without limits" are in early Christian thinking. There are echoes of these narrative tropes and motifs about the eradication of disability and a future without limits in the Microsoft commercial, and such ideas have been deeply influential in the formation of Western culture.[9]

Although pervasive in the reception history, these texts and tropes are not the only voices on disability in early Christianity. As I have argued in this book, the discourse on disability is much more polyphonic. Pseudo-Justin's insistence on the erasure of disability in the resurrection is challenged by the gospels' stories about Jesus's own resurrection body. According to the Gospel of Luke (24:39–40), as well as John (20:25–27), Jesus's risen body still has the marks of his crucifixion: a pierced abdomen and nail marks in his hands and feet. Jesus's resurrection body is not a perfectly able body but one bearing the marks of lived life as the primary signs of his identity and thus the proof of continuity. Moreover, as I have argued, Paul boasts of his nonnormative body (2 Cor 11–12). His much debated "thorn in the flesh" (2 Cor 12:7) should not be dismissed as a metaphor for temptation but understood as some sort of disability. I find it plausible that Paul had a somatic and social experience of difference that shaped his theological reflection.[10]

The Acts of Peter also challenges the typical healing narrative. In the Acts of Peter, there is a space for disability as something good, and there is an acceptance that healing does not always occur. Peter's daughter is better off as she is, and the widows have other abilities due to their visual impairment. It is seen as good for the believing community to have impaired

---

9. Eiesland, *Disabled God*, 70–75.

10. See also Yong, *Bible, Disability, and the Church*, 88–89.

members because they perform important functions. Although I hardly endorse the theology of this text (as I have noted, there are many challenging aspects from a feminist point of view), I think it is important to take note of the diversity in voices and perspectives that the early Christian texts offer.

8.3. Potential for Future Research

What is the potential of a disability perspective for biblical and early Christian scholarship? Polyphony may be a key word here, too. The research that has come out of this perspective so far has gone in several directions. Hector Avalos tried to schematize the earliest contributions (1990s–2007) and argued that there were three emerging approaches within biblical disability studies: a redemptionist approach, a rejectionist approach, and a historicist approach.[11] According to Avalos, in the redemptionist trajectory, the scholar seeks to redeem the biblical text by recontextualizing it for modern application; the rejectionist argues that the Bible has negative portrayals of disability that should be rejected in modern society; and a historicist approach is restricted to a historical examination of disabilities in the Bible.

These different trajectories are still identifiable trends within biblical disability studies, but in my opinion there is more of a continuum among them than Avalos allows for. My own approach in this book cannot be neatly placed within one of these trajectories. My research has a strong historicist component. I discuss disability terminology concepts and try to place them within their ancient literary and cultural framework. But I also go beyond the historicist examination of disability. I have critiqued the problematic aspects of connecting disability to sin (e.g., Mark 2:1–12; John 5:1–15) and its reception history, which has been very negative to people with disabilities.[12] I have also pointed to the symbolic and physiognomic uses of disability that stereotype people with disabilities and use them as a means to a theological end (e.g., Mark 7:24–30; John 9:1–41). With the editors of *This Abled Body*, I insist that "the Bible has negative portrayals of disability that should be rejected in modern society," which would place

---

11. Hector Avalos, "Redemptionism, Rejectionism, and Historicism as Emerging Approaches in Disability Studies," *PRSt* 34 (2007): 91–100.

12. Eiesland, *Disabled God*.

me in Avalos's rejectionist trajectory.[13] However, I have also made some potentially redemptionist points. I have suggested that the eunuch passages (Matt 19:12; Acts 8:26–40) can crip our conception of Jesus and that Paul's theology of weakness and madness has the potential to destigmatize differently abled bodies.

Hence, I find that all of these approaches to the Bible and disability have merit and that there is potential for exciting research in the years to come. From a historical perspective, there is a lot we still do not know about how people with various disabilities were treated in antiquity, how illnesses were conceptualized, and in what ways social and religious stigma were ascribed to various disabilities. Thus, a historical approach will in itself give new and useful knowledge about the biblical and ancient worlds. Such insights about representations of disability and the lives of people with disabilities in the Bible also contribute to the wider field of disability history.

I also think it is important to critique, along rejectionist lines, problematic aspects of disability that we find in the Bible. The Bible still has authority for Jews and Christians, and the problematic sides of its representations of disability and their ensuing theologies need to be exposed. For example, it is challenging for the ordinary Bible reader who has a modern understanding of medicine to make sense of the gospels' texts about demon possession and exorcism, as well as the stories about Jesus's miraculous healings. People with disabilities have critiqued Christian practices that use these biblical narratives to stigmatize and to one-sidedly focus on healing.[14] This is also a reason to look at early Christian texts across the divide between canonical and noncanonical. Noncanonical texts might reveal aspects of early Christian thinking that the canonical literature does not and underscore the diversity and polyphony of early Christian voices.

Nevertheless, I think there are aspects and traditions from the Bible that can be used in a constructive way in order to more fully include people with a variety of disabilities in religious communities and society. There is

---

13. Hector Avalos, Sarah J. Melcher, and Jeremy Schipper, introduction to *This Abled Body*, 6.

14. See, e.g., Julia Watts Belser, "Violence, Disability, and the Politics of Healing: The Inaugural Nancy Eiesland Endowment Lecture," *JDR* 19 (2015): 177–97; Belser and Morrison, "What No Longer Serves Us"; Moss, "Heavenly Healing"; Upson-Saia, "Resurrecting Deformity."

a need to develop a better disability theology, and biblical disability studies can also be a part of that conversation. But cross-disciplinarity should not stop there. Biblical scholarship using a disability perspective is also part of a wider scholarly conversation within disability studies. As I have tried to show in this book, I think biblical scholarship can contribute to a better understanding of the cultural negotiation of disability, both through history and today.

Bibliography

Primary Sources

"The Acts of John." Pages 303–43 in *The Apocryphal New Testament: A Collection of Apocryphal Christian Literature in an English Translation.* Edited by John K. Elliott. Oxford: Clarendon, 1993.

"The Acts of Peter." Pages 390–428 in *The Apocryphal New Testament: A Collection of Apocryphal Christian Literature in an English Translation.* Edited by John K. Elliott. Oxford: Clarendon, 1993.

The Apostolic Fathers. Vol. 2: *Epistle of Barnabas; Papias and Quadratus; Epistle to Diognetus; The Shepherd of Hermas.* Translated by Bart D. Ehrman. LCL. Cambridge: Harvard University Press, 2003.

Aretaeus. *The Extant Works of Aretaeus, the Cappadocian.* Translated by Francis Adams. Boston: Milford, 1972.

Aristotle. *Generation of Animals.* Translated by A. L. Peck. LCL. London: Heinemann, 1942.

The Digest of Justinian. Vol. 4. Translated by Alan Watson. Philadelphia: University of Pennsylvania Press, 1985

Eusebius. *Ecclesiastical History.* Vol. 2: *Books 6–10.* Translated by J. E. L. Oulton. LCL. Cambridge: Harvard University Press, 1932.

"Fragments of the Lost Work of Justin on the Resurrection." Translated by Rev. M. Dods. *ANF* 1:294–99.

Hippocrates. *Ancient Medicine; Airs, Waters, Places; Epidemics 1 and 3; The Oath. Precepts; Nutriment.* Translated by W. H. S. Jones. LCL. Cambridge: Harvard University Press, 1923.

———. *Nature of Man; Regimen in Health; Humours; Aphorisms; Regimen 1–3; Dreams; Heracleitus: On the Universe.* Translated by W. H. S. Jones. LCL. Cambridge: Harvard University Press, 1931.

———. *Prognostic; Regimen in Acute Diseases; The Sacred Disease; The Art; Breaths; Law; Decorum; Physician (Ch. 1); Dentition.* Translated by W. H. S. Jones. LCL. Cambridge: Harvard University Press, 1923.

Historia Augusta. Vol. 2. of Caracalla; Geta; Opellius Macrinus; Diadumenianus; Elagabalus; Severus Alexander; The Two Maximini; The Three Gordians; Maximus and Balbinus. Translated by David Magie. LCL. Cambridge: Harvard University Press, 140.

Horace. Satires; Epistles; The Art of Poetry. Translated by H. Rushton Fairclough. LCL. Cambridge: Harvard University Press, 1929.

———. Odes and Epodes. Translated by Niall Rudd. LCL. Cambridge: Harvard University Press, 2004.

Josephus. Jewish Antiquities. Vol. 7: Books 16–17. Translated by Ralph Marcus. LCL. Cambridge: Harvard University Press, 1963.

Lucian: On the Syrian Goddess. Edited and translated by J. L. Lightfoot. Oxford: Oxford University Press, 2003.

Lucian. The Passing of Peregrinus; The Runaways; Toxaris or Friendship; The Dance; Lexiphanes; The Eunuch; Astrology; The Mistaken Critic; The Parliament of the Gods; The Tyrannicide; Disowned. Translated by A. M. Harmon. LCL. Cambridge: Harvard University Press, 1936.

Pliny. Natural History. Vol. 8: Books 28–32. Translated by W. H. S. Jones. LCL. Cambridge: Harvard University Press, 1963.

Pausanias. Description of Greece. Vol. 4: Books 8.22–10. Translated by W. H. S. Jones. LCL. Cambridge: Harvard University Press, 1935.

Tacitus. Histories: Books 4–5; Annals: Books 1–3. Translated by Clifford H. Moore. LCL. Cambridge: Harvard University Press, 1931.

Secondary Sources

Abrams, Judith Z. Judaism and Disability: Portrayals in Ancient Texts from the Tanach through the Bavli. Washington, DC: Gallaudet University Press, 1998.

Abusch, Ra'anan. "Circumcision and Castration under Roman Law in the Early Empire." Pages 75–86 in The Covenant of Circumcision: New Perspectives on an Ancient Jewish Rite. Edited by Elizabeth Wyner Mark. Hanover: Brandeis University Press, 2003.

Albl, Martin. "'For Whenever I Am Weak, Then I Am Strong': Disability in Paul's Epistles." Pages 145–58 in This Abled Body. Rethinking Disability in Biblical Studies. Edited by Hector Avalos, Sarah Melcher, and Jeremy Schipper. SemeiaSt 55. Atlanta: Society of Biblical Literature, 2007.

Albrecht, Gary L., Katherine D. Seelman, and Michael Bury. "Introduction: The Formation of Disability Studies." Pages 1–8 in The Handbook *of Disability Studies*. Edited by Gary L. Albrecht, Katherine D. Seelman, and Michael Bury. Thousand Oaks, CA: Sage, 2001.

Anderson, Matthew R., and Karin B. Neutel. "The First Cut is the Deepest: Masculinity and Circumcision in the First Century." Pages 228–44 in *Biblical Masculinities Foregrounded*. Edited by Ovidiu Creanga and Peter-Ben Smit. Sheffield: Sheffield University Press, 2014.

Anderson, Paul N. *The Riddles of the Fourth Gospel: An Introduction to John*. Minneapolis: Fortress, 2011.

Atherton, Catherine. Introduction to *Monsters and Monstrosity in Greek and Roman Culture*. Edited by Catherine Atherton. Bari: Levante, 1998.

Avalos, Hector. *Illness and Health Care in the Ancient Near East: The Role of the Temple in Greece, Mesopotamia, and Israel*. Atlanta: Scholars Press, 1995.

———. *Health Care and the Rise of Christianity*. Peabody, MA: Hendrickson, 1999.

———. "Redemptionism, Rejectionism, and Historicism as Emerging Approaches in Disability Studies." *PRSt* 34 (2007): 91–100.

Avalos, Hector, Sarah J. Melcher, and Jeremy Schipper. Introduction to *This Abled Body: Rethinking Disability in Biblical Studies*. Edited by Hector Avalos, Sarah J. Melcher, and Jeremy Schipper. SemeiaSt 55. Atlanta: Society of Biblical Literature, 2007.

———. *This Abled Body: Rethinking Disabilities in Biblical Studies*. SemeiaSt 55. Atlanta: Society of Biblical Literature, 2007.

Baden, Joel S., and Candida R. Moss. *Reconceiving Infertility: Biblical Perspectives on Procreation and Childlessness*. Princeton: Princeton University Press, 2015.

Barclay, John M. G. "There Is Neither Young Nor Old? Early Christianity and Ancient Ideologies of Age." *NTS* 53 (2007): 225–41.

Barnes, Colin, Mike Oliver, and Len Barton. Introduction to *Disability Studies Today*. Edited by Colin Barnes, Mike Oliver, and Len Barton. Cambridge: Polity, 2002.

Barsch, Sebastian, Anne Klein, and Pieter Verstraete, eds. *The Imperfect Historian: Disability Histories in Europe*. Frankfurt: Lang, 2013.

Barton, Carlin A. *The Sorrows of the Ancient Romans: The Gladiator and the Monster*. Princeton: Princeton University Press, 1993.

Belser, Julia Watts. *Rabbinic Tales of Destruction: Gender, Sex and Disability in the Ruins of Jerusalem*. Oxford: Oxford University Press, 2018.

———. "Violence, Disability, and the Politics of Healing: The Inaugural Nancy Eiesland Endowment Lecture." *JDR* 19 (2015): 177–97.

Belser, Julia Watts, and Melanie S. Morrison. "What No Longer Serves Us: Resisting Ableism and Anti-Judaism in New Testament Healing Narratives." *JFSR* 27.2 (2011): 153–70.

Bengtsson, Staffan. "The Two-Sided Coin: Disability, Normalcy and Social Categorization in the New Testament." *SJDR* 18 (2016): 1–11.

Blundell, Sue, Douglas Cairns, Elizabeth Craik, and Nancy Sorkin Rabinowitz. "Introduction." *Helios* 40 (2013): 3–37.

Boys-Stones, George. "Physiognomy and Ancient Psychological Theory." Pages 19–124 in *Seeing the Face, Seeing the Soul: Polemon's Physiognomy from Classical Antiquity to Medieval Islam*. Edited by Simon Swain. Oxford: Oxford University Press, 2007.

Bradley, Keith. "The Sentimental Education of the Roman Child: The Role of Pet Keeping." *Latomus* 57 (1998): 523–57.

Brakke, David. *Demons and the Making of the Monk: Spiritual Combat in Early Christianity*. Cambridge: Harvard University Press, 2006.

Bremmer, Jan N. "Women, Magic, Place and Date." Pages 1–20 in *The Apocryphal Acts of Peter: Magic Miracles and Gnosticism*. Edited by Jan N. Bremmer. Leuven: Peeters, 1998.

Brewer, Douglas, Terence Clark, and Adrian Philipps. *Dogs in Antiquity: Anubis to Cerberus; The Origins of the Domestic Dog*. Warminster: Aris & Philipps, 2001.

Brown, Lerita M. Coleman. "Stigma: An Enigma Demystified." Pages 179–208 in *The Disability Studies Reader*. Edited by Lennard J. Davis. New York: Routledge, 2010.

Brown, Raymond E. *The Gospel according to John (I–XII)*. AB 29. New York: Doubleday, 1966.

———. *The Gospel according to John (XIII–XXI)*. AB 29A. New York: Doubleday, 1966.

Bruce, Patricia. "John 5:1–18 the Healing at the Pool: Some Narrative, Socio-historical and Ethical Issues." *Neot* 39 (2005): 39–56.

Buell, Denise Kimber. *Why This New Race: Ethnic Reasoning in Early Christianity*. New York: Columbia University Press, 2005.

Burke, Sean D. "Queering Early Christian Discourse." Pages 175–90 in *Bible Trouble: Queer Reading at the Boundaries of Biblical Scholarship*. Edited by Teresa J. Hornsby and Ken Stone. SemeiaSt 67. Atlanta: Society of Biblical Literature, 2011.

———. *Queering the Ethiopian Eunuch: Strategies of Ambiguity in Acts*. Minneapolis: Fortress, 2013.

Butler, Judith. *Gender Trouble: Feminism and the Subversion of Identity*. New York: Routledge, 1990.

Bynum, Caroline Walker. *The Resurrection of the Body in Western Christianity, 200–1336*. New York: Columbia University Press, 1995.

Byron, Gay L. *Symbolic Blackness and Ethnic Difference in Early Christian Literature*. London: Routledge, 2002.

Cadwallader, Alan H. "When a Woman Is a Dog: Ancient and Modern Ethology Meet the Syrophoenician Women." *BCT* 1.4 (2005): 35.1–35.17.

Callon, Callie. "Secondary Characters Furthering Characterization: The Depiction of Slaves in the *Acts of Peter*." *JBL* 131 (2012): 797–818.

Carter, Warren. " 'The Blind, Lame and Paralyzed' (John 5:3): John's Gospel, Disability Studies and Postcolonial Perspectives." Pages 129–50 in *Disability Studies and Biblical Literature*. Edited by Candida R. Moss and Jeremy Schipper. New York: Palgrave MacMillan, 2011.

Clark, Elizabeth A. *History, Theory, Text: Historians and the Linguistic Turn*. Cambridge: Harvard University Press, 2004.

———. *Reading Renunciation: Asceticism and Scripture in Early Christianity*. Princeton: Princeton University Press, 1999.

Clark-Soles, Jaime. "John, First-Third John, and Revelation." Pages 333–78 in *The Bible and Disability: A Commentary*. Edited by Sarah J. Melcher, Mikeal Parsons, and Amos Yong. Waco, TX: Baylor, 2017.

Cohen, Jeffrey Jerome. "Monster Culture (Seven Theses)." Pages 3–25 in *Monster Theory: Reading Culture*. Edited by Jeffrey Jerome Cohen. Minneapolis: University of Minnesota Press, 1996.

———. "Preface: In a Time of Monsters." Pages vii–xiii in *Monster Theory. Reading Culture*. Edited by Jeffrey Jerome Cohen. Minneapolis: University of Minnesota Press, 1996.

Collins, Adela Yarbro. *Mark: A Commentary*. Hermeneia. Minneapolis: Fortress, 2007.

———. "Paul's Disability: The Thorn in His Flesh." Pages 165–84 in *Disability Studies and Biblical Literature*. Edited by Candida R. Moss and Jeremy Schipper. New York: Palgrave Macmillan, 2011.

Conway, Colleen M. *Behold the Man: Jesus and Greco-Roman Masculinity*. Oxford: Oxford University Press, 2008.

———. " 'Behold the Man!' Masculine Christology and the Fourth Gospel." Pages 163–92 in *New Testament Masculinites*. Edited by Stephen D. Moore and Janice Capel Anderson. SemeiaSt 45. Atlanta: Society of Biblical Literature, 2003.

————. "Speaking through Ambiguity: Minor Characters in the Fourth Gospel." *BibInt* 10 (2002): 324–41.

Cotter, Wendy. *The Christ of the Miracle Stories: Portrait through Encounter*. Grand Rapids: Baker Academic, 2010.

Couey, J. Blake. "Prophets." Pages 215–73 in *The Bible and Disability: A Commentary*. Edited by Sarah Melcher, Mikeal Parsons, and Amos Yong. Waco, TX: Baylor University Press, 2017.

Culpepper, R. Alan. *Anatomy of the Fourth Gospel: A Study in Literary Design*. Philadelphia: Fortress, 1987.

Davis, Lennard J. *Bending over Backwards: Disability, Dismodernism, and Other Difficult Positions*. New York: New York University Press, 2002.

Dean-Jones, Lesley. *Women's Bodies in Classical Greek Science*. Oxford: Clarendon, 1994.

Demand, Nancy. *Birth, Death, and Motherhood in Classical Greece*. Baltimore: Johns Hopkins University Press, 1994.

Dewey, Arthur J., and Anna C. Miller. "Paul." Pages 379–426 in *The Bible and Disability: A Commentary*. Edited by Sarah J. Melcher, Mikeal C. Parsons, and Amos Yong. Waco, TX: Baylor University Press, 2017.

Edelstein, Emma J., and Ludwig Edelstein. *Asclepius: Collection and Interpretation of the Testimonies*. 2 vols. Baltimore: Johns Hopkins University Press, 1998.

Edwards, Martha L. "The Cultural Context of Deformity in the Greek World: Let There Be a Law That No Deformed Child Shall Be Reared." *AHB* 10.3–4 (1996): 79–92.

Eiesland, Nancy L. *The Disabled God: Toward a Liberatory Theology of Disability*. Nashville: Abingdon, 1994.

Eijk, Philip J. van der. "Cure and (In)curability of Mental Disorders in Ancient Medical and Philosophical Thought." Pages 307–38 in *Mental Disorders in the Classical World*. Edited by W.V. Harris. Leiden: Brill, 2013.

————. *Medicine and Philosophy in Classical Antiquity: Doctors and Philosophers on Nature, Soul, Health and Disease*. Cambridge: Cambridge University Press, 2005.

Elliott, John K. *The Apocryphal New Testament: A Collection of Apocryphal Christian Literature in an English Translation*. Oxford: Clarendon, 1993.

Eyler, Joshua R. *Disability in the Middle Ages: Reconsiderations and Reverberations*. Farnham: Ashgate, 2010.

———. "Introduction: Breaking Boundaries, Building Bridges." Pages 1–8 in *Disability in the Middle Ages: Reconsiderations and Reverberations*. Edited by Joshua R. Eyler. Farnham: Ashgate, 2010.

Fantham, Elaine, Helene Peet Foley, Natalie Boymel Kampen, Sarah B. Pomeroy, and H. A. Shapiro. *Women in the Classical World: Image and Text*. New York: Oxford University Press, 1994.

Fehribach, Adeline. "The 'Birthing' Bridegroom: The Portrayal of Jesus in the Fourth Gospel." Pages 104–27 in vol. 2 of *A Feminist Companion to John*. Edited by Amy-Jill Levine with Marianne Blickenstaff. 2 vols. London: Sheffield Academic, 2003.

Felton, D. "Rejecting and Embracing the Monstrous in Ancient Greece and Rome." Pages 103–32 in *The Ashgate Research Companion to Monsters and the Monstrous*. Edited by Asa Simon Mittman and Peter J. Dendle. Farnham: Ashgate, 2012.

Frayer-Griggs, Daniel. "Spittle, Clay and Creation in John 9:6 and some Dead Sea Scrolls." *JBL* 132 (2013): 659–70.

Furnish, Victor Paul. *II Corinthians*. AB 32A. Garden City, NY: Doubleday, 1984.

Garland, Robert. *The Eye of the Beholder: Deformity and Disability in the Graeco-Roman World*. Ithaca: Cornell University Press, 1995.

Garland-Thomson, Rosemarie. "Feminist Disability Studies." *Signs* 30 (2005): 1557–87.

———. "Integrating Disability, Transforming Feminist Theory." Pages 353–73 in *The Disability Studies Reader*. Edited by Lennard J. Davis. New York: Routledge, 2010.

———. *Staring: How We Look*. Oxford: Oxford University Press, 2009.

Gevaert, Bert, and Christian Laes. "What's in a Monster? Pliny the Elder, Teratology and Bodily Disability." Pages 211–30 in *Disabilities in Roman Antiquity: Disparate Bodies a Capite ad Calcem*. Edited by Christian Laes, Chris F. Goodey, and Martha Lynn Rose. Leiden: Brill, 2013.

Gilhus, Ingvild Sælid. *Animals, Gods and Humans: Changing Attitudes to Animals in Greek, Roman and Early Christian Ideas*. London: Routledge, 2006.

Glancy, Jennifer A. *Corporal Knowledge*. Oxford: Oxford University Press, 2010.

———. "Jesus, the Syrophoenician Woman and Other First Century Bodies." *BibInt* 18 (2010): 342–63.

————. *Slavery in Early Christianity*. Oxford: Oxford University Press, 2002.

Gleason, Maud W. *Making Men: Sophists and Self-Presentation in Ancient Rome*. Princeton: Princeton University Press, 1995.

Goffman, Erving. *Stigma: Notes on the Management of Spoiled Identity*. Harmondsworth: Penguin, 1968.

Goodey, Chris F., and Martha Lynn Rose. "Mental States, Bodily Dispositions and Table Manners: A Guide to Reading 'Intellectual' Disability from Homer to Late Antiquity." Pages 17–44 in *Disabilities in Roman Antiquity: Disparate Bodies a Capite ad Calcem*. Edited by Christian Laes, Chris F. Goodey, and Martha Lynn Rose. Leiden: Brill, 2013.

Goodley, Dan. *Disability Studies: An Interdisciplinary Introduction*. Los Angeles: Sage, 2011.

Gosbell, Louise A. "'The Poor, the Crippled, the Blind, and the Lame': Physical and Sensory Disability in the Gospels of the New Testament." PhD diss., Macquarie University, 2015.

————. *"The Poor, the Crippled, the Blind, and the Lame": Physical and Sensory Disability in the Gospels of the New Testament*. Tübingen: Mohr Siebeck, 2018.

Grant, Colleen C. "Reinterpreting the Healing Narratives." Pages 72–87 in *Human Disability and the Service of God: Reassessing Religious Practice*. Edited by Nancy L. Eiesland and Don E. Salier. Nashville: Abingdon, 1998.

Graumann, Lutz Alexander. "Monstrous Births and Retrospective Diagnosis." Pages 181–210 in *Disabilities in Roman Antiquity: Disparate Bodies a Capite ad Calcem*. Edited by Christian Laes, Chris F. Goodey, and Martha Lynn Rose. Leiden: Brill, 2013.

Grubbs, Judith Evans. "Abduction Marriage in Antiquity: A Law of Constantine (CTh. IX. 24. I) and Its Social Context." *JRS* 79 (1989): 59–83.

Haenchen, Ernst. *John 1: A Commentary on the Gospel of John Chapters 1–6*. Hermeneia. Philadelphia: Fortress, 1984.

————. *John 2: A Commentary on the Gospel of John Chapters 7–21*. Hermeneia. Philadelphia: Fortress, 1984.

Halberstam, Judith. *Skin Shows: Gothic Horror and the Technology of Monsters*. Durham, NC: Duke University Press, 1995.

Haley, Shelley P. "Be Not Afraid of the Dark: Critical Race Theory and Classical Studies." Pages 27–49 in *Prejudice and Christian Beginnings: Investigating Race, Gender, and Ethnicity in Early Christian Studies*.

Edited by Elisabeth Schüssler Fiorenza and Laura Salah Nasrallah. Minneapolis: Augsburg, 2009.

Harrill, J. Albert. "Invective against Paul (2 Cor 10:10), the Physiognomics of the Ancient Slave Body, and the Greco-Roman Rhetoric of Manhood." Pages 189–213 in *Antiquity and Humanity: Essays on Ancient Religion and Philosophy*. Edited by Adela Yarbro Collins and Margaret M. Mitchell. Tübingen: Mohr Siebeck, 2001.

Harris, William V. *Mental Disorders in the Classical World*. Leiden: Brill, 2013.

Harrocks, Rebecca. "Jesus' Gentile Healings: The Absence of Bodily Contact and the Requirement of Faith." Pages 83–101 in *The Body in Biblical, Christian and Jewish Texts*. Edited by Joan E. Taylor. London: Bloomsbury, 2015.

Hartsock, Chad. "The Healing of the Man with Dropsy (Luke 14:1–6) and the Lukan Landscape." *BibInt* 21 (2013): 341–54.

———. *Sight and Blindness in Luke-Acts: The Use of Physical Features in Characterization*. BINS. Leiden: Brill, 2008.

Henning, Meghan. "Paralysis and Sexualilty in Medical Literature and the Acts of Peter." *JLA* 8 (2015): 306–21.

Hester, J. David. "Queers on Account of the Kingdom of Heaven: Rhetorical Constructions of the Eunuch Body." *Scr* 90 (2005): 809–23.

Hill, Charles E. "Papias of Hierapolis." *ExpTim* 117 (2006): 309–15.

Horn, Cornelia B. "Suffering Children, Parental Authority and the Quest for Liberation? A Tale of Three Girls in the *Acts of Paul (and Thecla)*, the *Act(s) of Peter*, the *Acts of Nerseus and Achilleus*, and the *Epistle of Pseudo-Titus*." Pages 118–45 in *A Feminist Companion to the New Testament Apocrypha*. Edited by Amy-Jill Levine with Maria Mayo Robbins. London: T&T Clark, 2006.

Horn, Cornelia B., and J. W. Martens. *"Let the Little Children Come to Me": Childhood and Children in Early Christianity*. Washington, DC: Catholic University of America Press, 2009.

Howard, James M. "The Significance of Minor Characters in the Gospel of John." *BSac* 163 (2006): 63–78.

Hoyland, Robert. "A New Edition and Translation of the Leiden Polemon." Pages 329–464 in *Seeing the Face, Seeing the Soul: Polemon's Physiognomy from Classical Antiquity to Medieval Islam*. Edited by Simon Swain. Oxford: Oxford University Press, 2007.

Hughes, Bill. "What Can a Foucauldian Analysis Contribute to Disability Studies?" Pages 78–92 in *Foucault and the Government of Disability*.

Edited by Shelley Tremain. Corporealities. Ann Arbor: University of Michigan Press, 2005.

Hull, John M. *In the Beginning There Was Darkness: A Blind Person's Conversation with the Bible*. London: SCM, 2001.

Ipsen, Avaren. *Sex Working and the Bible*. Edited by Philip R. Davies and James G. Crossley. Bible World. London: Equinox, 2009.

Jeong, Dong Hyeon. "The Animal Masks of the Syrophoenician Woman and the Markan Jesus: Reading Mark 7:24–30 through a Postcolonial Animality Lens." Paper presented at the Society of Biblical Literature Annual Meeting, Boston, 20 November 2017.

Johnson, Luke Timothy. *The Acts of the Apostles*. SP 5. Collegeville, MN: Liturgical Press, 1992.

Jouanna, Jacques. "The Typology and Aetiology of Madness in Ancient Greek Medical and Philosophical Writing." Pages 97–127 in *Mental Disorders in the Classical World*. Edited by William V. Harris. Leiden: Brill, 2013.

Kafer, Alison. *Feminist, Queer, Crip*. Bloomington: Indiana University Press.

Kartzow, Marianne Bjelland. "'Asking the Other Question': An Intersectional Approach to Galatians 3:28 and the Colossian Household Code." *BibInt* 18 (2010): 364–89.

———. *Destabilizing the Margins: An Intersectional Approach to Early Christian Memory*. Eugene, OR: Pickwick, 2012.

———. *Gossip and Gender: Othering of Speech in the Pastoral Epistles*. Berlin: de Gruyter, 2009.

Kartzow, Marianne Bjelland, and Halvor Moxnes. "Complex Identities: Ethnicity, Gender and Religion in the Story of the Ethiopian Eunuch (Acts 8:26–40)." *R&T* 17 (2010): 184–204.

Keener, Craig S. *The Gospel of John: A Commentary*. 2 vols. Peabody, MA: Hendrickson, 2003.

Kelley, Nicole. "Deformity and Disability in Greece and Rome." Pages 31–46 in *This Abled Body: Rethinking Disabilities in Biblical Studies*. Edited by Hector Avalos, Sarah J. Melcher, and Jeremy Schipper. SemeiaSt 55. Atlanta: Society of Biblical Literature, 2007.

———. "'The Punishment of the Devil Was Apparent in the Torment of the Human Body': Epilepsy in Ancient Christianity." Pages 205–21 in *Disability Studies and Biblical Literature*. Edited by Candida R. Moss and Jeremy Schipper. New York: Palgrave Macmillan, 2011.

———. "The Theological Significance of Physical Deformity in the Pseudo-Clementine Homilies." *PRSt* 34 (2007): 77–90.

King, Helen. *Hippocrates' Woman: Reading the Female Body in Ancient Greece*. London: Routledge, 1998.

King, Karen. "Images of Aging and Immortality in Ancient Christianity." Pages 59–82 in *Metamorphoses: Resurrection, Body and Transformative Practices in Early Christianity*. Edited by Turid Karlsen Seim and Jorunn Økland. Berlin: de Gruyter, 2009.

Klauck, Hans-Josef. *The Apocryphal Acts of the Apostles: An Introduction*. Translated by Brian McNeil. Waco, TX: Baylor University Press, 2008.

Kleinman, Arthur. *Patients and Healers in the Context of Culture: An Exploration of the Borderland between Anthropology, Medicine, and Psychiatry*. Berkeley: University of California Press, 1980.

Kok, Jacobus. *New Perspectives on Healing, Restoration and Reconciliation in John's Gospel*. Leiden: Brill, 2016.

Konstan, David. *Friendship in the Classical World*. Cambridge: Cambridge University Press, 1997.

Koosed, Jennifer L., and Darla Schumm. "Out of the Darkness: Examining the Rhetoric of Blindness in the Gospel of John." Pages 77–91 in *Disability in Judaism, Christianity, and Islam: Sacred Texts, Historical Traditions, and Social Analysis*. Edited by Darla Schumm and Michael Stoltzfus. New York: Palgrave Macmillan, 2011.

Kristeva, Julia. *Powers of Horror: An Essay on Abjection*. New York: Columbia University Press, 1982.

Kudlick, Catherine J. "Disability History: Why We Need Another 'Other.'" *AHR* 108 (2003): 763–93.

Kuefler, Mathew. *The Manly Eunuch: Masculinity, Gender Ambiguity, and Christian Ideology in Late Antiquity*. Chicago: University of Chicago Press, 2001.

Laes, Christian, ed. *Disability in Antiquity*. RA. London: Routledge, 2017.

———. "Introduction: Disabilities in the Ancient World: Past, Present and Future." Pages 1–21 in *Disability in Antiquity*. Edited by Christian Laes. London: Routledge, 2017.

———. "Silent History? Speech Impairment in Roman Antiquity." Pages 145–80 in *Disabilities in Roman Antiquity: Disparate Bodies a Capite ad Calcem*. Edited by Christian Laes, Chris F. Goodey, and Martha Lynn Rose. Leiden: Brill, 2013.

———. "Silent Witnesses: Deaf-Mutes in Graeco-Roman Antiquity." *CW* 104 (2011): 451–73.

Laes, Christian, Chris F. Goodey, and M. Lynn Rose. "Approaching Disabilities *a Capite ad Calcem*: Hidden Themes in Roman Antiquity." Pages 1–15 in *Disabilities in Roman Antiquity. Disparate Bodies a Capite ad Calcem.* Edited by Christian Laes, Chris F. Goodey, and M. Lynn Rose. Leiden: Brill, 2013.

———, eds. *Disabilities in Roman Antiquity: Disparate Bodies a Capite ad Calcem.* Leiden: Brill, 2013.

Laqueur, Thomas. *Making Sex: Body and Gender from the Greeks to Freud.* Cambridge: Harvard University Press, 1992.

Lawrence, Louise J. *Bible and Bedlam: Madness, Sanism, and New Testament Interpretation.* LNTS. London: Bloomsbury T&T Clark, 2018.

———. *Sense and Stigma in the Gospels: Depictions of Sensory-Disabled Characters.* Oxford: Oxford University Press, 2013.

Lid, Inger Marie. "Disability as a Human Condition Discussed in a Theological Perspective." *Diaconia* 3 (2012): 158–71.

Liew, Tat-siong Benny. *Politics of Parousia: Reading Mark Inter(con)textually.* Leiden: Brill, 1999.

Linton, Simi. *Claiming Disability: Knowledge and Identity.* New York: New York University Press, 1998.

Luz, Ulrich. *Matthew 8–20: A Commentary.* Hermeneia. Minneapolis: Fortress, 2001.

Marcus, Joel. *Mark 1–8: A New Translation with Introduction and Commentary.* AB 27A. Garden City, NY: Doubleday, 2000.

Martin, Dale B. *The Corinthian Body.* New Haven: Yale University Press, 1995.

———. *Inventing Superstition: From the Hippocratics to the Christians.* Cambridge: Harvard University Press, 2004.

Marx-Wolf, Heidi, and Kristi Upson-Saia. "The State of the Question: Religion, Medicine, Disability and Health in Late Antiquity." *JLA* 8 (2015): 257–72.

McRuer, Robert. *Crip Theory: Cultural Signs of Queerness and Disability.* New York: New York University Press, 2006.

Meekosha, Helen, and Russell Shuttleworth. "What's So 'Critical' about Critical Disability Studies?" *AJHR* 15 (2009): 47–76.

Melcher, Sarah J. "A Tale of Two Eunuchs: Isaiah 56:1–8 and Acts 8:26–40." Pages 117–28 in *Disability Studies and Biblical Literature.* Edited by Candida R. Moss and Jeremy Schipper. New York: Palgrave Macmillan, 2011.

Melcher, Sarah J., Mikeal C. Parsons, and Amos Yong, eds. *The Bible and Disability: A Commentary*. Waco, TX: Baylor University Press, 2017.

Metzler, Irina, ed. *Disability in Medieval Europe: Thinking about Physical Impairment during the High Middle Ages, c. 1100–1400*. London: Routledge, 2006.

———. *A Social History of Disability in the Middle Ages: Cultural Considerations of Physical Impairment*. New York: Routledge, 2013.

Misset-van de Weg, Magda. "'For the Lord Always Takes Care of His Own': The Purpose of the Wondrous Works and Deeds in the *Acts of Peter*." Pages 97–110 in *The Apocryphal Acts of Peter: Magic, Miracles and Gnosticism*. Edited by Jan N. Bremmer. Leuven: Peeters, 1998.

Mitchell, Alexandre. "The Hellenistic Turn in Bodily Representations: Venting Anxiety in Terracotta Figurines." Pages 182–96 in *Disability in Antiquity*. Edited by Christian Laes. London: Routledge, 2017.

Mitchell, David T., and Sharon L. Snyder. *Narrative Prosthesis: Disability and the Dependencies of Discourse*. Ann Arbor: University of Michigan Press, 2001.

Mittman, Asa Simon. "Introduction: The Impact of Monsters and Monster Studies." Pages 1–16 in *The Ashgate Companion to Monsters and the Monstrous*. Edited by Asa Simon Mittman and Peter J. Dendle. Farnham: Ashgate, 2012.

Molinari, Andrea L. *"I Never Knew the Man": The Coptic Act of Peter (Papyrus Berolinensis 8502.4), Its Independence from the Apocryphal Acts of Peter, Genre and Legendary Origins*. Leuven: Peeters, 2000.

Moloney, Francis J. *The Gospel of John*. SP 4. Collegeville, MN: Liturgical Press, 1998.

Moore, Stephen D. *Empire and Apocalypse: Postcolonialism and the New Testament*. Sheffield: Sheffield Phoenix, 2006.

Moore, Stephen D., and Janice Capel Anderson. *New Testament Masculinities*. SemeiaSt 45. Atlanta: Society of Biblical Literature, 2003.

Moss, Candida R. "Christly Possession and Weakened Bodies: Reconsideration of the Function of Paul's Thorn in the Flesh (2 Cor 12:7–10)." *JRDH* 16 (2012): 319–33.

———. "Heavenly Healing: Eschatological Cleansing and the Resurrection of the Dead in the Early Church." *JAAR* 79 (2011): 991–1017.

———. "The Man with the Flow of Power: Porous Bodies in Mark 5:25–34." *JBL* 129 (2010): 507–19.

———. "Mark and Matthew." Pages 275–302 in *The Bible and Disability:*

A Commentary. Edited by Sarah J. Melcher, Mikeal C. Parsons, and Amos Yong. Waco, TX: Baylor University Press, 2017.

Moss, Candida R., and Jeremy Schipper. *Disability Studies and Biblical Literature.* Basingstoke: Palgrave Macmillan, 2011.

Moxnes, Halvor. *Putting Jesus in His Place: A Radical Vision of Household and Kingdom.* Louisville: Westminster John Knox, 2003.

Nanos, Mark D. "Paul's Reversal of Jews Calling Gentiles 'Dogs' (Phillipians 3:2): 1600 Years of an Ideological Tale Wagging an Exegetical Dog?" *BibInt* 17 (2009): 448–82.

Nash, Jennifer C. "Re-thinking Intersectionality." *FR* 89 (2008): 1–15.

Nutton, Vivian. *Ancient Medicine.* London: Routledge, 2004.

Økland, Jorunn. *Women in Their Place: Paul and the Corinthian Discourse of Gender and Sanctuary Space.* JSNTSup 269. London: T&T Clark, 2004.

Oliver, Michael. *The Politics of Disablement.* CTSWWS. Basingstoke: Macmillan, 1990.

Olyan, Saul M. "'Anyone Blind or Lame Shall Not Enter the House': On the Interpretation of Samuel 5:8b." *CBQ* 60 (1998): 218–27.

———. *Disability in the Hebrew Bible: Interpreting Mental and Physical Differences.* New York: Cambridge University Press, 2008.

Parkin, Tim G. *Old Age in the Roman World: A Cultural and Social History.* Baltimore: Johns Hopkins University Press, 2003.

Parrott, Douglas M., ed. *Nag Hammadi Codices V, 2–5 and VI: With Papyrus Berolinensis 8502.* Leiden: Brill, 1979.

Parsons, Mikeal C. *Body and Character in Luke and Acts: The Subversion of Physiognomy in Early Christianity.* Grand Rapids: Baker Academic, 2006.

Pearman, Tory Vandeventer. *Women and Disability in Medieval Literature.* Basingstoke: Palgrave Macmillan, 2010.

Perkins, Judith. *The Suffering Self: Pain and Narrative Representation in the Early Christian Era.* London: Routledge, 1995.

Pervo, Richard I. *Acts: A Commentary.* Hermeneia. Minneapolis: Fortress, 2009.

Pilch, John J. *Healing in the New Testament: Insights from Medical and Mediterranean Anthropology.* Minneapolis: Fortress, 2000.

Poirier, John C. "Another Look at the 'Man Born Blind' in John 9." *JRDH* 14 (2010): 60–65.

Rabinowitz, Nancy Sorkin. "Women as Subject and Object of the Gaze in Tragedy." *Helios* 40 (2013): 195–221.

Raphael, Rebecca. *Biblical Corpora: Representations of Disability in Hebrew Biblical Literature*. LHBOTS. London: Continuum, 2009.

Reinhartz, Adele. "'And the Word Was Begotten': Divine *Epigenesis* in the Gospel of John." *Semeia* 85 (1999): 83–103.

Reyes, Paulina de los, and Diana Mulinari. *Intersektionalitet: Kritiska reflektioner över (o)jämlikhetens landskap*. Stockholm: Liber, 2005.

Richlin, Amy. *Arguments with Silence: Writing the History of Roman Women*. Ann Arbor: University of Michigan Press, 2014.

———. Introduction to *Pornography and Representation in Greece and Rome*. Edited by Amy Richlin. New York: Oxford University Press, 1992.

———, ed. *Pornography and Representation in Greece and Rome*. New York: Oxford University Press, 1992.

Ringe, Sharon H. "A Gentile Woman's Story, Revisited: Rereading Mark 7.24–31a." Pages 79–100 in *A Feminist Companion to Mark*. Edited by Amy-Jill Levine with Marianne Blickenstaff. London: Sheffield Academic, 2001.

Ringrose, Kathryn M. *The Perfect Servant: Eunuchs and the Social Construction of Gender in Byzantium*. Chicago: University of Chicago Press, 2003.

Robertson, Jesse E. *The Death of Judas: The Characterization of Judas Iscariot in Three Early Christian Accounts of His Death*. New Testament Monographs. Sheffield: Sheffield Phoenix, 2012.

Rose, Martha L. *The Staff of Oedipus: Transforming Disability in Ancient Greece*. Ann Arbor: University of Michigan Press, 2003.

Samama, Evelyne. "The Greek Vocabulary of Disabilities." Pages 121–38 in *Disability in Antiquity*. Edited by Christian Laes. London: Routledge, 2017.

Sandahl, Carrie. "Queering the Crip or Cripping the Queer? Intersections of Queer and Crip Identities in Solo Autobiographical Performance." *GLQ* 9 (2003): 25–56.

Sandnes, Karl Olav. *Belly and Body in the Pauline Epistles*. SNTSMS 120. Cambridge: Cambridge University Press, 2002.

Sawyer, Deborah. "John 19.34: From Crucifixion to Birth, or Creation?" Pages 130–39 in vol. 2 of *A Feminist Companion to John*. Edited by Amy-Jill Levine. 2 vols. Sheffield: Sheffield Academic, 2003.

Schipper, Jeremy. *Disability and Isaiah's Suffering Servant*. BibRef. Edited by James Crossley and Francesca Stavrakopoulou. Oxford: Oxford University Press, 2011.

———. *Disability Studies and the Hebrew Bible: Figuring Mephibosheth in the David Story*. New York: T&T Clark, 2006.

———. "Joshua–Second Kings." Pages 93–120 in *The Bible and Disability: A Commentary*. Edited by Sarah Melcher, Mikeal Parsons, and Amos Yong. Waco, TX: Baylor University Press, 2017.

Schneemelcher, Wilhelm. "The Acts of Peter." Pages 285–316 in *New Testament Apocrypha*. Edited by Wilhelm Schneemelcher and R. McL. Wilson. Cambridge: James Clarke, 1991.

Schüssler Fiorenza, Elisabeth. "Introduction: Exploring the Intersections of Race, Gender, Status, and Ethnicity in Early Christian Studies." Pages 1–23 in *Prejudice and Christian Beginnings: Investigating Race, Gender, and Ethnicity in Early Christian Studies*. Edited by Elisabeth Schüssler Fiorenza and Laura Salah Nasrallah. Minneapolis: Fortress, 2009.

———. *Rhetoric and Ethic: The Politics of Biblical Studies*. Minneapolis: Augsburg Fortress, 1999.

Scott, Joan W. "Gender: A Useful Category of Historical Analysis." *AHR* 91.5 (1986): 77–97.

Seim, Turid Karlsen. "Descent and Divine Paternity in the Gospel of John: Does the Mother Matter?" *NTS* 51 (2005): 361–75.

———. "Motherhood and the Making of Fathers in Antiquity: Contextualizing Genetics in the Gospel of John." Pages 99–124 in *Women and Gender in Ancient Religions: Interdisciplinary Approaches*. Edited by Stephen P. Ahearne-Kroll, Paul A. Holloway, and James A. Kelhoffer. WUNT 263. Tübingen: Mohr Siebeck, 2010.

Shakespeare, Tom. "The Social Model of Disability." Pages 197–204 in *The Disability Studies Reader*. Edited by Lennard J. Davis. New York: Routledge, 2006.

Shauf, Scott. "Locating the Eunuch: Characterization and Narrative Context in Acts 8:26–40." *CBQ* 71 (2009): 762–75.

Siebers, Tobin. "Disability in Theory: From Social Constructionism to the New Realism of the Body." *ALH* 13 (2001): 737–54.

———. *Disability Theory*. Ann Arbor: University of Michigan Press, 2008.

Skinner, Marilyn B. *Sexuality in Greek and Roman Culture*. Malden, MA: Blackwell, 2005.

Smit, Peter-Ben. "Masculinity and the Bible: Survey, Models and Perspectives." *BRP* 2 (2017): 1–97.

Smith, Gregory A. "How Thin Is a Demon?" *JECS* 16 (2008): 479–512.

Smith, Jonathan Z. "Towards Interpreting Demonic Powers in Hellenistic and Roman Antiquity." *ANRW* 16.1:425–39.

Smith, Mitzi J. *The Literary Construction of the Other in the Acts of the Apostles: Charismatics, the Jews, and Women.* Eugene, OR: Pickwick, 2011.

Smith, William. *A Dictionary of Greek and Roman Antiquities.* London: John Murray, 1914.

Snyder, Sharon L., and David T. Mitchell. *Vital Signs: Crip Culture Talks Back.* Video documentary. www.youtube.com/watch?v=r5rWHA0KcFc.

Solevåg, Anna Rebecca. "Apostolic Power to Paralyze: Gender and Disability in the Acts of Peter." In *Marginalised Writings of Early Christianity: Apocryphal Texts and Writings of Female Authorship.* Edited by Outi Lehtipuu and Silke Petersen. BW. Atlanta: SBL Press, forthcoming.

———. *Birthing Salvation: Gender and Class in Early Christian Childbearing Discourse.* BINS. Leiden: Brill, 2013.

———. "Hysterical Women? Gender and Disability in Early Christian Narrative." Pages 315–27 in *Disability in Antiquity.* Edited by Christian Laes. London: Routledge, 2017.

———. "'Leap, Ye, Lame for Joy': The Dynamics of Disability in Conversion." In *The Complexity of Conversion.* Edited by Valerie Nicolet Anderson and Marianne Bjelland Kartzow. Sheffield: Sheffield Phoenix, forthcoming.

———. "Listening for the Voices of Two Disabled Girls in Early Christian Literature." Pages 287–99 in *Children and Everyday Life in the Roman World.* Edited by Christian Laes and Ville Vuolanto. London: Routledge, 2017.

———. "Monsteret Judas: Papias beskrivelse av Judas' død." *PNA* 31 (2016): 59–68.

———. "No Nuts? No Problem! Disability, Stigma, and the Baptized Eunuch in Acts 8:26–30." *BibInt* 24 (2016): 81–99.

———. "Prayer in Acts and the Pastoral Epistles: Intersections of Gender and Class." Pages 137–59 in *Early Christian Prayer and Identity Formation.* Edited by Reidar Hvalvik and Karl Olav Sandnes. Tübingen: Mohr Siebeck, 2014

———. "Salvation as Slavery, Marriage and Birth: Does the Metaphor Matter?" Pages 144–63 in *Bodies, Borders, Believers: Ancient Texts and Present Conversations; Essays in Honor of Turid Karlsen Seim on Her Seventieth Birthday.* Edited by Anne Hege Grung, Marianne Bjelland Kartzow, and Anna Rebecca Solevåg. Eugene, OR: Pickwick, 2015.

Sontag, Susan. *Illness as Metaphor and Aids and Its Metaphors*. London: Penguin Books, 2002.

Sorensen, Eric. *Possession and Exorcism in the New Testament and Early Christianity*. Tübingen: Mohr Siebeck, 2002.

Staley, Jeffrey L. "Stumbling in the Dark, Reaching for the Light: Reading Character in John 5 and 9." *Semeia* 53 (1991): 55–80.

Stewart, David Tabb. "Sexual Disabilities in the Hebrew Bible." Pages 67–88 in *Disability Studies and Biblical Literature*. Edited by Candida R. Moss and Jeremy Schipper. New York: Palgrave, 2011.

Stiker, Henri-Jacques. *A History of Disability*. Ann Arbor: University of Michigan Press, 1999.

Streete, Gail Corrington. *The Strange Woman: Power and Sex in the Bible*. Louisville: Westminster John Knox, 1997.

Swain, Simon. "Polemon's *Physiognomy*." Pages 125–201 in *Seeing the Face, Seeing the Soul: Polemon's Physiognomy from Classical Antiquity to Medieval Islam*. Edited by Simon Swain. Oxford: Oxford University Press, 2007.

———, ed. *Seeing the Face, Seeing the Soul: Polemon's Physiognomy from Classical Antiquity to Medieval Islam*. Oxford: Oxford University Press, 2007.

Theissen, Gerd. *The Gospels in Context: Social and Political History in the Synoptic Tradition*. London: T&T Clark, 2004.

———. *The Miracle Stories of the Early Christian Tradition*. Edinburgh: T&T Clark, 1983.

Thomas, Christine M. *The Acts of Peter, Gospel Literature, and the Ancient Novel: Rewriting the Past*. Oxford: Oxford University Press, 2003.

Thomson, Rosemarie Garland. *Extraordinary Bodies: Figuring Physical Disability in American Culture and Literature*. New York: Columbia University Press, 1997.

Thumiger, Chiara. "The Early Greek Medical Vocabulary of Insanity." Pages 61–95 in *Medical Disorders in the Classical World*. Edited by William V. Harris. Leiden: Brill, 2013.

———. "Mental Disability? Galen on Mental Health." Pages 267–82 in *Disability in Antiquity*. Edited by Christian Laes. London: Routledge, 2017.

Tischendorf, Constantin von, Max Bonnet, and Richard Adelbert Lipsius. *Acta Apostolorum Apocrypha*. 2 vols. Darmstadt: Wissenschaftliche Buchgesellschaft, 1959.

Tolbert, Mary Ann. *Sowing the Gospel: Mark's World in Literary-Historical Perspective*. Minneapolis: Fortress, 1989.

Tremain, Shelley. "Foucault, Governmentality and Critical Disability Theory." Pages 1–24 in *Foucault and the Government of Disability*. Corporealities. Ann Arbor: University of Michigan Press, 2005.

Trentin, Lisa. "Exploring Visual Impairment in Roman Antiquity." Pages 89–114 in *Disabilities in Roman Antiquity: Disparate Bodies a Capite ad Calcem*. Edited by Christian Laes, Chris F. Goodey, and Martha Lynn Rose. Leiden: Brill, 2013.

Turner, David M. *Disability in Eighteenth-Century England: Imagining Physical Impairment*. Hoboken: Taylor & Francis, 2012.

Tøssebro, Jan. "Introduction to the Special Issue of SJDR: Understanding Disability." *SJDR* 6.1 (2004): 3–7.

Upson-Saia, Kristi. "Resurrecting Deformity: Augustine on Wounded and Scarred Bodies in the Heavenly Realm." Pages 93–122 in *Disability in Judaism, Christianity and Islam*. Edited by Darla Schumm and Michael Stoltzfus. New York: Palgrave Macmillan, 2011.

Valentine, Katy. "Reading the Slave Girl of Acts 16:16–18 in Light of Enslavement and Disability." *BibInt* 26 (2018): 352–68.

Vander Stichele, Caroline, and Todd C. Penner. *Contextualizing Gender in Early Christian Discourse: Thinking beyond Thecla*. Edinburgh: T&T Clark, 2009.

———. "Gendering Violence: Patterns of Power and Constructs of Masculinity in the Acts of the Apostles." Pages 193–209 in *A Feminist Companion to the Acts of the Apostles*. Edited by Amy-Jill Levine with Marianne Blickenstaff. FCNTECW. London: T&T Clark, 2004.

Vlahogiannis, Nicholas. "Disabling Bodies." Pages 13–36 in *Changing Bodies, Changing Meanings: Studies on the Human Body in Antiquity*. Edited by Dominic Montserrat. London: Routledge, 1998.

Vogt, Kari. "'Becoming Male': A Gnostic and Early Christian Metaphor." Pages 170–86 in *The Image of God and Gender Models in Judaeo-Christian Tradition*. Edited by Kari Elisabeth Børresen. Minneapolis: Fortress, 1995.

Wainwright, Elaine M. "Of Dogs and Women: Ethology and Gender in Ancient Healing; The Canaanite Woman's Story—Matt 15:21–28." Pages 55–69 in *Miracles Revisited: New Testament Miracle Stories and Their Concepts of Reality*. Edited by Stefan Alkier and Annette Weissenrieder. Berlin: de Gruyter, 2013.

————. *Women Healing/Healing Women: The Genderization of Healing in Early Christianity*. Edited by Philip R. Davies. Bible World. London: Equinox, 2006.

Walters, Jonathan. "Invading the Roman Body: Manliness and Impenetrability in Roman Thought." Pages 29–43 in *Roman Sexualities*. Edited by Judith P. Hallett and Marilyn B. Skinner. Princeton: Princeton University Press, 1997.

Watson, David F. "Luke-Acts." Pages 303–32 in *The Bible and Disability: A Commentary*. Edited by Sarah Melcher, Mikeal Parsons, and Amos Yong. Waco, TX: Baylor, 2017.

Weissenrieder, Annette. *Images of Illness in the Gospel of Luke: Insights of Ancient Medical Texts*. Tübingen: Mohr Siebeck, 2003.

West, Mona. "The Story of the Ethiopian Eunuch." Pages 572–74 in *The Queer Bible Commentary*. Edited by Deryn Guest, Robert Goss, Mona West, and Thomas Bohache. London: SCM, 2006.

Williams, Craig A. *Roman Homosexuality: Ideologies of Masculinity in Classical Antiquity*. Oxford: Oxford University Press, 1999.

Williams, Gareth. "Theorizing Disability." Pages 123–44 in *Handbook of Disability Studies*. Edited by Gary L. Albrecht, Katherine D. Seelman, and Michael Bury. Thousand Oaks, CA: Sage, 2001.

Wynn, Kerry H. "Johannine Healings and the Otherness of Disability." *PRSt* 34 (2007): 61–75.

Yong, Amos. *The Bible, Disability, and the Church: A New Vision of the People of God*. Grand Rapids: Eerdmans, 2011.

Zeichmann, Christopher B. "Papias as Rhetorician: Exphrasis in the Bishop's Account of Judas' Death." *NTS* 56 (2010): 427–29.

Ancient Sources Index

Modern Authors Index